A Vanished Ideology

A Vanished Ideology

Essays on the Jewish Communist Movement in the English-Speaking World in the Twentieth Century

Edited by

Matthew B. Hoffman

and

Henry F. Srebrnik

Cover image by Joseph Lomoff was featured on the February 1931 cover of *Der Hammer*.

Published by State University of New York Press, Albany

Printed in the United States of America

For information, contact State University of New York Press, Albany, NY
www.sunypress.edu

Production, Diane Ganeles
Marketing, Michael Campochiaro

Library of Congress Cataloging-in-Publication Data

Names: Hoffman, Matthew (Matthew B.) editor. | Srebrnik, Henry Felix, editor.
Title: A vanished ideology : essays on the Jewish communist movement in the English-speaking world in the twentieth century / edited by Matthew B. Hoffman and Henry F. Srebrnik.
Description: Albany : State University of New York Press, 2016. | Includes bibliographical references and index.
Identifiers: LCCN 2016005978 | ISBN 9781438462196 (hardcover : alk. paper)
Subjects: LCSH: Jewish communists—History. | Communism—History.
Classification: LCC HX550.J4 V36 2016 | DDC 320.53/2089924—dc23
LC record available at https://lccn.loc.gov/2016005978

10 9 8 7 6 5 4 3 2 1

Contents

1

Introduction

Matthew Hoffman and Henry Srebrnik

As Jewish life in the late nineteenth and twentieth centuries became more economically and politically precarious, various movements arose which claimed they had found the "solution" to the political dilemmas facing the Jewish people. Some were religious, some frankly assimilationist, some completely universalistic and adherents of socialist doctrines, and some, of course, were nationalistic and Zionist. One political movement, though, combined elements of two strands, Marxist universalism and Jewish nationalism. This grouping of like-minded organizations, active mainly between 1917 and 1956, we have termed the Jewish Communist movement. It had active members throughout the Jewish diaspora, in particular in the various countries of Europe and North America, as well as in Australia, Palestine, South Africa, and South America. These were later interconnected on a global level through international movements such as the World Jewish Cultural Union, or *Alveltlekher Yidisher Kultur Farband* (YKUF), founded in 1937. YKUF, which operated mainly in Yiddish, created a great variety of newspapers and theoretical and literary journals, which allowed Jewish Communists to communicate, disseminate information, and debate issues such as Jewish nationality and statehood independently of other Communists. Though officially part of the larger world Communist movement, in reality the Jewish Communists developed their own specific ideology, which was infused as much by Jewish sources—Labour Zionism, the Jewish Labour Bund, the literature of such Yiddish poets and writers as I. L. Peretz and Sholem Asch—as it was inspired by the Bolshevik revolution.

While some Jewish revolutionaries actively distanced themselves from their Jewish backgrounds, others viewed involvement in Jewish left-wing and labour groups "as the preferred means of resolving both the class and ethnic oppression of Jews."[1] Their struggle to achieve a better world "overlapped with the liberation of the Jews—whether as individuals or as a people—from the thraldom of generations."[2] There were many Jews who wished to retain their Yiddish-based culture, and that too proved an acceptable option—as long as they managed to blend, within strict ideological limits, their ethnic identity with their "internationalist" and class-based politics.[3]

When the Soviet state emerged out of the ruins of the Tsarist empire, socialists throughout the world hailed it as the beginning of a new age. For many Jewish radicals, it also heralded the approaching end of some two millennia of persecution and marginalization. The formation of a multiethnic federation of socialist republics was, they maintained, the first step in the legal, social, and economic elimination of anti-Semitism. There was initial sympathy for the Russian revolutionaries who had overthrown the oppressive and anti-Semitic Tsarist autocracy. As one Jewish Communist exclaimed, "There was a tremendous joy and a tremendous friendship between the Gentiles and the Jews. We thought that this was like the Messiah came."[4] As time went on, the Jewish Communists depicted the Soviet Union as "the one country in which the Jews suffer no more," where "antisemitism is declared a crime," and where "Yiddish has been made one of the official state languages."[5] Visitors to the USSR came back full of enthusiasm, and Jewish intellectuals were especially uncritical.[6] Daniel Soyer has observed that many Jewish travelers who had left the Tsarist lands before World War I saw in the new USSR "not only their old home but their new spiritual homeland as well," an ideological fatherland as well as the "old country," a place "nostalgically associated with their families and their own youthful years."[7] For the east European immigrant generation, "Russia had very concrete personal as well as abstract symbolic meaning." After 1917 they could identify with the state as well as with their hometowns and Jewish communities.[8] "Through the blur of distance, time and utopian expectations, the Soviet Union became a dreamland of freedom and equality."[9] Thus was born a Jewish Communism with the Soviet Union at its center.

Jews in the Soviet Union, declared the Jewish left, were now liberated from a discriminatory economic and social system; they could cease occupying "middleman" economic positions in favor of agricultural and industrial pursuits. The transformation of "unproductive" Jews concentrated in trade, commerce, and financial "speculation" into artisans and farmers would deflect anti-Semitism. The *luftmensh*, the Jew without a trade or skill, eking out a living by his wits in the constricted world of the *shtetl*, the little hamlet, would soon be an historical memory. Jews would become economically, socially, and politically integrated, partners with the other Soviet nations in socialist construction. Even the pre-revolutionary *maskilim*, the enlightened Jewish intelligentsia, had called for the formation of a Jewish farming class in a back-to-the-land movement. Early Soviet propaganda used many of the same themes employed by Zionists, with scenes of muscular Jewish pioneers engaged in working the land, casting off their ghetto past to create healthy new lives on collective farms. The need for Jews to reject their role as "middlemen" and adjust their economic pursuits in order to become "productive" was a concern expressed by almost all Jewish social movements, from Zionism to Communism.

Jewish Communism as a Variant of Utopian Messianism

The world of Jewish socialism was a secular one and its discourse radical, yet its roots lay deep within the Jewish tradition, which, although far from monolithic, has always embodied a common thread, which Zvi Gitelman has called "the quest for utopia," a search to improve the world. Jewish Communists sought "to create both a Jewish socialist state and a socialist world."[10] Though there was much in Jewish life they opposed, from Orthodox Judaism to Zionism, these people did not turn to the Communist parties because they were alienated from the Jewish world, but rather because "of their urge to act for the sake of an improved society and to better the condition of the Jewish workers."[11] Typical were activists such as the writer Kalman Marmor, a delegate to several of the early Zionist congresses in Europe, a founder of the socialist-Zionist Poale Zion, and the first editor of the socialist *Yidisher Kemfer*. He came to the United States in 1906 at age 27, at first joined the Socialist Party, but threw in his lot with the Communist movement in 1920. "It was neither Marx nor Engels that made me a socialist. I was drawn towards socialism by the [Jewish biblical] prophets," he would remark many years later. "We were not simply socialists, but *Jewish socialists*."[12] He became a journalist and literary critic with the Communist Yiddish daily *Morgn-Frayhayt* in New York and a pedagogue with the schools of the International Workers Order (IWO). The east London trade unionist and Communist activist Mick Mindel put it succinctly: "To me being Jewish and being a socialist was a natural thing."[13] The members of the Jewish Communist movement were thus not assimilationists, at least not subjectively, unlike some Jews who were as individuals attracted to the mainstream, non-Jewish CPs. They saw no contradiction in participating in pro-Soviet Jewish organizations that, by working for an international transformation of society, would also promote Jewish interests.

The specific strand of Jewish radical socialism called Jewish Communism only emerged, of course, following the Russian Revolution and the founding of a Soviet state guided by the ideals of Marxism-Leninism. Genealogically it was the child and outgrowth of the larger socialist and left-Zionist Jewish milieu, already well organized and in full flower by the turn of the twentieth century. The many writers on the Jewish left, from Moses Hess through Vladimir Medem to Ber Borochov, had already been theorizing and debating the key national and class issues that the Communists would inherit when they broke with the rest of the Jewish socialist world. The Jewish socialist movements, whatever their theoretical or programmatic differences, were all obsessed—that is not too strong a word for it—with trying to solve the "national [read: Jewish] question" and "normalize" the situation of the Jews as a people. Unlike assimilationist Jews who internalized the post-Christian critique of the Jews as a fossilized, provincial caste group destined to integrate into the larger society once emancipated from their parochial religion and given the rights of citizenship (a view espoused by, say, Leon Trotsky or Rosa Luxemburg), Jewish Communists did see a collective and distinctive future for the Jews—or at least for the Jewish working class. They did not hold derogatory or "self-hating" views of the Jewish people, nor were they secular apostates, who renounced their Jewishness when becoming communists.

Jewish Communists sought not to supplant "Jewishness" with socialism and support for the USSR, but rather to augment their Jewish identity via Communism. Even when its members and organizations revolved around the Communist parties, it was nevertheless a specifically Jewish left movement, which, despite major disagreements, could be viewed as one of a family of socialist movements that included, among others, the Jewish Labour Bund, with its diaspora-oriented nationalist socialism and theories of national-cultural autonomy, and the Poale Zion and other socialist Zionist movements, who hoped to build a socialist Jewish *yishuv* (community) in Palestine.

Jewish Communists differed from the Bund in having a political center.[14] For them, the "homeland" would be the new USSR, because of the successful Bolshevik revolution that had made anti-Semitism a crime and had liberated Russian Jewry. It was logical to be pro-Soviet; after all, the revolution had been beneficial to the Jews of the Tsarist empire. And this conceptual framework was extended elsewhere: if socialism could liberate Jewry in Russia, the same social and political forces confronting capitalist states elsewhere would be "good for the Jews" in the same manner. Jewish Communists considered the Bolshevik Revolution a world-historical event of immense magnitude; it would usher in the realization of socialism throughout the world and thus lead to the transformation of Jewish life and society and the ultimate liberation of Jews everywhere. All of this inspired the theoreticians of the movement, who were remarkably critical of contemporary Jewish life in the diaspora, their deprecatory language exhibiting little sympathy toward the "bourgeois" milieu in which they operated. Later, during the 1930s and World War II, the benefit of being allied to a Soviet Union in the forefront of the battle against Hitlerism seemed to vindicate and make self-evident the Jewish Communist attachment to the Soviet Union.

The ideology of Jewish Communism was a combination of socialism and secular Jewish nationalism, though—and this is important to emphasize—the latter was often only a muted form of discourse, becoming more audible at critical moments such as the Second World War and the struggle for a Jewish state in Palestine. In any case, they affected one another in profound ways. Thus, proletarian Jewish culture (especially in Yiddish) for Jewish Communists constituted the most authentic expression of being Jewish, of a secular *Yidishkayt*. The Yiddish language and its literature were perceived as the primary vehicle of Jewish continuity, hence the importance given to a secular and radical Yiddish school system and to Yiddish cultural production. Indeed, poets and novelists and essayists, I. L. Peretz being an obvious example, often had pride of place over political figures. Rejecting religious and traditional Judaism, the Jewish Communists believed they could advance their cultural self-identity within a Marxist-Leninist framework. Even while being part of a larger Communist "family," the extensive network of groups fashioned by the Jewish Communists enabled them to create what Arthur Liebman has called a "communist-oriented subculture"[15] that was largely independent of the Communist Party. The Jewish Communist movement created its own fraternal organizations, with active members throughout the Jewish diaspora, in particular in various countries in Europe, North and South America, Australia, Palestine (later Israel), and South Africa.

Some might call these Jewish movements "pro-Soviet" rather than "Communist," and of course they were. But that is a distinction without a difference, because by the 1930s the Communist parties themselves were to a large extent doing Moscow's bidding and so were also "pro-Soviet" organizations. They called themselves Communist, and while the Jewish front organizations did not use that word, often preferring "progressive," they were all part of the same communist apparatus emanating from the Kremlin.

Moreover, we define these Jewish movements as communist, even if they were not so officially, because almost all of the main figures that actually organized and led them were members of Communist parties and followed the Soviet "line" on all important issues—even condoning, as the New York Yiddish daily the *Frayhayt* did, the 1929 pogrom against Jews in Hebron and the 1939 Molotov-Ribbentrop Pact. These organizations all operated under the auspices of their respective Communist parties and were, in the final analysis, bureaucratically tied (sometimes in "hidden" ways) to the Soviet Union. In Canada, Jewish Communists organized the United Jewish People's Order, in the United States, the Jewish People's Fraternal Order, in Britain, branches of the Workers' Circle. They published books and journals, and operated schools and camps. They were part of a wider cradle-to-the-grave world of Yiddish secular immigrant organizations. Indeed, one could be part of this movement without formal adherence to the party. And that whole "Communist solar system" would remain firmly tied to the Soviet Union (as opposed to China or other breakaway Communist states) through much of the Cold War and beyond.

But the Jewish Communist movements were not simple extensions of Communist parties; a majority of their members were neither Communist Party members, nor even Communists. Like the other Jewish left movements, the Jewish Communists had a deep feeling for Jewish history and emerged from the same historic and economic conditions as the other Jewish socialist movements of the time. They all were products of the Jewish enlightenment or *haskala*, the growth of Yiddish as a language of culture and literature, the proletarianization and impoverishment of the Jews in the Russian Pale of Settlement before 1917, and the organization of Jews into trade unions and other resistance organizations as a response to pogroms and persecution. Jewish Communism was, as were the other leftist Jewish groups, a movement of an oppressed nationality, in a sense a movement for a people in exile who had yet to create a socialist Jewish state or even become part of a diaspora state where Jews would have internal freedom as a people. All sought in one manner or another to liberate Jews from the oppressive aspects of diasporic exile, which was felt as a dialectical antithesis to "homeland" and redemption via socialism. And all of them initially supported the

1917 Russian revolutions and the overthrow of Tsarist autocracy, which had legitimized and even legalized anti-Semitism, numerous economic, political, and residential restrictions on Jewish life, and pogroms and violence.

The perspective of the Jewish Communists was, even if not articulated in such terms, oftentimes closer to the historic Jewish narrative of exile and redemption than to so-called "scientific socialism" and class struggle and, while ostensibly concentrating on organizing on "the Jewish street" alone, it was just as much concerned with the worldwide situation of Jews, especially after the rise of fascism, the Holocaust, and the eventual formation of the state of Israel. Their historical heroes and "role-models," and even their ideological mentors, were as likely to be Jewish radicals and literary figures in Europe or the United States as non-Jews of the left. The Jewish Communists saw themselves as part of a larger movement, active in Canada, the United States, Mexico, Argentina, Britain, France, South Africa, and even Palestine itself, all working for socialism in the interests of the Jews as a people—a very different perspective from that of the non-Jewish Communist parties. Indeed, one Jewish Communist in the United States had even been brazen enough in 1920 to broach the idea of "an alliance of Jewish Communist bodies the world over," a Jewish section of the Communist International, or Comintern—an offer rebuffed by the Soviets as somewhat smacking of nationalism if not indeed Zionism![16] More internationally minded than most other people on the left, and being especially interested in what was transpiring in what for a large number was their place of birth, their "old country," now suddenly a "new socialist state," they especially sought contact with Soviet Jewish bodies such as the *Evsektsiya*, the Jewish Section of the Soviet Communist Party (CPSU) in the 1920s, and the Jewish Anti-Fascist Committee (JAFC) in the 1940s. While Jewish liberation throughout the diaspora was the long-term goal, the short-term Communist frame of reference was remarkably similar to that of Zionism: emancipation and rejuvenation, the creation of a "new" Jew, would initially occur in one country. Not, of course, in the Land of Israel, but rather in the USSR, particularly in Birobidzhan, in the Soviet Far East.

Again, it is extremely important to emphasize that the movement was a contradiction, whether its members realized it or not; it was *Jewish*, its focus was on Jews and the Jewish world, yet it tied itself to a non-Jewish ideology. It was for a long time able to overcome this dilemma by its uncritical support of those Soviet nationality policies that involved autonomous Jewish jurisdictions, at first in the Crimea, Belarus, and Ukraine, and later in the territory set aside for Soviet Jews in Birobidzhan; as well, it took at face value Soviet opposition to anti-Semitism. Still, this tension—between the concern for Jews and the voluntary self-subjection to Communist Party discipline by the leadership—often led to major problems, in particular in relation to the Jewish *yishuv* in Palestine. Thus, the dilemma, never really resolved, that confronted Jewish Communists: how to "square the circle" between their desire to improve the life of the Jewish "masses," while needing to conform to the dictates of the international Communist movement, as interpreted by its ideological and political leadership in the Soviet Union. As mentioned, they suffered a major setback in 1929, following the murder of Jews by Arabs in Hebron, which Moscow considered an "anti-imperialist" act. Even worse were their rationalizations around the 1939 Nazi-Soviet Pact. Many individual members quit at those times, while those who stayed on were often conflicted, in a sense having personally internalized their own ideological predicament. (Nor did this dilemma remain an issue with their children and grandchildren: most of those who stayed on the left became New Leftists or social liberals, while others rejoined mainstream Jewish communities. Still others, of course, left the Jewish world altogether.)

The Birobidzhan Project

Birobidzhan, a sparsely populated area of 13,895 square miles (36,490 square kilometers) in the Amur-Ussuri district of the Far Eastern Territory of the USSR, just north of Manchuria, was set aside by the Soviets as an area for Jewish settlement in 1928, twenty years before the Zionist establishment of the state of Israel. It was, in part, the result of Vladimir Lenin's nationality policy, which stated that each of the national groups that formed the Soviet Union would receive a territory in which to pursue cultural autonomy in a socialist framework. Jews in Birobidzhan were to possess their own administrative, educational, and judicial institutions. For the Jewish Communists, the idea was to create a new Soviet Zion, where a proletarian Jewish culture could be developed. Yiddish, rather than Hebrew, would be the national language, and a new socialist literature and arts would replace religion as the primary expression of culture. This would broaden Jewish culture and create a new Jewish spirit.[17]

The Birobidzhan project is probably best understood in the context of that form of Jewish nationalism known as territorialism, a proto-Zionist doctrine that preached the formation of a sovereign Jewish collective in a suitable territory anywhere in the world, and not necessarily in the Land of Israel. From the time of the great upheavals in Russia's Pale of Settlement after 1881, these proposals addressed the lack of civil rights and political exclusion of Jews in the diaspora. The solutions included emigration to and settlement in rural, agricultural areas in Argentina, Australia, Canada, and the United States, among many other places, and even the creation of a Jewish polity in Uganda. So the proposal of a Jewish entity in Birobidzhan aroused wide interest among those who sought a solution to Jewish statelessness, especially among those enamored of the Soviet state or Communist ideology.

In much the same way as Zionist organizations considered themselves support groups for the building of a Jewish commonwealth in Palestine, so did the Jewish Communists propagandize on behalf of the new Jewish Autonomous Region in Birobidzhan, forming groups such as the ICOR (Association for Jewish Colonization in the Soviet Union—*Gezelshaft far Yidishe Kolonizatsye in Ratn-Farband*) in Canada and the United States, ICOS (Organization for Jewish Colonization in Soviet Russia—*Organiztsye far Yidishe Kolonizatsye in Sovyet-Rusland*) in Great Britain, and GEZERD (named for the Soviet organization, Association for the Settlement of Jewish Toilers on the Land—*Alfarbandishe Gezelshaft farn Aynordenen Oyf Erd Arbetndike Yidn in F.S.S.R.*) in Australia and South Africa.

The well-regarded journalist B. Z. Goldberg of the New York Yiddish daily *Der Tog,* who favored the Birobidzhan idea, in 1928 declared it more important than the colonization ongoing in Argentina and Palestine. "[Theodor] Herzl almost took Uganda in the wilds of Africa," he observed. What would Herzl have said had the Tsar offered him Birobidzhan, "and on such terms!" Goldberg suggested that Jews should not pass up this opportunity.[18]

By the mid-1930s a massive propaganda campaign was underway to induce Jewish settlers to move to Birobidzhan. Some of these efforts incorporated the standard Soviet propaganda tools of the era, and included Yiddish-language posters and novels describing a socialist utopia. Posters from the 1930s resemble Zionist literature from the same era, exhorting diaspora Jewry to help build a Jewish land—in Russia. The propaganda impact was so effective that several thousand Jews immigrated to Birobidzhan from outside of the Soviet Union in the 1930s. In 1934 it was officially elevated to the status of a Jewish Autonomous Region. During that time, the Jewish population of the region peaked at almost one-third of the total: some 41,000 Jews had relocated to Birobidzhan. Some spoke optimistically of an eventual Jewish majority of perhaps a million people. It was hoped the region would evolve into a full-fledged Soviet socialist republic, similar to, say, Armenia, Azerbaijan, Kazakhstan, or Ukraine. Hence, the Birobidzhan projects tapped into the subterranean but very powerful secular nationalist sentiments of the Jewish Communist movement.

This worldview, which combined socialism, Yiddishism, and secular nationalism, was part of the ideological baggage that left Eastern Europe along with the massive immigration of east European Jews, and was thus transferred to the countries discussed in this book. As Paul Buhle has recounted, "a Messianic radicalism among the immigrant Jewish workers . . . allowed Communism to appeal to some of the deepest traditions of the community."[19] "Utopian and quasi-messianic visions were . . . endemic to the East European [Jewish] style of politics."[20] This "messianic" aspect of the ideology, as evidenced in the rhetoric of Jewish Communists as they marshalled support for a new Zion, would replace the old Judaic ideal of a return to the Land of Israel with an idealized Soviet Russia as the new "promised land."

The Apogee of Jewish Communism

The period from the mid-1930s to the late 1940s proved to be the historical "moment" for the Jewish Communists. As a result of political developments in the international arena, they benefited from a favourable political climate. In 1935 the Communist International (Comintern), in an attempt to counter the growth of fascism and Nazism, decided to allow Communist parties considerable leeway in their efforts to attract wider segments of their populations, calling for a new "Popular Front" to combat fascism. One such attempt was an appeal to minorities along openly ethnic lines; Jewish Communists were encouraged to assume political and moral leadership of broad alliances within their respective communities.

In the United States especially, the new Popular Front policy initiated a major shift in the attitude of the Jewish Communists, as they began to openly embrace Jewish culture and topics of general Jewish interest that had previously been considered taboo. The pages of the Yiddish Communist press during the Popular Front era were filled with calls for unity among the Jewish masses, campaigns against anti-Semitism, and a renewed interest in secular Yiddish culture, largely absent during the previous period.[21] This was all part of their attempt at establishing the Communists as mainstream leaders in American Jewish life, friendly to Jewish issues. They would no longer define themselves simply as Yiddish-speaking workers, but as *Jewish* Communists, who were an integral part of the larger Jewish community.

Within the next decade, Jewish Communists would become involved in "popular front" campaigns on behalf of anti-fascist struggles in Spain and elsewhere. They called attention to the destruction of the Jews of Eastern Europe. They were in the forefront of support for the Soviet Union in its struggle against Hitler. During World War II, they took their political cue from the Moscow-based Jewish Anti-Fascist Committee, and helped sponsor the 1943 tour of the Soviet Jewish emissaries Itzik Fefer and Shloime Mikhoels to Canada, the United States, Mexico, and Britain. By 1945, most were also favorably disposed toward a Jewish state, and were instrumental in moving the world Communist movement in that direction. This relatively short-lived but favorable conjuncture of ethnic and class forces, whereby their ideological tenets and Jewish interests were to a large extent congruent, enabled Jewish Communists in several countries to post a number of electoral and ideological victories in constituencies with significant Jewish populations.

In the July 1945 British general election, Phil Piratin, a Communist candidate, was elected to Parliament from the predominantly Jewish constituency of Mile End, Stepney. That autumn, the Stepney Communist Party won ten seats on the borough council, and the following spring, two seats on the London County Council. In the Cartier riding of Montreal, Fred Rose, running for the Labor-Progressive (Communist) Party, won election to the House of Commons in 1943 and 1945; two LPP candidates, including J. B. Salsberg, won seats in the 1945 Ontario provincial election. In the United States, Leo Isacson, running on behalf of the Communist-dominated American Labor Party, won election in 1948 to the House of Representatives from the largely Jewish 24th Congressional District in the Bronx, New York. And South Africa witnessed the election, in November 1948, of Sam Kahn, a leading Communist Party theoretician. (He was actually elected by Black Africans in Cape Province.) The movement was also very active in the Jewish communities of Argentina, France, Mexico, and Uruguay.[22]

The Demise of Jewish Communism

Jewish Communism remained a significant force in Jewish life until the mid-1950s when its demise was swift and far-reaching with much of the Jewish Communist orbit crashing to the ground. For, unlike the other leftist Jewish movements, Jewish Communism was itself a political and ideological paradox that would doom it in the end. Although largely built around its own autonomous institutions and operating in its own language, Yiddish, and organizing a Jewish socialist life, it remained (until 1956) voluntarily under the discipline of a non-Jewish state, and a world Communist movement, that would prove to be a major enemy of the Jewish people. In a sense, the ideological basis of the movement, Marxism-Leninism, had always required a "suspension of disbelief" on the part of Jewish Communists. Ideologically, they managed for a few decades to survive in the interstices between the Jewish and Communist worlds. After all, when it came to many of the major works of Marxist writers and political actors, from Marx himself through Lenin and Stalin, their characterizations of Jews were, to say the least, uncharitable, and their polemics often downright anti-Semitic. This vulnerability would prove to be the movement's Achilles heel. The USSR was the pole of reference for Jewish Communists, mainly because of that new state's supposed positive relationship to its Jewish population, and only secondarily because of its supposed economic and political accomplishments. And when that proved to have been a delusion by the mid-1950s, the vast majority of Jewish Communists, forced to choose between their *Jewish* and their *pro-Soviet* attachment to socialism, overwhelmingly chose the former. Belonging to the CP was, even if they felt deep commitment, a contingent and utilitarian, not a basic, element of their identity. It was contingent on their belief that Soviet-style socialism would solve the "Jewish question."

In February 1956, Nikita Khrushchev, leader of the Soviet Union, delivered a speech to the 20th Congress of the Communist Party in which he denounced the crimes committed by Joseph Stalin and his associates. Stalin's anti-Semitic campaigns, which had intensified after 1948, were also finally acknowledged. The Warsaw Yiddish Communist newspaper *Folks-shtime* in April 1956 published articles about the extent and virulence of Stalin's anti-Semitism. All of this came as a shock to Jewish Communists in the western countries. They were already becoming ideologically marginalized within the larger Jewish communities after the establishment of the state of Israel in 1948 and the disillusionment with the Soviet Union greatly accelerated the process. Within a matter of years, the movement virtually vanished. Apart from the failure of Jewish colonization efforts in the Soviet Far East, by the 1950s most American Jews were aware that in Russia the Jewish alliance with victorious Communism that had been entered into with great enthusiasm by some sectors of Soviet Jewry had ended in the destruction not only of traditional Jewish life, something which the Jewish left had, after all, actually desired, "but in the destruction of nearly all aspects of autonomous Jewish life."[23]

For so many decades, the Jewish Communists had defended the USSR: after all, how could a state that had granted Jews national rights in Birobidzhan, allowed for the development of Yiddish-language institutions, and defeated Nazism, have betrayed the Jews? But after Stalin's death and the denunciation of his totalitarian policies by Nikita Khrushchev, when the depth of Soviet anti-Semitism and the forced assimilation policies directed at Soviet Jews under Stalin had become clear, it was too powerful a contradiction to ignore or rationalize. As well, the Birobidzhan project, as so much else, had been exposed as largely fraudulent and a complete failure. The so-called Jewish Autonomous Region was a large "Potemkin village."[24]

Revelations of anti-Semitism in the highest ranks of the Soviet Communist hierarchy also led to defections on the part of "fellow-travelers." The "Jewish problem" was more deep-rooted and difficult of solution than the heady propaganda of the 1930s produced by the Jewish Communist movements had ever imagined. Perhaps the coup de grace was the creation of the state of Israel, to which most overseas Jewish efforts henceforth would be directed. Internationalism seemed a harder faith to sustain after the death of six million Jews. Despite the Allied victory, it had become apparent that European Jewry had been the true losers of the war—and that none of the allied powers had been overly concerned with the crematoria. Many Jews drew the conclusion that the catastrophe was due to statelessness and lack of sovereignty, a condition Israel would at least partially rectify, but which Birobidzhan could not.

The Jewish Communist movement could thus no longer serve as a Jewish diaspora support group for a state that had not only failed to "solve the Jewish question," but had arguably made conditions worse for its Jewish citizens, certainly in terms of cultural and political freedom, a state that turned out to be one that had perpetuated the marginal and exilic condition of Jews rather than liberating them from it. This was indeed a watershed, and after 1956 the contours of Jewish and non-Jewish Communism would speedily diverge, even amongst those who did not immediately quit the Communist parties and renounce Communism altogether. Further shocks were to follow: the unconditional and uncritical Soviet support of the Arab side in the 1967 Arab-Israeli Six-Day War, and a year later the Soviet destruction of a reformist government in Czechoslovakia and the "anti-Zionist" campaigns in Poland, which drove out the remainder of Polish Jewry, including many who had remained loyal to Communism.

The remaining Jewish sympathizers in pro-Communist movements would now be forced to withdraw overt support from any Communist

Party that continued to remain loyal to the Soviet Union. In the end, their Jewish identities trumped their support for the Soviet Union. After all, the Jewish Communists had finally come to recognize that the Soviet Union had proved to be a major danger both to those Jews living under the harsh rule of Communism in the USSR and, later, in Soviet-dominated eastern European countries. As well, given Moscow's increasingly vicious anti-Zionism and support of Arab Middle Eastern countries, it was a danger to those Jews living in Israel itself.

The demise of Jewish Communism was a part of the passing of an entire era in Jewish life. As the state of Israel became the central and most important feature of post-war Jewish life, Birobidzhan receded into the mists of dim memory. The Jewish Communists, for all of their ideals, their cleverness, and their efforts, were never able to prove that a Soviet Jewish republic had actually emerged in the Far East. As Israel's star rose, so did pro-Soviet groups ossify and wither away. The Jewish Communist movement had become caught in the ambiguity, indeed contradictions, of their own ideology: a pro-Soviet internationalism combined with an interest in Jewish national regeneration; support for a Zionist-style enterprise in far-off Siberia but opposition to Zionism itself.

In any case, the Jewish community in the immediate post-war world was a very different place than it had been in the 1930s and 1940s. Jews were moving out of the old downtown neighborhoods and into the suburbs; they were leaving the workforce in the garment industries and entering business and the professions. Jewish Communists found it difficult to reestablish their institutions and gain a hearing for their ideas in these newer areas of settlement. The increasingly bourgeois socioeconomic position of Ambijan's own membership, which had prospered greatly during World War II, made it difficult for the organization to even retain the loyalty of those already in the movement. The dream of a Jewish culture grounded in Communist-inspired political values now appeared absurd.

Finally, there was a large influx of Holocaust survivors into Australia, Canada, and the United States after World War II: most were more traditionalist in culture and religion and harbored few illusions about the USSR and the new people's democracies, in which many had spent periods of time. More recent Jewish immigration from the Soviet Union and its successor states brought further waves of people who were living proof of the failure of the Bolshevik experiment. All these changes shifted the community away from the far-left politically. "The older Yiddish-socialist subculture could not survive this constellation of forces, nor . . . could Communists and other radicals find effective ways of challenging it."[25] As for the broader Jewish community, its interests by the 1960s centered around Israel; most Jews had come to see the USSR as an enemy of the Jewish people and its state.

Some of the Jewish Communists who had been involved with the various support movements would continue their pro-Soviet activities in a much-diminished Communist world; the YKUF and a few other remnants survived the 1950s. They had devoted their entire lives to the movement and remained within its self-contained walls. They belonged to a party that was stronger than any religion. But even after breaking with the international Communist movement, the Jewish Communists would never be able to shake off the stigma in the wider Jewish community of having been a pro-Soviet movement. Lamented Shirley Novick, widow of the former editor of the New York-based Yiddish Communist newspaper, the *Frayhayt*, "We believed in the party like religious Hasidim."[26] Little wonder then, that by the 1960s, they had faded into an insignificant sect.

Irving Howe has remarked that many Jewish Communists were "marked by a deep ambivalence toward everything Jewish. . . . They declared themselves internationalist, even cosmopolitan, in outlook and concerned mostly with raising the class consciousness of all workers, yet they could not escape the impulse common to many immigrant Jews of building a hermetic community of their own."[27] Such "aging immigrants could not give up a lifetime of psychological investment," observed Arthur Hertzberg, and they were, as Paul Lyons wrote about Philadelphia Jewish Communists, "reluctant to abandon [their] protective if shrinking subculture."[28] The Communist Party, observed Nathan Glazer, "was their entire life" and itself had become, as Maurice Isserman put it, "a comfortable retirement home."[29]

To be fair, for some, Communism also retained an ethical core, the search for social justice, and it remained a noble endeavor that had become a barbarous totalitarianism for specific reasons relating to the Soviet leadership, in particular Stalin. A few began to look at other "models," especially China and Cuba. But these countries would be of no particular interest to most Jews who had become Communists or pro-Communists specifically because they were Jewish and the USSR had "solved the Jewish question." As an "ethno-political" movement, after 1956 "Jewish Communism" had virtually ceased to exist.

This book examines the flowering of Jewish Communism in the Anglophone countries of Australia, Canada, Great Britain, South Africa, and the United States. It places the Jewish Communist movement within the historical context of a Jewish left subculture. Other countries where the movement flourished include Argentina, Brazil, Cuba, France, Mexico, and Uruguay, which were also nations with considerable east European Jewish immigration. That story must await another book.

In our volume, Matthew Hoffman looks at Yiddish-language Communists in the United States. Also in America, Jennifer Young provides a study of the Jewish People's Fraternal Order, while Genady Estraikh examines the career of Paul Novick, the long-time editor of the Communist *Frayhayt.*

Henry Srebrnik focuses on the work of pro-Soviet Jewish organizations in Canada, while Ester Reiter concentrates on women in the Canadian Jewish Communist movement, and on the political activities of the United Jewish People's Order. Stephen Cullen discusses the nature of Jewish involvement with Communism in Britain while Philip Mendes provides an overview of the organizations founded by Jewish Communists in Australia. Finally, David Saks describes the political work of a number of influential Jewish Communists active in the struggle against apartheid in South Africa; some lived to see it finally toppled. The concluding chapter sums up our work.

Notes

1. Philip Mendes, "The Rise and Fall of the Jewish/Left Alliance: An Historical and Political Analysis," *Australian Journal of Politics and History* 45, No. 4 (1999): 497. In his expanded study of the disproportionate historical contribution of Jews to the political Left, Mendes attributes the association of Jews with the Left to a combination of four factors: class and ethnic oppression; Jewish cultural values; Left support for Jewish equality; and the urbanization and intellectualism of Jews. See *Jews and the Left: The Rise and Fall of a Political Alliance* (London: Palgrave Macmillan, 2014), 5–18.

2. Anita Shapira, "'Black Night—White Snow': Attitudes of the Palestinian Labor Movement to the Russian Revolution, 1917–1929," in *Essential Papers on Jews and the Left*, ed. Ezra Mendelsohn (New York: New York University Press, 1997), 241.

3. The literature on Marxist attitudes, both positive and negative, toward the national aspirations of the Jewish people is truly enormous. See Enzo Traverso, *The Marxists and the Jewish Question: The History of a Debate (1843–1943)*, trans. Bernard Gibbons (Atlantic Highlands, NJ: Humanities Press, 1994). See also Walker Connor, *The National Question in Marxist-Leninist Theory and Strategy* (Princeton, NJ: Princeton University Press, 1984); Ronaldo Munck, *The Difficult Dialogue: Marxism and Nationalism* (London: Zed Books, 1986); and Ephraim Nimni, *Marxism and Nationalism: Theoretical Origins of a Political Crisis* (London: Pluto Press, 1991) for a survey of historic Communist positions on nationality.

4. David Leviatin, *Followers of the Trail: Jewish Working-Class Radicals in America* (New Haven, CT: Yale University Press, 1989), 98.

5. Matthew Hoffman, "The Red Divide: The Conflict Between Communists and their Opponents in the American Yiddish Press," *American Jewish History* 96, No. 1 (2010): 22, citing Moyshe Olgin, "The Only Way Open For Jews," *Morgn-Frayhayt*, November 3, 1936.

6. Zosa Szajkowski, *Jews, Wars, and Communism* Vol. I: *The Attitude of American Jews to World War I, the Russian Revolutions of 1917, and Communism (1914–1945)* (New York: Ktav, 1972), 408–12.

7. Daniel Soyer, "Back to the Future: American Jews Visit the Soviet Union in the 1920s and 1930s," *Jewish Social Studies* 6, No. 3 (2000): 125–26, 130.

8. Daniel Soyer, "Soviet Travel and the Making of an American Jewish Communist: Moissaye Olgin's Trip to Russia in 1920–1921," *American Communist History* 4, No. 1 (2005): 1, 3–5, 20.

9. Gennady Estraikh, "The Yiddish-Language Communist Press," in *Dark Times, Dire Decisions: Jews and Communism* (*Studies in Contemporary Jewry* 20), eds. Dan Diner and Jonathan Frankel (New York: Oxford University Press, 2004): 66.

10. Zvi Gitelman, "Introduction," in *The Quest for Utopia: Jewish Political Ideas and Institutions Through the Ages*, ed. Zvi Gitelman (Armonk, NY: M. E. Sharpe, 1992), x–xi.

11. Bat-Ami Zucker, "The 'Jewish Bureau': The Organization of American Jewish Communists in the 1930s," in *Modern History: Bar-Ilan Studies in History III*, ed. Michael J. Cohen (Ramat-Gan, Israel: Bar-Ilan University Press, 1991), 146.

12. Sholem Shtern, "Bageygenishn un shmusen mit Kalman Marmor," *Yidishe Kultur* 43, No. 5 (1981): 14 (emphasis in original). For more on Marmor, see his biography, *Mayn Lebns-geshikhte*, 2 vols. (New York: YKUF, 1959).

13. Mick Mindel, "Socialist Eastenders," *Jewish Socialist* 6/7 (1986): 26.

14. *Doikayt* ("here-ness") was the Bundist principle that called for Jews "to remain in the Diaspora and fight for their national and political rights rather than waste their proletarian energy on building a Jewish state." It was anti-Zionist but was also opposed to the Communist project in the Soviet Union. Gennady Estraikh, "Professing Leninist Yiddishkayt: The Decline of American Yiddish Communism," *American Jewish History* 96, No. 1 (2010): 56.

15. Arthur Liebman, *Jews and the Left* (New York, 1979), 305.

16. Melech Epstein, *The Jew and Communism: The Story of Early Communist Victories and Ultimate Defeats in the Jewish Community, U.S.A. 1919–1941* (New York: Trade Union Sponsoring Committee, 1959), 78.

17. An excellent overview of the entire project is provided by Allan Laine Kagedan, *Soviet Zion: The Quest for a Russian Jewish Homeland* (New York: St. Martin's Press, 1994), and Robert Weinberg, *Stalin's Forgotten Zion: Birobidzhan and the Making of a Soviet Jewish Homeland. An Illustrated History, 1928–1996* (Berkeley: University of California Press, 1998).

18. B. Z. Goldberg, "Tsvishn 'icor'-mentshn," *ICOR* 1, No. 1 (1928): 2–4.

19. Paul Buhle, "Jews and American Communism: The Cultural Question," *Radical History Review* 23 (Spring, 1980): 11, 14.

20. Jonathan Frankel, "Modern Jewish Politics East and West (1840–1939): Utopia, Myth, Reality," in Gitelman, *The Quest for Utopia*, 84.

21. See Bat-Ami Zucker, "American Jewish Communists and Jewish Culture in the 1930s," in *Modern Judaism* 14, No. 2 (May, 1994), 175–85, for an in-depth look at the transition from the Third Period to the Popular Front in terms of Jewish Communist approaches to Jewish culture.

22. For a detailed account of this history, see Henry Srebrnik, *London Jews and British Communism, 1935–1945* (London: Vallentine Mitchell, 1995); *Jerusalem on the Amur: Birobidzhan and the Canadian Jewish Communist Movement, 1924–1951* (Montreal and Kingston: McGill-Queen's University Press, 2008); and *Dreams of Nationhood: American Jewish Communists and the Soviet Birobidzhan Project, 1924–1951* (Boston: Academic Studies Press, 2010).

23. Ezra Mendelsohn, *On Modern Jewish Politics* (New York: Oxford University Press, 1993), 119.

24. Ezer Goldberg, "A Yubl vos vert nisht Gefeyert: 25 Yor fun der Birobidzhaner Autonomer Gegnt," *Unzer Tsayt* 10 (1959): 30.

25. Paul Lyons, "Philadelphia Jews and Radicalism: The American Jewish Congress Cleans House," in *Philadelphia Jewish Life, 1940–1985*, ed. Murray Friedman (Philadelphia: Temple University Press, 2003), 61.

26. Interview with Shirley Novick, New York, June 13, 1996.

27. Irving Howe, *World of Our Fathers: The Journey of the East European Jews to America and the Life They Found and Made* (New York: Simon and Schuster, 1976), 330.

28. Arthur Hertzberg, *The Jews in America: Four Centuries of an Uneasy Encounter: A History* (New York: Simon and Schuster, 1989), 265; Paul Lyons, *Philadelphia Communists, 1936–1956* (Philadelphia: Temple University Press, 1982), 165.

29. Nathan Glazer, *The Social Basis of American Communism* (Westport, CT: Greenwood Press edition, 1974), 165; Maurice Isserman, *If I Had a Hammer . . . : The Death of the Old Left and the Birth of the New Left* (New York: Basic Books, 1987), 24.

2

"At What Cost Comrades"?

Exploring the Jewishness of Yiddish-Speaking Communists in the United States

Matthew Hoffman

At a Memorial Meeting in New York on November 23, 1940, honoring the one-year anniversary of the death of Moyshe Olgin, the long-time editor of the Yiddish Communist daily, *Morgn-Frayhayt* (*Morning Freedom*), Earl Browder, the general secretary of the American Communist Party, commemorated Olgin's life. In the speech he gave, entitled "In Memory of a Great Jewish Leader," Browder referred to Olgin as "a great American Communist, a great leader of the Jewish people, and a great man" seeing him as both a "true son of the Jewish people [and] a true communist."[1] Browder affirmed the dual identity of Olgin as being both fully Jewish and fully communist at once, not seeing these identities as mutually exclusive, but as reinforcing each other, one not being privileged above the other.

Just over a year prior to this meeting, a few weeks before Olgin died, S. Margoshes, the prominent editor of the popular Yiddish daily, *Der Tog* (*The Day*), excoriated Olgin, as a "so-called Jewish leader" and a Jewish anti-Semite "at one with Father Coughlin [and] Fritz Kuhn," both notorious anti-Semites.[2] He claimed that Olgin's writing was "sheer Nazi propaganda," which should be "treated only in the same fashion we treat the fulminations of a Streicher, of a Goebbels."[3] This kind of scathing denunciation of Olgin, and the Jewish Communists in general, was fairly common in the Yiddish press; the *Forverts*, *Tog*, and others—socialists, Zionists, and traditionalists alike—had for years condemned the Jewish Communists as traitors to Jewish life, betrayers of the Jewish tradition, and enemies of the Jewish people."[4]

Which side was more accurate? How should we understand Olgin and his comrades? These two divergent perspectives on Moyshe Olgin, and Yiddish-speaking Communists more generally, raise a variety of crucial questions about the identity of Jewish Communists and the nature of Yiddish Communist culture. What was the relationship between being a communist and being a Jew? Were these two things mutually exclusive or inextricably linked? Did this change as communist policy evolved? Was there some kind of cost or trade-off to one's Jewishness (*yidishkayt*), however defined, in becoming a communist? What was the Yiddish-speaking Communists' vision of Yiddish culture in America and how did they conceive of this culture in terms of its *yidishkayt*, especially vis-à-vis their commitment to communist internationalism as defined by the Party? What were the central challenges that the leading Yiddish Communist ideologues like Olgin faced in their attempt to combine communist internationalism and Yiddish culture? After all, these were persistent questions, asked both by communists and their opponents, since the Party's establishment in America in 1921, and by numerous scholars who have analyzed this relationship between Jewishness and communism.[5]

In this chapter I attempt to illustrate that despite their commitment to communism and opposition to Jewish particularism, the Yiddish-speaking Communists created a uniquely Jewish form of communist culture. This holds true from the inception of the party onwards, despite ideological shifts in the Communist Party (CP) line. Whether during the formative years of American Communism (1921–1928), the ideologically rigid and politically militant Third Period (1928–1935), or the ideologically looser Popular Front era (1935–1939 and 1941–1945), the leading Yiddish-speaking Communist intellectuals created a distinctively Jewish form of communist culture and identity, unlike other forms of both Jewish and communist identity, which was often at odds with both mainstream Jewish and communist leadership. By focusing here especially on Jewish Communist intellectuals like Olgin (1878–1939), Kalman Marmor (1876–1956), and Moyshe Katz (1885–1960), and looking at the period when the communist line was most hostile to any particularistic forms of ethnic or national identity—from 1925 to 1935—we can see how these Yiddish-speaking Communists forged what they believed to be a true union of communism and *yidishkayt*: a progressive, proletarian culture in Yiddish for Jewish workers.

For these Jewish Communists, their commitment to Yiddish and to maintaining an ethnic/national form to their expression of communism was consistent with their understanding of communist internationalism and the idea of "national in form, socialist in content" that was a pillar of the Leninist Nationality policy of the Soviet Union. Much as David Shneer has argued in his work on Yiddish and the creation of a Soviet Jewish culture,[6] I argue that these Jewish Communists were building on earlier Jewish reformist traditions, such as the Haskalah and the Bund, in merging a new ideology—in this case communism—with a revised form of Jewish culture and identity. Whereas the Jewish Communists, at least until the Popular Front era, rejected a sense of Jewish nationalism or Jewish national identity in favor of a class-based identification with the Jewish working masses, they still eschewed a completely universalistic and assimilationist approach that would have included the rejection of Yiddish and the Communist Jewish subculture of groups and institutions that they created. Yiddish may have been seen by some of them as a purely expedient means of propagandizing to the Jewish masses (as it was by Maskilim and Bundists at first), but even when faced with pressure from within the CP, from both Jewish and non-Jewish Communists who favored linguistic assimilation and the amalgamation of Jewish workers with the native-born, they fought vigorously to maintain a Yiddish Communist identity with its unique cultural expressions and institutions.

Unlike many who argue that communist policy suppressed an authentic Jewish identity and culture, especially when the Party came out against Jewish causes or movements,[7] I propose that, ironically, it was especially during the most ideologically rigid or "repressive" periods (1925–1935) that the most distinctive form of Jewish Communist identity was created. After 1935 and the adoption of the Popular Front, many scholars have shown how the Jewish Communists embraced a more explicitly open Jewish cultural identity, even cooperating with non-communist groups in Jewish cultural endeavors.[8] Yet, I argue that after the Popular Front begins, the communists' form of Jewishness becomes much less distinctive and more similar to other forms of left-wing Jewish identity and culture. Indeed, it was when the most stringent attempt to separate the Jewish Communists from any traditional forms of Jewish identity and culture occurred that the most innovative combination of communism and *yidishkayt* took place.

From its inception in 1921, the Jewish Section, or later, Bureau, of the Central Committee of the Communist Party USA (CPUSA) played a major role in the growth and development of the Communist Party in the United States. Jewish intellectuals, writers, labor leaders, and the Jewish "toiling masses" helped establish the Communist Party as a significant political force on the American scene, especially in the Depression era leading up to World War Two.[9] Yet, from the outset, the nature of the "Jewish" or "national" element of the Jewish Bureau was a constant source of tension for American Jewish Communists as well as for the Party as a whole. For Jews, even the long-time secular socialists who formed the intellectual base of the Jewish section of the Party, they had to navigate between embracing communist internationalism in its peculiar Americanized form on the one hand, and any expression of Jewish particularism on the other. Before joining the Party, many Jews, like Moyshe Olgin and his peers, had been active in the Bund and other Jewish socialist or socialist-Zionist groups that had championed secular Yiddish culture.[10] So, despite their new ideological commitment to proletarian internationalism and staunch opposition to "bourgeois" forms of nationalism, like Zionism, they retained a strong attachment to the Yiddish language and various forms of secular Yiddish culture, an attachment that was certainly strained at times by their allegiance to the Communist Party, but never severed.

For its part, the Central Committee of the CPUSA was initially supportive of foreign-born members of the Party having their own language sections or federations, with various expressions of culture in those languages, as long as they essentially adhered to the Party line. By the end of the 1920s however, there was a shift in the Party's attitude toward Americanization, part of a larger trend of Bolshevization, and they pushed the foreign-language sections to adopt English and to amalgamate with native-born workers.[11] The new CP policy toward national groups, laid out in the 1930 "Resolution on Language Work," was to downplay any kind of nationalism while allowing for foreign-language publications and activities solely as a way to bolster the "revolutionary struggles of the working class in the United States."[12] The Party's new line combined Marxist internationalism with a "Melting Pot" approach to American society that brought pressure on Jewish Communists to avoid any expression of Jewish particularism, including secular Yiddish culture. So, what did the Yiddish-speaking Communists do? How did they reconcile their dual commitments to Yiddishism and communism—to being Jewish and communist in meaningful ways at one and the same time? And how did the CP leadership understand the relationship between communism and Jewishness?

Leading scholars of American Jewish Communists, especially the Yiddish-language section of the CPUSA in the interwar years, have long pointed to the ever-present tension between Jewish and Communist identities. In his important study of Jewish Communists, Tony Michels argues that "the Yiddish-speaking immigrant communist movement . . . should be understood within the context of deep-seated conflicts within the immigrant Jewish community. At the heart of these conflicts was a fundamental tension in modern Jewish politics . . . between particularistic and universalistic goals and political strategies."[13] In the case of the Yiddish Communist newspaper, the *Frayhayt*, Michels asserts that from early on there was a constant tension between tight Party control of the paper and its own "political and cultural autonomy," which included the "promotion of Yiddish culture."[14] He claims that "from 1923 onward, the Yiddish-speaking communist movement would continually have to negotiate between its cultural goals and the political dictates of the party."[15] Ultimately, Michels concludes that his study shows "how individuals joined the party with idealistic visions of a radicalized, Yiddish culture that were compromised or quashed altogether by the prerogatives of the party leadership and, by extension, the Soviet Union."[16] While I agree that this may have been the case for some Jewish Communists, especially in the early years of the Party, I think that it tends to downplay the possibility that Jewish Communists like Olgin or Marmor did not see their "cultural goals" as being wholly at odds with the political dictates of the Party. Olgin's desire to create a truly proletarian Yiddish culture largely conformed to Party ideology as well as his own uniquely Jewish cultural goals.

Others have tried to show how this fundamental tension led to a synthesis of Jewish and Communist identities and ideologies. In his study of Jews and American Communism, Paul Buhle argues that Yiddish-speaking radicals had "the sense of Communism as realization of 'national' (or ethnic) and international aspirations simultaneously. To Yiddish-speaking Communist recruits, Bolshevism did not imply 'national nihilism,' but rather the advance of cultural self-identity in a movement recast according to Leninist faith."[17] I would suggest that Olgin and many of his contemporaries fit this mold rather well. Like Michels however, Buhle, too, argues that the Party made this kind of Jewish-Communist synthesis quite difficult. He posits that the ideological rigidity of communism in the late 1920s and 30s (before the Popular Front era) did much to quash the creativity and imaginativeness of radical Yiddish culture in that period. Buhle claims that this sent less ideologically committed artists out of the communist camp or curtailed the creative careers of ideologues like Moyshe Olgin.[18] Again, this claim is somewhat subjective. Was Olgin's creative career curtailed because of the CP's rigid ideological and political orientation? During these years he was, I would argue, very creatively merging communist proletarian culture with a new form of secular Jewish identity. While Buhle convincingly demonstrates that the merging of culture and politics was the secret strength of Yiddish Communism,[19] he does not fully explore the extent to which ideologically committed Jewish Communists were able to realize "ethnic and international aspirations simultaneously," even during the more rigid Third Period.

Others, such as Ezra Mendelsohn, have argued against the existence of this type of hybrid Jewish-Communist identity altogether. Mendelsohn proclaims that the Communist Party, especially the "Jewish sections" within it, functioned as "halfway houses, positioned between the ultimately doomed ghetto and a future of universal brotherhood."[20] In other words, the Jewish Communists' support for the "proletarian, Yiddish-speaking Jewish nation" was only temporary, an expedient means of transforming working-class Jews into communist cosmopolitans for whom the Yiddish language and Jewish culture have no inherent worth or viable future.[21] According to this theory, the communists simply used Jewish culture as a way to manipulate the Jewish street. In some cases, this may have been true, but as a theory for understanding Jewish communism more broadly, it is faulty. I suggest that for the leading figures of Yiddish-language communism in America—Moyshe Olgin, Kalman Marmor, Moyshe Katz, and others—Mendelsohn's model is mistaken. As we shall see below, their commitment to a hybrid identity of communism and secular *yidishkayt* was more deeply rooted and genuine than Mendelsohn's theory supposes.

At times, these figures redefined their understanding of secular Yiddish culture, but their commitment to it was abiding and formed a core of their cultural and intellectual vision. As Bat-Ami Zucker has argued about these Yiddish-speaking Communists, especially in the 1930s, "though they considered themselves loyal communists and adhered to communist beliefs, they never let go and kept proclaiming that they belonged to the Jewish people. Their use of Yiddish, and the Jewish content of their cultural and educational activities speak for the conscious preservation of their Jewishness."[22] Indeed, I would add that unlike the more assimilated, English-speaking, American Jewish Communists, such as Ben Gitlow or Jay Lovestone (as well as many others), the Yiddish-language Communists always retained strong links to their Jewish ethnicity and cultural identity. They wanted to bring communism to the Yiddish-speaking, immigrant workers, not simply to the American working classes.

Many, like Mendelsohn, who questioned the Jewish cultural allegiances of the Jewish Communists often pointed to the fact that Jewish Communist culture was completely controlled by and subservient to the dictates of the Communist Party, whether the Comintern in Moscow, or the Central Committee in New York.[23] This theory alleges that Jewish Communists were only interested in Jewish or Yiddish culture when the Party told them (or allowed them) to be; they slavishly followed the Party line at all times, even when it was in stark contrast to perceived Jewish interests or issues. On the one hand, I agree that leading Yiddish Communists, like Olgin, Marmor, and Katz, were outwardly loyal to the Party line on all important issues until the day they died (1939, 1956, and 1960, respectively). The same could be said for the important Yiddish Communist organs, led by the *Frayhayt*. In some cases, especially concerning the issues of Zionism and Palestine, the CP line and the Jewish Communists' support for it, clearly put them at odds with the vast majority of Yiddish-speaking Jews in America. On the other hand, I would argue that the Yiddish Communist leaders and Yiddish Communist periodicals, consistently maintained a commitment to secular Yiddish culture in ways they felt coalesced with, or at least did not blatantly contradict, the prevailing communist policies of the day, even when other leaders of the Party felt otherwise. They did not simply pretend to be interested in secular Yiddish culture as an expedient means to "dupe Jewish workers into joining the Party."[24] They believed that they were merging the best of both traditions and ideologies—secular *yidishkayt* and communism.

Throughout the 1920s and early 1930s, most of Olgin's articles and essays on the cultural front focused on creating and developing a proletarian literature and culture in Yiddish for the Jewish working class.[25] His vision was very much in line with the Yiddish-speaking Communists in the Soviet Union who attempted to create a Soviet Jewish culture that followed the Leninist model of "national in form, socialist in content."[26] Olgin saw Yiddish as a vehicle through which to create proletarian culture for the Yiddish-speaking masses; it was "an instrument for class struggle."[27] Other than his use of Yiddish and focus on the Jewish working class, Olgin typically rejected national themes or elements of Jewish culture that were not class-conscious (except for during the Popular Front era). Especially during the militant Third Period, but even to an extent earlier, Olgin attempted to forge a proletarian Yiddish culture that distinguished itself from what he deemed to be purely "national" forms of Jewish culture, including the cultural work of other socialist Jewish parties, such as the Bund. A former Bundist himself, Olgin became critical of the Bund for not fighting for a truly proletarian culture, claiming that on the cultural front, the Bund, unlike the communists, was not class-conscious.[28]

In the same vein, Marmor and other leading Yiddish Communist ideologues attempted to set apart their conceptualization of a class-oriented culture in Yiddish from other left-wing forms of Yiddish culture. They criticized secular Yiddishists, like Khaim Zhitlovsky and others, whom they saw as working for a common, national Jewish culture that was not concerned with class differences. According to Marmor, "for the Yiddishists, as for the Zionists, language and culture are abstract ideals, a kind of shrine around which they can unite boss and worker as one people with the same 'national interests.' "[29] Against this approach, the communists sought to replace the existing forms of national Jewish culture with a new, proletarian Yiddish culture for the Jewish worker. According to this perspective, Yiddish was not to be celebrated because it was the national language of the Jews, rather, it was only valuable as long as it served to "mobilize the toiling masses in their struggle against capitalism."[30] Olgin, Marmor, and their comrades tried to create a revolutionary culture in Yiddish that was based on Marxist-Leninist principles.

So, was this, as Mendelsohn postulates, just an expedient means of transforming working-class Jews into communist cosmopolitans for whom the Yiddish language and Jewish culture have no inherent worth or viable future?[31]

I would argue not. By creating this culture in Yiddish, and establishing cultural institutions for Jews in Yiddish, these Jewish Communists, very deliberately, stamped this culture as Jewish, not simply a universal communist culture in which Jews could participate. This type of "communist cosmopolitan" culture already existed in the United States, and many Jews did participate in it as English-speaking Communists who happened to be Jews.

Instead of adopting this assimilationist model, part of the Yiddish-speaking Communists' effort to create a progressive, proletarian culture in Yiddish involved establishing a number of cultural organizations within the Yiddish-speaking, Jewish immigrant orbit, forming what Arthur Liebman has called a "communist-oriented subculture."[32] Some of these organizations included musical groups (*Frayhayt Gezangs Farayn*), Jewish workers' clubs, a Jewish workers' university, a Yiddish proletarian theatre company (*Arbeter teater farband* or ARTEF), a fraternal order for radical Jewish workers, the International Workers Order (IWO), Yiddish schools for workers' children (*Arbeter orden shuln*), and summer camps for Jewish workers and their families.[33] These groups both promulgated communist ideals and provided radical, Yiddish-speaking Jews—many of whom were not necessarily identified as communists—a common cultural experience. In his discussion of this Jewish Communist-oriented subculture, Liebman observed that for Yiddish-speaking Communists, "their immersion in a Yiddish Communist subculture had produced a rather loyal following for the Party in general and for Yiddish Communism in particular. The role of ideology and politics, however, in the post-World War II era was undoubtedly subordinate to the decades-long social network that they had forged."[34] Although Liebman was not focusing solely on the Third Period years, but also on the Popular Front era and beyond, his observation helps to demonstrate that the very existence of such a pervasive cultural and social framework for Yiddish-speaking, Communist-oriented Jews, regardless of its ideological content, worked to create a distinctively Jewish-Communist culture. Paul Buhle also argued that it was this particularistic, ethnic cultural component of American Jewish Communism that made it such a popular movement among Jewish immigrants.[35]

Communist intellectuals such as Olgin, Marmor, and Katz played a large role in these communist-affiliated cultural organizations, often editing or writing for their official journals, or serving as secretary or director of the institution itself. For example, Kalman Marmor served as president of the ARTEF and editor of its official journal, *Artef*; he became the cultural director of the IWO upon its establishment in 1930, the editor of its Yiddish journal, *Der Funk* (*The Spark*), and the director of its Yiddish school network; he was a faculty member of the Jewish Workers' University (and in the late 1930s, served as its director), and a regular contributor to the *Morgn-Frayhayt* and to the Communist Yiddish monthly, *Der Hamer* (*The Hammer*). Olgin, too, was an important figure within this larger Jewish Communist cultural world; besides serving as the founding editor of the *Frayhayt* in 1922 and then again from 1929–1939, he also edited *Der Hamer* from 1926 to 1939, and played a leading role in the ARTEF, the Jewish Workers' clubs, the Jewish Music Alliance (*Yidishen muzik farband*), the IWO and the IWO Yiddish schools and summer camps, and the Yiddish Proletarian Writers' Union (Proletpen).[36]

Some scholars have suggested that Olgin's active involvement in building Jewish Communist institutions might have actually hindered his importance and power within the CP. On this point Harvey Klehr suggests that "although he served on the Central Committee for a number of years, Olgin never became a power within the Party, handicapped by his reluctance to surrender his interest in Jewish affairs."[37] This reflects the fact that many within the Party, Jews and non-Jews alike, frowned upon the building up of separate, foreign-language cultural institutions along ethnic or national lines, especially during the Third Period.[38] Despite this, Olgin, Marmor, Katz, and others, invested a tremendous amount of time and energy in creating a separate, Yiddish-speaking cultural network for Jewish Communists in the 1920s and early 1930s, instead of abandoning their "Jewish cultural work" in favor of general Party work in English.[39] These Yiddish-speaking Communists pushed the boundaries of Third-Period communism by maintaining this ethnic, cultural component as a distinctive and integral part of their radicalism.

One of the linchpins of Jewish Communist ideology and a major factor in the Yiddish-speaking Communist subculture was support for the Soviet Union. The Soviet Union was the *axis mundi* for communist parties worldwide in the years following the Bolshevik Revolution, often depicted in romantic, glowing terms as a socialist utopia and workers' paradise. American Communists were no different in this regard, and a pro-Soviet orientation and strong connection to the Soviet Union were major aspects of American communism. However, for the Yiddish-speaking Communists, the Soviet Union was more than a flawless, socialist utopia, it was a *Jewish* utopia as well. From the early 1920s until 1956 and the revelation of Stalin's crimes against the Soviet Jews, the Yiddish-language Communist press and cultural organizations consistently championed the Soviet Union, in part, as the solution to the Jewish national question. All Yiddish-language Party organs and intellectuals emphasized the fact that the Soviet Union outlawed anti-Semitism and brought equal rights to Jews as a national minority with its own Yiddish-language culture and institutions, which the Soviet state supported.

Moreover, the ICOR (*Gezelshaft far Yidishe Kolonizatsye in Ratn-Farband*), a non-partisan organization with close ties to the Party was formed in 1924, both to promote Jewish agricultural colonization in the Soviet Union as well as to advocate for the Soviet Union among left-wing Jews in America.[40] The ICOR quickly became an integral part of the Jewish Communist subculture, sponsoring public talks, organizing mass demonstrations in support of the Soviet Union, publishing pro-Soviet brochures, and eventually publishing its own journal *Nailebn* (*New Life*), from 1935 to 1950.[41] Especially after 1928 and the initiation of the Soviet plan to resettle Jews in their own national autonomous region in Birobidzhan (in the Soviet Far East), the ICOR and its communist supporters looked to the Soviet Union as the land of Jewish national emancipation.

Yiddish Communist leaders like Olgin, Marmor, Katz, and others tirelessly campaigned for the Birobidzhan settlement project and continually reiterated their central message that the Soviet Union was a panacea for the

Jews *qua* Jews. In a 1930 ICOR publication entitled *Di lage fun di yidn in Sovetn-Farband* ("The Position of Jews in the Soviet Union"), *Frayhayt* contributor, Paul Novick, who took over as *Frayhayt* editor after Olgin died in 1939, incorporated a plethora of facts and figures to demonstrate how the Soviet Jews were thriving economically and culturally. In his forward, which he titled "To the Jewish masses in America," Novick began by declaring that the Soviet Union was "the first and only government in history that does everything in its power to improve the life of the Jewish masses."[42] Likewise, in his many articles and speeches about the Soviet Union, Olgin often highlighted the Jews' positive treatment and progress there. In an article on Jews and non-Jews in the Soviet Union, Olgin began by musing, "I often think: where in the world is there the same kind of equality between Jews and non-Jews as in the Soviet Union?"[43] In another article, Olgin made a claim similar to Novick's, writing that "anyone who has seen the life of the Jewish masses under the hammer and sickle would surely conclude that 'the Bolsheviks gave the Jews absolute freedom, the likes of which they had never before experienced in history.' "[44] These are just a few of the countless examples of Yiddish-speaking Communists using specifically Jewish criteria in their support for the Soviet Union; their seemingly internationalist position was, at least in part, inspired by national-ethnic considerations.[45]

There were still other ways in which the proletarian culture of the Yiddish-speaking Communists was informed by Jewish cultural concerns. Despite eschewing "national" forms of Jewish culture, these Yiddish Communist intellectuals, led by Olgin and Marmor, also maintained an ongoing interest in Yiddish literary history.[46] Throughout his communist period (1921–1939), Olgin wrote works of literary criticism on many leading Yiddish writers. Writing solely in Yiddish Communist publications, Olgin published numerous studies of classical Yiddish authors, such as Mendele, Peretz, and Sholem Aleichem, who were not "revolutionary writers" in the communist sense, in which he tried to identify "unconscious" proletarian elements in their works.[47] Marmor was also a scholar of Yiddish literature, who published authoritative studies of leading Yiddish poets, especially the early generation of American socialist-oriented poets, such as David Edelstadt, Joseph Bovshover, and Morris Winchevsky.

In an essay on Sholem Aleichem that appeared in the *Frayhayt* on May 25, 1929, Olgin acknowledged that although he was solidly middle class, Sholem Aleichem was an "historical figure that the working class had adopted as part of its literary heritage," adding that there were "parts of this heritage that the worker must discard as well as many pearls that will enrich him."[48] In other words, the Jewish Communists needed to recuperate Sholem Aleichem by focusing on the class-conscious elements in his writing, and rejecting the bourgeois aspects.[49] This begs the question: why would Olgin, who was concerned with building a proletarian culture for the Jewish working class, focus on bourgeois Jewish writers like Sholem Aleichem? I would suggest that Olgin and Marmor were mining Yiddish literature and culture to create a "useable past" that conformed to their own class-conscious, revolutionary paradigm. Instead of focusing exclusively on communist or class-conscious literature—past and present—these Yiddish-speaking communists persisted in engaging with forms of non-communist Jewish culture. They actively sought out those aspects of Jewish history, culture, and literature that they felt conformed to their own class-conscious view. I would argue that Olgin's interest in making Sholem Aleichem "kosher for communists"[50] demonstrates his ongoing attempt to merge the particular and the universal, to bring together his communist ideology and his attachment to secular *yidishkayt*. In many ways, this kind of selective, ideologically driven use of the Jewish past was quite common in other modern Jewish movements as well, especially Zionism.

If, as Michels and others have claimed, the Yiddish-speaking Communists were forced to negotiate between their "cultural goals and the political dictates of the party," then to what extent were their agenda and the content of their cultural organs determined by Party dictates? Were the Yiddish-speaking Communists, as their contemporaneous opponents and many contemporary scholars have charged, completely subservient to the political demands of the Party at the expense of their Jewish loyalties? To begin to answer these questions we must first keep in mind that Jewish Communists were among those in the Party exercising such control, so this issue should not be viewed in such binary terms as "CP equals non-Jews," and "Yiddish communists equals Jews."[51] There were many prominent Jewish members of the Central Committee, both Yiddish-speaking, and more assimilated Jews.[52] Moreover, the secretary of the Jewish Bureau of the Party, a position always held by a Yiddish-speaking Jew, was responsible for making sure that Yiddish-language Communist organs and cultural activities fell in line with CP policies.[53] A figure like Joseph Sultan, who was secretary of the Jewish Bureau in the 1930s, was both a Party official and a committed Yiddish cultural activist for his entire career.[54]

From almost the inception of the CPUSA in the early 1920s, the fact of Party control of its affiliated cultural organs, especially the communist press, is easy to establish. It is exceedingly clear from numerous communiqués sent to the communist paper editors that the Party exercised strict control over what appeared in its papers, including the English-language *Daily Worker*, as well as foreign-language papers like the *Frayhayt*.[55] In the case of the *Frayhayt*, it began as an independent-minded, communist paper steeped in Yiddish secular culture. Yet, from shortly after its founding in 1922, the *Frayhayt* editors worked in close cooperation with the Agitprop department of the Central Committee of the Party, which determined particular content to include in the communist dailies. For example, a letter to the *Frayhayt* editors on November 4, 1925, chastised the paper for including an article that was critical of the Proletarian Art Theatre. The letter's author ("General Secretary, District Two") declared "please arrange that no such attack shall appear in the future against any organizations that consist of Party members."[56] Clearly, particular editorial opinions and even theatre reviews were subject to Party suppression, and this was not an isolated instance, but an ongoing policy. For instance, in a letter to *Frayhayt* editor, Melech Epstein, from January 12, 1928, the Party district organizer chided the *Frayhayt* for not publishing any notice of Party membership meetings and wanted to ensure that "enough pressure may be brought upon your editorial staff to correct situations like this."[57] These kinds of rebukes were quite common. The papers were expected to serve as effective and obedient voices of the Party.

The type of material to be suppressed or included might have changed from period to period, but Party control over content in Party organs was a constant. These Party intercessions were not just limited to general "dos and don'ts," and often spelled out very detailed directions on what to include. A letter from June 7, 1932 to the foreign-language editors of the communist press gave specific directions on translating a review of Communist presidential candidate, William Z. Foster's book *Towards Soviet America* and how to adapt the review to suit the "special needs" of the foreign-language readers, as well as suggestions for promoting the book among workers.[58] Newspaper contents as well as the attendance of Party meetings and the giving of public lectures were tightly regulated and organized by the Party's Central Committee; disciplinary actions were threatened for lack of compliance.

Besides playing such a censorial role with the press, the Party also maintained close control over the cultural work of its leading intellectuals, such as Kalman Marmor. Throughout the 1920s and '30s, Marmor received numerous directives from the Central Committee and Agitprop department to attend meetings and to give public speeches, in Yiddish, on pre-selected topics. The Party called on Marmor to give lectures on a variety of subjects, ranging from famous Yiddish writers like Mendele and Sholem Aleichem, to class struggle in Jewish history, to lofty themes like "the role of science in human progress." Clearly, the inclusion of explicitly Jewish cultural topics was acceptable, as long as the Party had some oversight as to which topics they were. Marmor's speeches at gatherings such as this did not need to be pre-approved, but if a public speech or article in the *Frayhayt* deviated from the Party line in some way, there was typically a letter to the speaker or the editor, or the Jewish Bureau leaders, calling attention to such deviations and threatening consequences if they continued. In one letter to Marmor from October 17, 1925, the Jewish Section secretary, B. Lifshitz, informed him that the Agitprop department of the Jewish Section of the Party wanted to review all of the lecture topics being assigned to "change them as needed so they conformed more to the current political conditions."[59] This verifies that the Party could control the topics of lectures given under its auspices, though, ultimately, Marmor, or other speakers, still had final word as to what to include in their public talks.

Marmor was also ordered to address anti-religious "mass meetings" at Jewish workers' clubs and other venues, during the Jewish High Holidays, especially on Yom Kippur. In a letter from August 3, 1926, Lifshitz notified Marmor that he would be addressing an anti-religious meeting on Yom Kippur at one workers' club, and the following week he would be the featured speaker at a "Sholem Aleichem evening" at another workers' club.[60] This demonstrates the type of Jewishly engaged secularism that Marmor and Yiddish Communists like him often promoted. Opposition to Jewish religion, expressed in Yiddish to Jewish workers on Yom Kippur, followed by an evening celebrating Sholem Aleichem, typifies the peculiar hybrid of Marxism and secular *yidishkayt* that Marmor, Olgin, and other Yiddish Communist intellectuals advocated, and the Party, at least at times, endorsed.

How should we understand this kind of close Party oversight? Did the Yiddish Communists themselves feel like they were being censored or controlled by some kind of external force? Or was it that as members of a common community—the Party—they realized that their actions in service of common goals would of course be monitored, regulated, and critiqued? In many cases, I believe it was the latter. Indeed, in its own annual reports to the Central Committee of the Party, the Jewish Bureau saw itself as working for and on behalf of the Party as a whole. For example, the 1932 Report of the Jewish Bureau makes it clear that its job is to carry out Party directives in its various member organizations and publications:

> [T]he particular task of the bureau is to mobilize the whole membership of these organizations for every Party campaign, for every movement in the class struggle under the leadership of the Party . . . In addition to the specific cultural activities of such organizations as the Workers Schools, Workers Musical Alliance, Artef, Proletpen, and Jewish Workers University, all of the mass organizations mentioned conduct wide cultural activities in the form of lectures, forums, courses, etc., the content and form of these activities being controlled by the Bureau.[61]

This does not mean that items of "Jewish content" were prohibited, but it does establish that Yiddish Communist cultural organizations functioning under the auspices of the Jewish Bureau and the CP Central Committee, and ultimately the Comintern, were seen as both explicitly political and cultural in function. Commitment to the Party and commitment to Yiddish culture were not seen as mutually exclusive, but as reinforcing each other.

Along these lines, the same 1932 report refers to the *Morgn Frayhayt* as "the most important single institution under the supervision of the Jewish Bureau" adding that the *Morgn Frayhayt* is also "regarded as one of the most important weapons of the Party in its general campaigns. It is recognized by the Party as a paper which extends its influence over the broad masses and has the most devoted following among them. Indeed, the influence of the Morning Freiheit extends beyond the limits of our organized followers, reaching a wide periphery of sympathizers."[62] We must be careful to remember that this statement is in an official report to the Central Committee, where it is more likely that the political accomplishments of the *Frayhayt* would be emphasized over the quality of the Yiddish poetry published on its pages. Nonetheless, we should not discount the sincerity of the Jewish Bureau or members of the *Frayhayt*, who viewed the paper as a powerful weapon in the revolutionary class struggle. Nor should we assume that every contributor to the *Frayhayt* shared this political commitment to the same degree. Yet, communist political commitments did not preclude a genuine and ongoing interest in Yiddish culture as intrinsically valid.

In spite of such close oversight by the Party, up until 1929 many prominent, non-communist, Yiddish writers, including M. L. Halpern, H. Leyvik, Avrom Reisen, and countless others, contributed to the *Frayhayt*, which originally conceived of itself as a champion of Yiddish culture and literature, not merely a Party organ. The *Frayhayt* valued high Yiddish literature and paid good royalties for it, which attracted top writers, even if they were not communist. Melech Epstein presented a number of reasons why talented non-communist writers were drawn to the *Frayhayt* in its early years. He suggested that its high regard for quality Yiddish literature, its connection to the Soviet Union with its resurgent Yiddish culture of the 1920s, and its support of literary evenings and other cultural forums, all helped attract leading writers to the *Frayhayt*.[63] Thus, the *Frayhayt* was in the thick of the Yiddish cultural scene in America, notwithstanding its close cooperation with the Party. This all changed with the initiation of the Third Period of Communism that began in the summer of 1928 with the Comintern's call to oppose all forms of cooperation with the organs of capitalism, i.e., all non-communists, who were now seen by the Party as social fascists and counter-revolutionaries.[64]

In the context of American Yiddish culture, it was during the summer of 1929 when the dividing lines between communists and non-communists became solidified with the so-called "Great Break" following the Arab riots in Palestine in August of that year.[65] While the new, more militant orientation of Third Period Communism had already caused a rift between communists and non-communist sympathizers at the *Frayhayt*,[66] the conflict over the communists' response to the Arab riots finalized this split. After initially referring to the Arab Riots in Hebron, in which approximately sixty Jews were killed, as Pogroms and blaming the crisis largely on British imperialism, the *Frayhayt* was rebuked by the Party for "crass Right-Wing deviation" and accused of taking a position no different "from the stand of the Jewish nationalist, Zionist, and the capitalist press."[67] Subsequently, the *Frayhayt* radically changed its position on the riots, blaming the "Zionist-Fascists" for provoking the uprising and siding with the "revolutionary Arab masses" in their struggle against the forces of imperialism.[68] While the Yiddish-speaking Communists had been consistently anti-Zionist from the beginning, by supporting the Party line on the Arab uprisings, they were seen as crossing a "red line," choosing the Party over the Jewish people.

This led to the defection of most non-communist writers from the *Frayhayt*, and the ostracization of the *Frayhayt* and Jewish Communists in general, by much of the Yiddish press, socialist and Zionist alike. Indeed, the storm against the *Frayhayt* was great in the *Forverts* and throughout the non-communist Yiddish left, involving incendiary polemics, boycotts, mass protests and demonstrations, and even mock trials against the *Frayhayt*.[69] Throughout the Yiddish-speaking community, the *Frayhayt* and the Jewish

Communists in general were fiercely condemned for their revised position on the Arab riots and their ongoing denunciations of Zionism. Their zeal in following the Party line had upset the precarious balance between their communist and their Jewish allegiances.

Yet, as we have witnessed above, even the "Great Break" did not lead to the communists abandoning Yiddish culture or altogether. In fact, in many ways, it was after 1929 that key components of the Jewish Communist subculture were firmly established or bolstered. As the Jewish Communists were completely cut off from the cultural organizations and groups of non-communist Jews, they compensated by reinforcing and expanding their own communist cultural network, much of which had been in place prior to 1929. Even though the numbers of their supporters might have dwindled, the leaders of the Yiddish Communist movement did not embrace assimilation or turn away from the ethnically Jewish character of their communist subculture. Shortly after the Arab riots and the ensuing controversy, the Yiddish Communist writers' union, or Proletpen, was formed to disassociate the communist writers from non-communists who had been writing for the *Frayhayt* and other communist organs.[70] Besides helping to facilitate the break with the non-communists, the Proletpen also aimed to advance the Yiddish-speaking Communists' longstanding goal of creating a proletarian, internationalist communist culture in Yiddish, rather than a "Jewish" culture.

The Yiddish poet and publicist Moyshe Nadir, a long-time *Frayhayt* contributor who sided with the communists in the 1929 dispute, summed up the Yiddish Communists' stance thus, "we are against Jewish culture or Judaizing the culture, but we are for culture in Yiddish, with all the beauty, vitality, and richness of our cultural treasures."[71] In other words, Nadir was rejecting Jewish religion and traditions and any semblance of a national Jewish culture in favor of a secular, socialist-oriented culture for Jews in Yiddish. This approach became the norm in the Yiddish Communist press and culture of those years. Any topics that pointed to a Jewish national culture or Jewish particularism of any sort were downplayed or eschewed. Yet, the Yiddish Communist leadership took more and more steps to create this uniquely Jewish proletarian culture and its supporting cultural and social networks.

One of the major building blocks of this new proletarian Yiddish culture was the Communist-affiliated Yiddish-language schools (*Arbeter orden shuln*), run by the Jewish section of the International Workers Order or

IWO, which had been founded in 1930 by the left-wing faction of the socialist Workmen's Circle.[72] The IWO was officially non-partisan, but its leaders and ideology were by and large communist. In his 1931 booklet outlining the mission of the IWO, Olgin explained that one of the main purposes of the IWO Yiddish schools was to bring proletarian culture to the Jewish workers' children in Yiddish.[73] However, against accusations that the IWO schools were "assimilationist" because of their militantly proletarian orientation, Olgin declared that "we do not renounce Jewish history or the history of Jewish literature, as our adversaries say. We simply want to illuminate the study of history and literary history with a Marxist analytical perspective."[74] The schools offered students a selective exposure to Jewish history, mostly that of immigration and labor movements, selected Yiddish literature, and a strong emphasis on communist teachings and principles. The degree of explicit Jewish content in the schools' textbooks varied, with books from the Third-Period years being exceptionally limited in Jewish topics, while textbooks from the Popular Front era contained more Jewish topics and authors.[75]

Concerning the IWO Yiddish schools, Roger Keeran has documented that themes in the Yiddish textbooks included the plight of the Jewish working-class, conflicts with religious Jews, bosses, police, landlords, and attacks on the Jewish religion. They also celebrated socialist figures in history (Marx, Lenin, etc.), heroes of American labor history (Haymarket martyrs, Sacco and Vanzetti, etc.), and Jewish life in the Soviet Union and the successes of the Russian Revolution. Keeran concludes, "in short, the textbook represented what might be called communist political culture, rather than Jewish culture."[76] We see, however, that there was a special focus on Jewish life and ethnicity, whether in America or the Soviet Union, which put the IWO Yiddish school curriculum somewhat at odds with the Third Period vision of American Communism. As Bat-Ami Zucker concluded in her analysis of the Jewish Communist schools, "the network of schools, by teaching even selected Jewish subjects in Yiddish—albeit under strict Party supervision and control—facilitated the development of a Jewish identity."[77] This reveals the distinctive nature of Communist Jewish culture. Indeed, as Keeran rightly observed, the IWO's effort to maintain a distinct Yiddish culture over against a more assimilationist approach was criticized by the CP's 1930 "Resolution on Language Work," which accused the IWO's Yiddish-language schools of "developing national culture" and "giving insufficient attention to the political and economic struggles of the working class in the United States."[78]

For the IWO, and the Jewish Communists more broadly, this kind of Party criticism may have led them to minimize Jewish content to an extent, but it did not deter them from developing a thriving network of Yiddish schools for Jewish children, numbering a little over one hundred schools and about 8,000 pupils by 1936.[79] Even when Yiddish-speaking Communists railed against "nationalist" or "bourgeois" forms of Jewish culture they could not, or would not, remove the secular, ethnic type of *yidishkayt* that informed the IWO Yiddish schools as well as most Yiddish Communist cultural products and organizations. Yiddish Communist intellectuals, like Olgin and Marmor, or IWO Jewish section leader, Reuben Saltzman, still maintained a sense of Jewish ethnic and cultural identity that, even during the Third Period, informed the hybrid form of Jewish Communist culture they created.

There are also examples of devoted Yiddish-speaking Communists fighting back against the Party, or at least particular groups within it, when they felt that certain essentials of their cultural identity were being challenged, such as Yiddish itself. I have already mentioned that beginning in 1929 the Party urged the foreign-language sections to Americanize and adopt English as much as possible. Among Jewish Communists themselves this produced real tensions. The committed Yiddishists of the *Frayhayt* and the Jewish Bureau were being increasingly challenged by English-speaking, American-born Jewish Communists, and well as non-Jewish Communists, to give up Yiddish for English.

One such example of this conflict is recounted in an undated letter from the summer of 1933 from Moyshe Katz, a co-editor of the *Frayhayt* and staunch Party man, to the secretary of the Jewish Bureau, Joseph Sultan. Writing in English (possibly because of the institutional purpose of the letter), Katz described to Sultan his experience of being invited to be a guest speaker from the *Frayhayt* at the Communist adult summer colony, Camp Nitgedaiget, and being told not to speak "Jewish" (Yiddish). He explained that the camp leaders were trying to phase out the use of Yiddish at the camp, so that more English-speaking workers might attend. Katz was incensed by this rejection of Yiddish at a camp that, as Katz observed, "is composed at least 99% of Jewish workers," and he complained to Sultan that this attitude reflected a broader trend in American Communist circles that needed to be stopped. He offered Sultan more examples of how the "Jewish language is being persecuted in the camp," and concluded his letter by declaring that "all the above mentioned facts constitute deviation from the Party line and of the line of the Leninist national policy which is the line of our party as much as of any other section of the Comintern."[80]

Also in 1933, Katz openly addressed the issue of segments of the CP coming out against the *Frayhayt* and separate Jewish enclaves within the party, complaining in the *Frayhayt* that "non-Jewish Communists spoke disparagingly of the paper and of Jewish work."[81] Besides exposing a severe tension between assimilationist and Yiddishist orientations among Jewish (and non-Jewish) Communists in 1933, this reveals that, for Katz, a proper understanding of communist policy actually supported his pro-Yiddish position. In the letter, he referred numerous times to "Leninist national policy" and the "Leninist-Stalinist line on the national question," and the idea of communist culture being "socialist in content and national in form," to support this position. Even during the militant phase of Third Period Communism, when the Jewish Communists distanced themselves strenuously from all things smacking of Jewish particularism or nationalism, communists like Katz opposed linguistic assimilation for Yiddish-speaking Jews, seeing it as being inherently anti-communist.

There is evidence that this Yiddish-English tension existed at the grassroots level as well, not just among leading communist intellectuals like Katz. In a letter to the Jewish Bureau Central Organization Department from the National Initiative Committee of the CP, dated March 21, 1935, the issue of the various Jewish fractions resisting English-language work was raised. The National Initiative Committee was trying to organize women in a campaign against sales tax. The letter explained to the Jewish Bureau that "we feel it is the duty of our councils already in existence, to make strenuous efforts to organize English speaking councils . . . however, our first experience in this drive met with strong opposition on the part of the Jewish Bureau."[82] The National Initiative Committee recognized the need to organize among "Negro" and "Americanized" women, and felt that the "narrow environment" of the foreign-language councils, such as the Jewish Bureau, was limiting this effort. The letter goes on to report a conflict that occurred at a Communist conference in Boston on March 10, 1935, in which Jewish speakers rejected the call for English-speaking councils, claiming that "the New York councils are out to break the Jewish-speaking councils of Boston."[83] This letter reveals the tension that continued to exist within the Party as of 1935 over the use of foreign languages, especially Yiddish. It shows that many Jewish Communists resisted the move to English-language work within official Party groups or organizations that had been part of the Jewish Bureau of the Party.

How did non-Jewish Communist leaders view the synthetic identities of Yiddish Communists like Olgin and Marmor? Earl Browder, the general secretary of the CPUSA, had a close working relationship with Moyshe Olgin, at least starting in 1936, when Browder ran the first time for president on the Communist ticket. Olgin campaigned rigorously for Browder, often appearing with him at public events, party conventions, and the like, and even writing an English-language biographical sketch of Browder in one of his campaign booklets. For his part, Browder frequently addressed Jewish audiences under the auspices of the Jewish Bureau or the *Frayhayt*. From 1936 until he was forced out of the Party almost a decade later, his speeches and articles appeared often in Yiddish translation in the *Frayhayt* and he read the Yiddish press, both the *Frayhayt* and its "bourgeois" opponents, in English translations. At Olgin's funeral in November of 1939, Browder was one of the featured speakers.

At the beginning of this article, we saw how in his speech at Olgin's one-year Memorial service Browder affirmed Olgin's hybrid identity as being both fully Jewish and fully communist at once, calling him "a great American Communist, a great leader of the Jewish people, and a great man."[84] Browder viewed Olgin as a true leader of the Jewish people, in part, because of his fervent support for the Soviet Union, unlike the "bourgeois and social-democratic Jewish misleaders" who "heaped calumny and incitement" on the Soviet Union, not seeing the "liberating role of the Soviet Union . . . for the Jews and for all mankind."[85] So, in this sense, Olgin was a good Jewish leader because of his communism, which determined his attitude toward the Soviet Union, and not in spite of it.

Another prominent Communist leader, V. J. Jerome, the long-time editor of the journal *The Communist* and a prominent figure within the Party, eulogized Olgin in similar terms. Representing the National Committee of the Party at the unveiling of Olgin's monument on October 19, 1941, Jerome read a speech entitled "Homage to an American Bolshevik." Like Browder's, Jerome's homage to Olgin captures the hybrid nature of his Jewish-Communist identity:

> Olgin was an internationalist. By upholding the constructive heritage of nationhood, against those who sought to debase it from within through chauvinism, and against those who sought to destroy from without through fascist subjugation, Olgin the Leninist was a great American, as he was a great Jew.[86]

Jerome's tribute to Olgin outlines the tripartite poles of his identity—Leninist, American, Jew—all working together in perfect harmony. In this reading,

Olgin's communism did not erase Olgin's Jewishness; it helped him forge a new distinctive identity that was Communist and Jewish at once.

Obviously, those like the anti-Communist Yiddish editor, Margoshes, who compared Olgin to Nazis and anti-Semites, had a very different assessment of the Jewish Communists' relationship to Jewishness and Jewish culture. Many contemporary scholars have been similarly skeptical of the communists' Jewishness, seeing it as insincere or at least subjugated to their communist loyalties. However, in this chapter I have tried to show that the Yiddish-speaking Communists had a much more complex identity than their critics have given them credit for. While some might claim that the hybrid Communist-Jewish culture that they created was simply "Communism in Yiddish," I believe that this misses the point. By choosing to create a communist culture in Yiddish for Jewish immigrant workers in the United States, I propose that Yiddish-speaking Communist intellectuals like Olgin and Marmor spearheaded a movement that created a uniquely Jewish form of communist culture. It diverged in significant ways from both the norms of non-communist, left-wing Jewish culture and from the mainstream of American Communism at the time, while simultaneously incorporating substantial aspects of both.

Notes

1. "In Memory of a Great Jewish Leader," Earl Browder Papers, R-7070, Reel 9, Folder 261, Tamiment Collection, New York University.

2. S. Margoshes in *Der Tog*, October 21, 1939, 1.

3. Ibid.

4. See Matthew Hoffman, "The Red Divide: The Conflict Between Communists and their Opponents in the American Yiddish Press," *American Jewish History* 96, No. 1 (2010).

5. See, for example, Nathan Glazer, *The Social Basis of American Communism* (New York: Harcourt, Brace & World, 1961), 132 ff., where he addresses the question of the relationship between Jewishness and communism for Jewish Communists in America.

6. David Shneer, *Yiddish and the Creation of Soviet Jewish Culture: 1918–1930* (Cambridge: Cambridge University Press, 2004).

7. See, for example, Tony Michels, "Socialism With a Jewish Face: The Origins of the Yiddish-Speaking Communist Movement in the United States, 1907–1923" in *Yiddish and the Left: Papers of the Third Mendel Friedman International Yiddish Conference*, eds. Gennady Estraikh and Mikhail Krutikov (Oxford: Legenda Press, 2001); Paul Buhle, "Jews and American Communism: The Cultural

Question," in *Radical History Review* 23 (Spring, 1980); and Ezra Mendelsohn, *On Modern Jewish Politics* (New York: Oxford University Press, 1993).

8. See, for example, Bat-Ami Zucker, "American Jewish Communists and Jewish Culture in the 1930s," in *Modern Judaism* 14, No. 2 (May, 1994); Arthur Liebman, *Jews and the Left* (New York: Wiley, 1979); and Melech Epstein, *The Jew and Communism: 1919–1941* (New York: Trade Union Sponsoring Committee, 1959).

9. See Albert Fried, *Communism in America: A History in Documents* (New York: Columbia University Press, 1997) for an overview of American communism during this period.

10. Kalman Marmor had been active in Zionist circles since 1899 and was a founding figure of the *Poalei Zion* (Workers of Zion), before abandoning Zionism for socialism and Yiddish cultural work in America. Likewise, Moyshe Katz had been active in left-wing Zionist circles in Russia and Palestine in the early twentieth century and was active in Yiddish cultural circles as well.

11. See Glazer, 46–56, for more on the process of Americanization and Bolshevization of the Party, especially its impact on the foreign-language sections of the CP.

12. Roger Keeran, "National Groups and the Popular Front: The Case of the International Workers Order," in *Journal of American Ethnic History* 14 (Spring, 1995): 27. See *Thesis and Resolutions for the Seventh National Convention of the Communist Party of U.S.A.* March 31–April 4, 1930, 79–84.

13. Tony Michels, "Socialism with a Jewish Face: The Origins of the Yiddish-Speaking Communist Movement in the United States, 1907–1923" in *Yiddish and the Left: Papers of the Third Mendel Friedman International Yiddish Conference*, eds. Gennady Estraikh and Mikhail Krutikov (Oxford: Legenda, 2001), 25. See also Michels, *A Fire in their Hearts: Yiddish Socialists in New York* (Cambridge, MA: Harvard University Press, 2005), 217–50, where he looks at the founding of the Jewish Communist movement in the context of the split between right-wing and left-wing Jewish socialists.

14. Ibid., 26.

15. Ibid.

16. Ibid., 50, n. 8.

17. Paul Buhle, "Jews and American Communism: The Cultural Question," in *Radical History Review* 23 (Spring, 1980): 18.

18. See Buhle, 25.

19. Ibid., 20.

20. Ezra Mendelsohn, *On Modern Jewish Politics*, 28.

21. Ibid., 27–28.

22. Bat-Ami Zucker, "American Jewish Communists and Jewish Culture in the 1930s," in *Modern Judaism* 14, No. 2 (May 1994): 182.

23. This was a persistent claim by contemporary opponents of Jewish Communists, such as *Forverts* editor, Abe Cahan, and *Tog* editor, S. Margoshes. See Hoffman, "Red Divide," for examples of these claims.

24. Cahan, Margoshes and others leveled this charge of "duping the Jewish masses" repeatedly. See, for example, Hoffman, "Red Divide," 27.

25. See M. Olgin, *Kultur un Folk* [*Culture and the People*] (New York: YKUF, 1949), 41–157, for a posthumous collection of his essays from 1923 until 1939 that lays out his vision of a proletarian Yiddish culture. In his introduction to *Kultur un Folk*, Paul Novick claims that Olgin "fought a never-ending battle for a progressive [Yiddish] culture," 21.

26. See David Shneer, *Yiddish and the Creation of Soviet Jewish Culture: 1918–1930*, for an innovative and in-depth study of the distinctive Yiddish culture that Soviet Jewish intellectuals created in the 1920s.

27. Olgin, "*Mir un Yiddish*" ("Yiddish and Us"), *Frayhayt*, May 14, 1928, in *Kultur un Folk*, 139. All translations from Yiddish primary sources are mine. Olgin had a public debate with Khaim Zhitlovsky on December 9, 1928, on the question of whether the Yiddish language and culture should be just a means to reach socialism, or an end in itself. Olgin argued there for a separate proletarian culture in Yiddish, while Zhitlovsky envisioned a broader, more inclusive Yiddish culture.

28. Olgin, *Kultur un Folk*, 20.

29. Kalman Marmor, "*Der ort fun kultur-arbet*" ("The Place of Cultural Work"), September 20, 1931, *Morgn-Frayhayt*.

30. Moyshe Olgin, "*Kent ir di Morgn-Frayhayt?*" ["Do You Know the Morning Frayhayt?"] (New York: Morgn Frayhayt, 1932), 18.

31. See Mendelsohn, 27–28.

32. Arthur Liebman, *Jews and the Left* (New York, 1979), 305.

33. See Liebman, 305–25, for an overview of some of the main communist-affiliated cultural organizations.

34. Liebman, 315.

35. See Buhle, 11–12.

36. For Olgin's role in the founding of the Proletpen, see Gennady Estraikh, *In Harness: Yiddish Writers' Romance with Communism* (Syracuse, NY: Syracuse University Press, 2005), 92–98. For more on the Proletpen writers, see Dovid Katz's introduction to *Proletpen: America's Rebel Yiddish Poets*, eds. Amelia Glaser and David Weintraub (Madison: University of Wisconsin Press, 2005), 3–24. For Olgin's role in the founding of myriad communist-associated cultural organizations, see P. Novick's introduction to *Kultur un Folk*, 21.

37. Harvey Klehr, *The Heyday of American Communism: The Depression Decade* (New York: Basic Books, 1984), 383.

38. See Melech Epstein, *The Jew and Communism: 1919–1941*, 253–54, and Liebman, 492–97, for a discussion of the impact of Americanization and Bolshevization trends on the Jewish section of the Party.

39. There were many Jewish Communists, such as Israel Amter and Alexander Bittelman, who were fluent in Yiddish, but chose to work mostly in English and become major powers within the Party.

40. For an historical overview of ICOR and its place among American Jewish Communists, especially in regard to support for Birobidzhan, see Henry Srebrnik, *Dreams of Nationhood: American Jewish Communists and the Soviet Birobidzhan*

Project, 1924–1951 (Boston: Academic Studies Press, 2010). See also Srebrnik's "Diaspora, Ethnicity and Dreams of Nationhood: American Jewish Communists and the Birobidzhan Project," in *Yiddish and the Left: Papers of the Third Mendel Friedman International Yiddish Conference,* eds. Gennady Estraikh and Mikhail Krutikov (Oxford: Legenda, 2001), 80–108.

41. Moyshe Katz was one of the founding editors of *Nailebn,* and Olgin, Marmor, and other prominent Yiddish Communist writers were regular contributors. However, the *Naileben* editorial line claimed that the ICOR was non-partisan, not a communist organ, and that its main aims were to combat fascism and anti-Semitism, cooperate with Jewish pioneers in Birobidzhan, and promote friendship with the Soviet Union.

42. P. Novik, *Di lage fun di yidn in Sovetn-Farband: Faktn un tsifern* ["The Position of the Jews in the Soviet Union: Facts and Figures"] (New York: ICOR, 1930), 1.

43. Moyshe Olgin, "*Yidn un nit-yidn in Sovetn-Farband*" ["Jews and Non-Jews in the Soviet Union"], 1934, in the posthumous collection of Olgin's essays on the Soviet Union, *Sovetn-Farband* (New York: Morgn Frayhayt, 1944), 169.

44. Olgin, "*Der yid iz oyfgerikht gevorn*" [The Jew Became Prosperous"], 1934, in *Sovetn-Farband,* 174.

45. It should be noted here that much of the Jewish Communists' praise of the Soviet Union and its positive treatment of Jews served apologetically to refute the numerous anti-Soviet charges found in the anti-communist press, led primarily by Abe Cahan and the *Forverts.*

46. Olgin was formally trained as a literary scholar, receiving a PhD from Columbia in Russian literature.

47. See Olgin's *Kultur un Folk* for a collection of his literary essays from the early 1920s through 1939, which includes essays on Mendele, Sholem Aleichem, Peretz, Morris Rosenfeld, H. D. Nomberg, as well as on several later leftist or proletarian poets, and even the communist cartoonist, William Gropper, 161–319.

48. Ibid., 166.

49. This was true in most of Olgin's essays on pre-revolutionary or non-communist writers; he would criticize them from a proletarian perspective, but also highlight those qualities of their oeuvre that he saw as redeemable.

50. I borrow this concept of "kosher for communists" from Anna Shternshis and her book, *Soviet and Kosher: Jewish Popular culture in the Soviet Union, 1923–1939* (Bloomington: Indiana University Press, 2006), in which she provides a fascinating study of the hybrid, innovative nature of Communist-Jewish popular culture in the Soviet Union.

51. David Shneer makes this point in his discussion of Soviet Yiddish culture as well: "In fact, within the Soviet Yiddish intelligentsia, it is very hard to tell the difference between the Bolshevik propagandist and the Jewish cultural activist," Shneer, 4.

52. See Harvey Klehr, *Communist Cadre: The Social Background of the American Communist Party Elite* (Stanford, CA: Hooever Institution Press, 1978), 37–52, for a discussion of Jewish leadership in the Party.

53. See Bat-Ami Zucker, "The Jewish Bureau: The Organization of American Jewish Communists in the 1930's," in *Bar-Ilan Studies in History III: Modern History* (Ramat-Gan, 1991), 135–47, for an overview of the organization and function of the Jewish Bureau and how it fit within the CPUSA structure.

54. For more on Sultan's commitment to Yiddish culture, see Zucker, "American Jewish Communists," 181.

55. See Kalman Marmor archive, RG 205, folder 453 ff., YIVO Institute for Jewish Research, New York.

56. Ibid., folder 476.

57. Ibid., folder 454.

58. Ibid., folder 453.

59. Ibid., folder 456.

60. Ibid.

61. CPUSA Archives, R-7548, Reel 214, Folder 2754, 3, Tamiment Collection, New York University.

62. Ibid.

63. Epstein, 104.

64. See Albert Fried, *Communism in America: A History in Documents*, 93–109, for an overview of Third Period Communism.

65. See Gennady Estraikh, *In Harness: Yiddish Writers' Romance with Communism*, 96–97.

66. Gennady Estraikh, "The Yiddish-Language Communist Press," in *Dark Times, Dire Decisions: Jews and Communism*, ed. Jonathan Frankel (Oxford: Oxford University Press, 2004), 70.

67. Epstein, 224.

68. Ibid., 225–26.

69. See Epstein, 225–33.

70. See Estraikh, "In Harness," 97. As Epstein points out, "the staff of the *Frayhayt* was expelled from the Yiddish Writers' Union for anti-Jewish activities" (Epstein, 229), another reason for the creation of a separate communist writers' union.

71. Zucker, "American Jewish Communists and Jewish Culture in the 1930s," 177. This came from an article Nadir wrote upon the founding of the Proletpen, appearing in the *Frayhayt* on September 14, 1929.

72. See Liebman, 310–15, for background on the founding of the IWO.

73. Moyshe Olgin, "*Der Internatsyonaler Arbeter Ordn: geshikhte, program, taktik*" ["The International Workers Order: History, Program, Tactics"] (New York: Internatsyonaln Arbeter Ordn, 1931), 53–55.

74. Ibid., 55.

75. In the fourth-grade textbook from 1934 (*Arbeter Shul: Lernbukh farn ferter yor*, New York, 1934), there are only five explicitly Jewish items in the 210-page book, with a few entries on Jewish Communist organizations, and dozens of entries on communist figures, songs, and important historical events. The third-grade textbook from 1934 is much the same. In contrast, the second-grade textbook from

1939 (*Mayn Bukh*, New York, 1939) contains at least fifteen entries from famous Yiddish writers, such as Mendele, Peretz, Sholem Aleichem, and Avrom Reisen, as well as entries about such writers.

76. Keeran, 32.

77. Zucker, "American Jewish Communists and Jewish Culture in the 1930s," 179.

78. Keeran, 28.

79. According to the January, 1937 issue of the official organ of the IWO Jewish schools, *Proletarische Derziung* ("Proletarian Education"), there were 114 Yiddish schools operating by 1936 compared to 56 in 1931.

80. CPUSA Archives, R-7548, Reel 247, Folder 3178, Tamiment Collection, New York University.

81. Cited in Epstein, 254.

82. CPUSA Archives, R-7548, Reel 292, Folder 3786, Tamiment Collection, New York University.

83. Ibid.

84. "In Memory of a Great Jewish Leader," Earl Browder Papers, R-7070, Reel 9, Folder 261, Tamiment Collection, New York University.

85. Ibid.

86. V. J. Jerome, "Homage to an American Bolshevik," in *Olgin Album* (New York: Morgn Frayhayt, 1941), 27, found in the Bund Archive "American Communism," RG 1400, YIVO Institute for Jewish Research, New York.

3

The Scorched Melting Pot

The Jewish People's Fraternal Order and the Making of American Jewish Communism, 1930–1950

Jennifer Young

On an evening in late May 1945, as Americans celebrated the end of the war in Europe, thousands of Jews gathered at New York's Madison Square Garden to mark the fifteenth anniversary of the Jewish People's Fraternal Order (JPFO), a left-wing fraternal organization. The event included speeches by prominent figures such as Rabbi Stephen Wise, Sholem Asch, and Marc Chagall, and the performance by more than 100 children from the JPFO's Yiddish schools in a ballet entitled, "Moses, the Liberator." The speakers struck a sober note, emphasizing the immediate need for American Jews to work together to rebuild postwar Jewish culture. Sholem Asch announced to the audience, "The Jewish people still lives, my friends." Whenever Jews gather, they would now carry the spiritual legacy of the Jews whom Hitler destroyed, Asch declared: "Their mantles have fallen upon our shoulders, and we are responsible for the continuation of the golden chain of the culture which they have created."[1] Rubin Saltzman, the JPFO's general secretary, congratulated members on their work in forging unity among the Jewish people, especially during the crisis brought about by the war. "Our Order is highly conscious of the high responsibility which the present time demands of us all," he proclaimed.[2] After fifteen years of fighting for the Jewish working class, Saltzman predicted, the JPFO's next great task would be to unite with all Jews to build the Jewish future.

Closely tied to the Communist Party of the United States (CPUSA), the JPFO emerged out of internecine battles within the Jewish labor movement in the 1920s. After increasing its membership and prominence exponentially in the 1930s, the JPFO sought to expand its role on the world stage during the war years. In 1944, after its previous request to join had been denied, the JPFO won admission to the American Jewish Conference, a communal body representing a wide range of Jewish organizations.[3] The Conference sought to create a new structure for American Jewish leadership in postwar reconstruction and international policy. Its representatives sought to overcome ideological differences and work together as a united front. Wise had championed the JPFO's admission to the Conference, arguing in 1944 that it would be "unwise for American Jewry to exclude a Jewish group on the grounds of its Communist views, when an attempt is being made to bring all the Jews of the world, including those of Soviet Russia, into the great circle of Jewish fellowship."[4] At Madison Square Garden, Rabbi Wise explained to the almost 18,000 attendees his role in admitting the JPFO to the Conference, and underlined the importance of including Jewish Communists within the Conference as a symbol of Jewish unity: "We had no choice, we had to admit you," Wise said. "You are Americans, you are Jewish, you are fraternal . . . we had not the right to question you about your political, your ideological, or your ethical or social views . . . You said to us, *ivri anachnim* [*sic*] [We are Jews]—that is enough for us."[5]

Besides Wise's commitment to Jewish unity, he also recognized the more practical advantage of working with the JPFO: claiming 50,000 members and possessed of an efficient fundraising engine, the JPFO could quickly raise large sums of money for postwar reconstruction. At Madison Square Garden, JPFO leaders presented Wise with a check for $75,000 for his work with the Jewish Council for Russian War Relief. At the same time, they presented Mrs. Moses Epstein, the president of Hadassah, with a check for $40,000 for a Jewish children's home in Palestine.[6]

Despite these auspicious beginnings, the alliance between communists and the American Jewish establishment would prove to be short-lived. In April 1947, the JPFO was placed on United States Attorney General Tom Clark's List of Subversive Organizations, an outgrowth of President Truman's "loyalty program" designed to identify potential communists employed by the federal government. In short order, the JPFO was expelled from most Jewish community organizations in the country. While the American Jewish Conference dissolved in 1948, in that same year the JPFO was expelled from the American Jewish Congress, another major communal body, which charged the JPFO with incomplete support for civil rights and Israel, and for denying abuses against Jews in the Soviet Union.[7] In 1950, in one well-known case, the Jewish Community Council of Los Angeles conducted an internal trial and ultimately expelled the L.A. branch of the JPFO from within its ranks, due to fears that it would spread communist influence throughout the community. Local JPFO leaders angrily denounced the ouster by a "handful of men" who "damn[ed] as un-Jewish all who disagree with them."[8] The optimism and careful diplomacy of 1945 had disappeared, replaced by fear, anxiety, and resentment from all sides. Was the JPFO for communism, or for Jews? Even its leaders were not always sure of the answer.

The JPFO's brief moment of political integration, and its long rise and rapid fall from grace into relative obscurity, reflects the tenuous position of American Jewish Communists in the American Jewish community, and within its historiography. While many scholars have noted the JPFO's divisive role within mid-century Jewish life, few have treated the subject in depth.[9] This chapter provides an overview and timeline of the JPFO's activities, focusing primarily on the organization's support for social security and civil rights. The JPFO's support for these goals was inextricably tied to its political analysis of assimilation, and its programmatic articulation of the role that minority cultures and languages could play in American political life. Fighting against what they called the "melting pot" ideology, or political and economic exploitation expressed as a false promise of prosperity and security, JPFO leaders created a mass movement centered on promoting Yiddish language and culture as a form of anticapitalism. Throughout the Depression and New Deal years, and in the early years of the Cold War, they pushed to expand the boundaries of the welfare state and to achieve what they believed to be a more equal, and therefore a more truly American, economic and social system.

The JPFO grew out of, and alongside, the International Workers Order (IWO), a fraternal insurance organization founded in 1930 by a group of Jewish leftists in New York. Rubin Saltzman (1890–1959), the IWO's founding secretary and later general secretary of the JPFO, was born in Brest-Litovsk during the Tsarist regime, the son of a shoemaker. He became a Bundist as a teenager, participating in revolutionary activity that resulted in a three-year exile to Siberia.[10] In 1911, Saltzman arrived in the United States, and soon became an active member of the socialist fraternal order, the Workmen's Circle (known in Yiddish as the *Arbeter Ring*).[11] As a member of the Workmen's Circle national education committee, and, later, the national executive board, Saltzman became part of the "young guard" that wished to develop a stronger political stance within the organization. He also helped to establish several of the first Yiddish secular schools in the United States, in 1915.[12] While the Workmen's Circle regulations mandated that every member must join a union and must vote for a political party that stood for socialism, "old guard" delegates to the 1920 convention of the Workmen's Circle voted to abolish this rule. The "young guard" members rejected this proposed change, leading to a protracted leadership struggle within the organization.

In the fall of 1921, socialist journalists Moyshe Olgin (1878–1939) and Paul (Peysakh) Novick (1892–1989) left the Yiddish daily *Forverts*, and the following year, established the *Frayhayt* as a left-wing alternative. From this point onwards, the *Frayhayt* would serve in many ways as an anchor for the Jewish Communist fraternal movement through the rest of the twentieth century, until the *Frayhayt* ultimately ceased publication in 1988. In the mid-1920s, the left-wing faction of the Workmen's Circle sought to bring their organization's ideology closer in line with the pro-Soviet revolutionary fervor of the *Frayhayt* and its contingent. The tensions within the Workmen's Circle built until sixty-four branches of the Workmen's Circle were expelled in 1926, leading to the construction of rival cultural institutions, including the *Umparteyishe Yidishe Shuln* [non-partisan Yiddish schools], a rival network of Yiddish schools, and a children's summer camp, *Kinderland.* Throughout the 1930s and 1940s, Jewish Communists built networks of Jewish affiliation via the rapidly expanding circles of fraternal groups, periodicals, choirs, camps, schools, and cooperative housing projects, in locations as diverse as rural New Jersey, Philadelphia, and Los Angeles.

In February 1930, Saltzman and others officially issued a call for the establishment of a new Jewish fraternal order that would rival the Workmen's Circle. In March 1930, this organization was duly recognized by the Insurance Department of the State of New York, and legally titled the International Workers Order (though known primarily at this time by its Yiddish name, *Internatsiyonaler Arbeter Ordn*). While IWO members venerated the Soviet Union and modeled their ideal of a Soviet America on the supposed economic and social equality found in Soviet Russia, they grounded their political aspirations in the American context, especially in campaigns for comprehensive social security reform as a first step toward a robust communist movement in the United States. Their overall goal was to deploy culture as a tool to fight capitalism's power to "alienate, discriminate, and segregate."[13]

The close relationship between the IWO and the Communist Party, which later came under intense scrutiny by the courts, was by no means covert in the IWO's early days. Prominent communist leaders such as Max Bedacht, Samson Milgrom, and William Weiner took on public leadership roles in the IWO,[14] and the IWO ran frequent campaigns to raise money for the Party and for the *Daily Worker*, the Communist Party's daily newspaper.[15] The IWO also supported communist candidates for state and federal office.[16] In a 1931 IWO membership campaign, the winner of a contest to sign up the most new members for their lodge won a trip to the Soviet Union alongside the IWO's official delegation.[17]

In order to attract a broader membership base beyond Workmen's Circle dissidents, the IWO intended at the outset to bring non-Jewish groups into its fraternal structure—hence its use of the term "international." In May 1931, the 5,000-member Slovak Workers Society entered into an amalgamation agreement with the IWO, and in 1932, the IWO absorbed the membership of a 20,000-member Hungarian fraternal association. As the Order divided into linguistic subsections, Saltzman moved from general secretary of the IWO as a whole to head of the Jewish section, later named the Jewish People's Fraternal Order, or JPFO (*yidisher folks-ordn*). Throughout the 1930s, new national sections were established, as Italians, Poles, Ukrainians, Romanians, and Croatians set up their own societies, followed by Serbs, Carpatho-Russians, Finns, Greeks, and Czechs, and a Spanish-language section, comprised primarily of Mexicans and Puerto Ricans. By 1950, the IWO consisted of fourteen national sections, including the Douglass-Lincoln Society, a Black fraternal society, and a constellation of smaller lodges that did not have sufficient membership to establish a formal society. These smaller groups represented almost every immigrant group in the country, from Chinese and Japanese lodges in California and an Arabic-language lodge in Michigan, to Portuguese lodges in Massachusetts. The IWO also organized an English-language section, a youth section, and a women's section, the Emma Lazarus Division, which was entirely Jewish.

The IWO achieved great success in organizing industrial workers, especially in New York's garment industry and the Pennsylvania anthracite mining region, where workers were particularly prone to tuberculosis. Every IWO member held an insurance policy, typically one that cost about $6 per year to cover a family (about $59 in 2014 dollars).[18] All IWO members were insured at rates based on age, rather than by race or profession, at a time when both Blacks and miners paid higher insurance costs at corporate insurance companies.[19] As a preventative health measure, the IWO introduced yearly chest X-rays, which often caught cases of incipient tuberculosis when the patient still had a chance to recover and return to work. Doctors regularly made house calls, bringing their X-ray machines with them. Patients were sent to the IWO's TB sanitarium in Liberty, New York, and were granted a special $600 "T.B. benefit," an extension of sick benefits to $20 a week for thirty weeks, which covered the entire cost of room, board, and daily doctor's visits at the sanitarium. During their stay, patients' dues would be paid for out of a special IWO sick fund, so that they would not fall behind on payments. Under special IWO medical services plans, IWO members in New York in the 1930s paid thirty-five cents per month in health insurance, and were entitled to receive medical care from a doctor either at an office or in the home. This policy also covered spouses and all children up to the age of eighteen. Under these plans, top specialists at respected hospitals performed major surgery for $75, a significantly lower rate than most plans.[20] The quality and affordability of this care provided the IWO with a powerful organizing tool, one that the Communist Party could, by its nature, never possess. Thus, the Party relied on the IWO as a vital link in the chain connecting workers, via the Order, to the Party.

The symbiosis between the IWO and the Party was made clear in the IWO's internal guidelines. Recognizing that a majority of Americans would never hold membership in the Communist Party itself, the Communist Party of the United States (CPUSA) hoped that the IWO, as a mass membership organization, would attract the widest possible population. Bringing in a racially, politically, religiously, and nationally diverse group, and developing intimate ties amongst them, was the primary goal of communist leadership within the IWO. "The development of such friendships must be fostered through the institution of club life in all branches," stated a CPUSA guideline to the IWO leadership: fraternal insurance must be a "task of revolutionary leadership," since these benefits made the IWO attractive for people who would not be attracted by any other kind of organization under communist leadership.

> An effective club life, in turn, makes these masses seek in the Order not only protection through insurance but also friendship, social life, entertainment, advice on daily problems, and so forth . . . presenting the tremendous possibility of Bolshevik work presented to the Communists as the leaders of the IWO. We can influence and educate these masses; we can overcome their mutual prejudices which capitalist education has generated in them through racial, religious or political mis-education; we

> can make these masses an active force in the struggle for progress and class consciousness.[21]

The relationship between the Party and the IWO continued to develop through the 1930s. While the Party considered IWO membership to be a conduit to development of communist cadres, it also recognized that many workers, both immigrant and native-born, would not develop sufficient class consciousness to become communists. The function of the fraternal order, therefore, would be to organize these workers to support a more progressive society overall, thus paving the way for eventual communist governmental leadership.

In 1929, as part of its "Third Period" policy shift, the Communist Party established the Trade Union Unity League (TUUL), which would serve as the Party's organizing engine for the first half of the 1930s. The TUUL served as an umbrella organization of industrial unionism, following a strategy of setting up radical unions to compete with existing unions, rather than creating communist factions within existing organizations. In this sense, the IWO functioned as a "dual union" alongside the Workmen's Circle, competing in the fraternal insurance field. In this era, thematically dubbed "Towards a Soviet America," both the Party and the IWO focused on the struggle to organize within the labor movement. At the second IWO national convention in Chicago, 1933, Saltzman proclaimed the IWO's plan to increase membership within industrial unions, or as he termed it, a policy of *mitn ponem tsum shap* (orienting toward the shop).[22] He also underscored the necessity of fighting Zionism and social democracy, and of defending Jews in Poland against "pogroms," as necessary revolutionary duties.[23]

As the Depression worsened, the Communist Party began organizing mass rallies to focus public attention on the plight of the working class. But after Franklin Delano Roosevelt's election, change was on the horizon.

Like the CPUSA, the IWO faced a policy adjustment in the summer of 1935. At the Communist International (Comintern)'s Seventh Congress, communist leader Georgi Dimitrov declared that the threatening rise of fascism across Europe determined that combating fascism would now become the communist movement's immediate priority. Dimitrov called for all Communist Parties to immediately form a coalition of interests across the spectrum of society; communists would now work alongside workers, farmers, intellectuals, and the bourgeoisie in order to save social democracy. Rather than focusing on the didactic task of creating class-consciousness among workers, communists were now instructed to "speak the language of the masses," thereby creating cohesion in the face of a common threat. Adopting the slogan, "Communism is Twentieth Century Americanism," the CPUSA dissolved the Trade Union Unity League and utilized the newly formed Congress of Industrial Organizations as a means of mass organization.

The immediate effects of these changes in JPFO policy are clearly evident in the materials produced for the Yiddish school network. Almost overnight, the language of class war was replaced with the language of Jewish peoplehood. In examining this shift, it becomes evident that the transition from class-based language to a focus on Jewish culture under threat became a powerful tool for building the JPFO as a whole. It also suggests an underlying continuity between Third Period and Popular Front approaches within the JPFO: an emphasis on building a relationship between the immigrant generation and their American-born children, and a concern to transmit a common set of progressive values over time.

The JPFO's School and Cultural Director, Itshe Goldberg, oversaw the changes in the Yiddish schools. Born in 1904 into a middle-class family in Apt (Opatow), Poland, Goldberg spent his youth in Warsaw and immigrated with his family to Toronto after World War I. After working in a Workmen's Circle *shule* (supplementary school) in Toronto, Goldberg moved to Philadelphia to teach in the left-wing Yiddish schools there.[24] In 1932, he moved to Harlem to teach in a JPFO *mitlshul* (middle school). Goldberg would eventually become the JPFO's cultural theorist, as well as its leading pedagogue. He continued to refine his arguments for the importance of Yiddish as a minority culture and language in the postwar U.S. throughout the 1930s.

In January 1935, the JPFO founded its own Yiddish pedagogical journal, *Proletarishe Dertsiung* (*Proletarian Education*). Both Goldberg and Saltzman served on the editorial board. Following Lenin's dictum that "there is no such thing as apolitical education,"[25] the journal proclaimed its pedagogical aims: teaching not only knowledge and language, but shaping the consciousness of the child so that he would become an active agent in the struggle of his class. The first issue underlined the proletarian message of the Third Period, as applied to the classroom: "the notion that a school can serve all [socioeconomic] classes is a lie," one writer proclaimed. Education must have one primary goal: tying the working class child to the working class. Yiddish must be used strategically, as a tool of class struggle, Goldberg and a colleague stated.[26] Contrasting the JPFO's proletarian Yiddish culture against the cultural nationalism of "Yiddishists," who believed in elevating

Yiddish culture as a value in itself, he argued that the category of "Yiddish literature" was a false distinction, since no literature could exist outside of the class struggle. Elevating the "folk" and language could only serve nationalist and chauvinist interests, not the working class.[27] This message remained constant in other JPFO *shule* pedagogical materials. A curriculum outline for the early 1930s stated that parents who sent their children to yeshivas and other nationalistic schools poisoned the children with religion, oppression, national hate, and racial segregation. The Boy Scouts were also singled out for disapprobation for their militarism, seen as rooted in American patriotic chauvinism. Furthermore, American popular culture was suspect, according to this analysis, because its cheap movies and yellow press all helped to prepare the child for the false notion that anyone in America could achieve his or her dreams.[28]

The IWO's educators argued that only the IWO *shules* could prepare working-class children to take a strong, active role in the working class, and could unite working-class children with working-class parents. After the introduction of Popular Front policy, *Proletarishe Dertsiung* ceased almost entirely to use the term *arbeter masn* (working class), replacing it instead with *yidishe masn* or *yidishe folk* (Jewish people). At the same time, the JPFO's curriculum displayed a new emphasis on Jewish traditions and holidays, as well as on modern literary sources such as Sholem Aleichem and I. L. Peretz. These changes were in direct contradiction to the excoriation of "culture for its own sake" in the early 1930s; they were also an indication that JPFO leaders were attempting to develop a more direct connection between Jewishness and "progressive" politics.

The transformation in the JPFO's *shule* curriculum also indicated a growing anxiety regarding fascism abroad and right-wing reaction at home, and an ongoing critique of the ways in which capitalist culture required the sacrifice of native language, group cohesion, local loyalties, and a sense of belonging to a collective. A 1937–38 JPFO curriculum plan stated that fascism and anti-Semitism forced the masses of Jewish workers to think deeply about the problems of Jewish life, and especially about the problem of educating children. Thus, according to this document, the role of JPFO schools was to bind together parents and children, to bring them both into the movement. "Upon us lies the great undertaking of serving the interests of the Jewish workers and *folks-masn*, and therefore . . . [we also carry] the great responsibility of carrying out our work in the best possible method," the document stated. In assessing the success of the previous school year, it concluded: "The deepening of teaching of Yiddish language, literature, history, and expansion of the study of social studies and workers' problems achieved good results both in the knowledge of the children and in the satisfaction of parents. . . ." Each school, therefore, should actively take part in cultural work, in order to build the "united Yiddish cultural front."[29]

Further signifying a shift toward a populist Jewish cultural identity, in 1939 *Proletarishe Dertsiung* changed its name to *Heym un Dertsiung* (*Home and Education*), and began publishing a short English section. These disjunctures of presentation and terminology, however, underlined an enduring continuity: Jewish parents and educators were deeply concerned for their children to have knowledge of Jewish language, traditions, and culture. In the first issue of *Heym un Dertsiung*, JPFO teacher Irving Garbati argued that there were two principal motives of parents in sending their children to IWO schools: the desire of the Jewish people to teach their American-born children the traditions, language, and history of their parents, and to "imbue their children with the ideals of progressive humanity." He wrote:

> The Jewish people saw their children being torn away from them spiritually and emotionally by the 'melting pot.' They saw their children being subtly inculcated with the sneering attitude towards 'foreigners.' To some of the more far-sighted parents it was a question of group perpetuation, of a struggle for existence; true, an ideological and cultural struggle, but a struggle nevertheless. And can we deny to a people the desire to safeguard their culture and their language? Can we dare to say to a people: 'In America only one language and culture are permitted. You have been allowed to come here by the grace of those who have emigrated here before you, and when you die there will be no living trace left of your language, your tradition, your literature, your culture?[30]

The critique of assimilation and the melting pot would continue through the 1940s, as the JPFO leadership struggled to come to terms with the war.

In August 1939, after the signing of the Hitler-Stalin non-aggression pact, the JPFO struggled to retain members who were shocked and disturbed to see the Soviet Union working on behalf of Nazi interests, especially after Hitler's invasion of Poland in September of that year. The leadership of the IWO stressed that the most important issue to consider was the "non-aggression" aspect of the pact, and that the Soviet Union hoped to delay an escalation of tensions as long as possible. They argued that the rush to fight a new world war was spurred by the military and political ruling class, who would benefit financially from the conflict.[31] After dedicating themselves to anti-fascist work, boycotts of German goods, and even protests resulting in arrests in front of the German consulate, JPFO members challenged the JPFO's official support of the pact. In late 1939, an internal splinter group emerged. Joining together with dissenting members of the Communist Party and others who left the *Frayhayt* due to its support of the Pact, these members created the League Against Fascism and Dictatorship. While leveling a strong critique against the IWO's leadership, they announced that their intention was not to break with the Order, but rather to reform it from within. The group planned to hold leafleting sessions, lectures, and protest meetings. "We, the members of the 'temporary committee' of Order members . . . have now united and organized an action committee of IWO members against the Stalin Hitler Pact," their leaflet read. Their critique focused on the power elite at the IWO's top echelons: "We know that the careerists will, like always, remain loyal [to the CP], which has the power and controls the jobs and the apparatus of the Order. We appeal not to these people, but to the honest people who have not yet lost the ability to think for themselves." The "League" encouraged JPFO members to not let the JPFO leadership speak in their names.[32] It is difficult to discern exactly how many members left the IWO due to its support of the Pact. However, in 1940, the IWO's membership dropped from 161,000 to 155,000; this was not only a steep decline, considering years of growth, but it was the first net decline in membership since the IWO was founded.[33]

The IWO's support for the pact was not merely theoretical; the IWO also produced some propaganda in support of the pact, including a cartoon published in the IWO's national monthly magazine, *Fraternal Outlook* in October 1940, depicting President Roosevelt as a warmonger, and an article entitled "The People of America Must Wage Peace," published in May 1941.[34] After Hitler broke the pact in June 1941 by invading the Soviet Union, the IWO quickly reversed course and responded with support for the war. *Fraternal Outlook* published an article in the July 1941 edition entitled, "All Aid to the People's Fight Against Fascism." Quoting the national executive board's statement in support of the war, the article states: "Thus the war no longer involves merely the interests of the few who profit from imperialistic exploitation . . . Hitler is now waging war against the people of the world. The war now assumes an altogether different character."[35] After the attack on the Americans by the Japanese at Pearl Harbor later that year, thousands of IWO members enlisted, and the IWO put all of its significant organizational apparatus into supporting the war effort.

The IWO focused some of its home-front efforts in combating prejudice against Italian and German Americans, emphasizing their role in the fight against fascist regimes in their home countries, but the Order did not speak out in support of Japanese Americans. In February 1942, President Roosevelt signed Executive Order 9066, which provided a legal basis for the establishment of internment camps. The IWO remained silent, issuing no formal criticism of this legislation, despite the presence of Japanese lodges in California. The internment of thousands of Japanese Americans was not covered in *Fraternal Outlook*, nor was it highlighted in the *Fray-hayt*. The CPUSA not only supported Japanese internment, it suspended the memberships of its Japanese-American members. It is worthwhile to note, however, that Japanese-American communists, on the whole, did not break with the CPUSA during this period. They argued that the larger common goal of anti-fascism dictated the temporary acceptance of a racist policy, since it was a better alternative than living under the fascist regimes of Germany or Japan.[36] The question of support for Japanese Americans was not entirely absent, however, from Order-wide discussions of the war. In a national conference of English-speaking lodges in July 1944, Ethel Stevens, an IWO leader from Oakland, praised Japanese Americans, some of whom were members of her lodge in Oakland, as "loyal, hard-working Americans," subject to "eminently unfair persecution." She compared these members favorably against some members of the IWO's local Hungarian lodges, which had fallen prey to pro-Nazi sympathies.[37] The case of the IWO's silence over Japanese internment indicates the close correspondence between official CPUSA policy and IWO policy. It also suggests that IWO members felt comfortable expressing their opinion without fear of suppression from the Party, although evidently, in this case, criticism from the membership level did not result in an official change in policy.

During the Hitler-Stalin pact period, the IWO had reorganized its national sections, moving to emphasize their cultural contributions as American ethnic groups and to deemphasize their linguistic similarities. This change in policy reflected the fact that, by this time, the majority of IWO members were American born or raised. Restructuring the national sections to place more emphasis on internal cultural autonomy, the leadership reasoned, would lead to more and better opportunities to mobilize around key legislative campaigns for social security and civil rights. In February 1941, the general executive board officially instructed national section leaders to "begin functioning as fraternal organizers and leaders of their national groups, not merely organizers of people speaking their language."[38] The goal, according to the IWO's general secretary Max Bedacht, was to promote the cultural work within each national group, and, in turn, to "respect each other's cultural endeavors."[39] Ultimately, Bedacht argued, this work within and across IWO sections would not only help unite and build the Order, it would further strengthen the ultimate goal of an extensive national social security program.

In order to coordinate the new work in the national sections, the IWO brought in Herbert Benjamin, a prominent Communist Party operative. Benjamin, born in 1900 in Chicago to Lithuanian-Jewish immigrants, had led Hunger Marches on Washington in the early 1930s. Benjamin undertook two principal substantial tasks at this time—to oversee the reorganization of the national sections, and, at the same time, to launch a major social security campaign that would engender widespread support among Americans for a stronger welfare state.

In 1941, Benjamin authored an IWO pamphlet entitled, "Our Plan for Plenty," which outlined a plan for a guaranteed minimum yearly income for all Americans. Constructed to deal with the problem of widespread unemployment alongside the large-scale accumulation of profits, the plan articulated a response that would create more wealth equality in the United States. Although the United States is "the richest country in the world," it was yet "a nation of poor people," Benjamin wrote, due to an "unjust distribution of our national income."[40] The premise of his solution was simple:

> Each American family and individual who is willing to engage in useful labor or service should be entitled to a minimum income sufficient to provide the necessities and comforts of modern life as a minimum share in the abundance of which our country is capable . . . the government in the interest of the general welfare and in pursuance of its obligation to those governed, must assure and/or provide such a minimum by means of direct grants, supplements and services.[41]

Calling upon Congress to authorize payments from the Federal Treasury through the Social Security Board, Benjamin proposed that every family of three be guaranteed an income of at least $1,200 a year (almost $20,000 in current U.S. dollars). Appropriations of government funds to be redirected to address the immediate needs for housing, slum clearance, and public health programs, Benjamin argued, would be one more step to address the equality imbalance. The task of the IWO was to bring these ideas to the lodges and neighborhoods of the IWO's membership, to mobilize a mass campaign. While the Plan received some criticism from within the Order as an attempt to provide "panaceas," instead of revolution, Benjamin argued that the plan represented an attempt to "simplify and dramatize certain policies in terms believed to be more easily understood in a mass organization with a membership of varied political composition and development."[42] In other words, the IWO was following its policy of developing "class consciousness" within workers, encouraging them to accept such ideas as income equality readily, thus laying the groundwork for communist political mobilization.

IWO organizers moved swiftly to publicize the "Plan for Plenty" among workers, and to link it to the IWO's stance on the war, as well as to its support for national minority groups within the United States. At a territorial district convention in Scranton, New Jersey, in November of 1940, JPFO member and organizer, Sam Pevzner, delivered a report from the IWO's general executive board to a coalition of anthracite miners. Explaining the Order's position on the Hitler-Stalin Pact, he proclaimed, "We members of the IWO must organize ourselves to Keep America Out of War." While people in the South, especially Blacks, were starving, war could only serve the interests of those who sought to profit it from it. At the same time, he introduced the concept of the IWO's "Plan for Plenty," and laid out plans for organizing a campaign around social security reform. He also emphasized the IWO's backing of a current anti-lynching bill, and pledged support to the American Committee for the Protection of Foreign-Born, which organized the legal defense for deportation and denaturalization cases.[43] Wartime prejudice against immigrants grew, even as the foreign-born themselves increasingly identified with the United States. The IWO, in close consultation with the Party, moved to restructure national sections to serve a wider role in mobilizing American-born and raised members.[44]

In a long article in *Fraternal Outlook* published in February 1941, Benjamin attacked the superiority of white Americans who used their ancestry as a justification for their claim on wealth and privilege, and their concomitant discrimination against ethnic and racial groups. Benjamin argued that the industrial and cultural contributions of national groups were "vital and significant to American life," and that immigrants to the United States were the true American patriots, not the Anglo-Saxon ruling elite. Racism and discrimination, claimed Benjamin, often originated from "the small minority who claim ownership of the wealth of America," who seek justification to exclude others from their riches. The "truly democratic, progressive American people," especially the working class, never considered "ancestry" the test of Americanism, but "cherished the wealth of cultural and social traditions accumulated by their forbears." Consciously echoing and reversing the words of Theodore Roosevelt, who told the Knights of Columbus in 1915 that there was no place for "hyphenated Americans" in the United States, Benjamin declared that, today, hyphenated Americans were not recent immigrants, but thoroughly integrated into American ways of life. These hyphenated Americans, he argued, "can and will carry forward the progressive traditions of the national group movements."[45]

Benjamin quoted the lyrics to *Ballad for Americans*, a popular cantata that had just been performed by the IWO's American People's Chorus and soloist Paul Robeson at a sold-out performance sponsored by the IWO's New York City Central Committee at Manhattan Center, in February, 1941. The IWO's unofficial anthem, the cantata musically narrated the story of American democracy from 1776 onwards. Invoking Lincoln, the soloist/narrator proclaims, "[a] man in white skin can never be free / while his black brother is in slavery. . . ." Interrogating the narrator, the chorus repeatedly asks him, "Say, we still don't know who you are, mister . . . are you an American?" until the narrator finally declares, "Am I an American . . . ?! I'm just an Irish, Negro, Jewish, Italian . . . Spanish, Russian . . . Czech and double-check American!"[46] The cantata's lyrics, emphasizing the importance of "hyphenated Americans," echoed the IWO's philosophy: national culture and identity among Americans helped to strengthen group identity, and strong group identity served as the basis for empathy and identification across linguistic, cultural, and class divisions, leading to more effective political mobilization. Furthermore, as the cantata illustrated, IWO leaders believed that fighting to end racism benefited whites as much as Blacks; white ethnic groups therefore had the duty to strengthen their own communities as part of the central battle against capitalism.

This philosophy was reflected in the activities undertaken at the lodge level; the JPFO encouraged their lodges to take an active part in Negro History Week, and, apart from all other fraternal activities, sponsored events related to Black culture. These efforts were most evident in New York City, which had the largest concentration of JPFO lodges. The largest of the JPFO's some 400 lodges across the country was lower Manhattan's Lincoln Steffens Lodge, with over 1,000 members in 1950.[47] The lodge provided a stream of social, cultural, and political opportunities for its members: it organized cultural programs around Jewish holiday themes, lectures on Israel and American Jewish history, legislative campaigns for national healthcare and fair employment practices, and organized spaghetti dinners, piano recitals, polka dances, and card parties. Since the IWO placed strong emphasis on racial integration, the IWO often sponsored concerts and pageants featuring Black celebrities such as Paul Robeson, Pearl Primus, and Josh White. In keeping with this emphasis, the Lincoln Steffens lodge sponsored an annual contest honoring progressive Black artists, actively promoted Negro History Week, and advocated for passage of anti-lynching and poll tax laws.

The passage of the Smith Act, or Alien Registration Act, in 1940, provided a major occasion for mobilization of both foreign and American-born members of the IWO, and created a further opportunity to build "unity" between the IWO's Black and immigrant cohorts. The act allowed for the deportation of a non-citizen who had been a member of a subversive group at any time since their arrival in the United States. As fear of arrest, internment, and deportation rippled through the national groups, the IWO's committee for organizing Blacks suggested that discussion of the effects of anti-alien legislation among national groups was a useful way to raise awareness of issues facing Blacks. Moran Weston, the IWO's director of Negro Work, also suggested that the IWO's campaign against the poll tax be compared with the struggle to repeal anti-alien legislation; since foreign-born Americans now had an even more intimate understanding of the harassment, intimidation, and arbitrary application of the law due to the Smith Act, he argued, they could particularly understand the effects of Jim Crow racism on Black Americans. It was no coincidence that a key proponent of poll taxes was Representative Howard W. Smith of Virginia, sponsor of the Smith Act, he concluded.[48]

As the war in Europe escalated, IWO leaders continued to link foreign-born Americans and Blacks in the common fight against fascism. In May 1943, Saltzman, Weston, and others on the IWO's Committee on Negro Work, proposed a resolution stating that, "other minority and foreign-born groups who are frequently the subject of undemocratic attacks are becoming increasingly aware that they must support the demands of the Negro people for complete democratic rights, if they are to secure and preserve these rights for themselves." The common interest between vulnerable and persecuted groups also served as a catalyst for organizing postwar social security campaigns.

After President Roosevelt introduced his social and economic "bill of rights" in 1944, the IWO hoped that the time was right to fight for far-reaching reform of health insurance. The Wagner-Murray-Dingell Bill, introduced in 1943 and then again in 1945, was the first comprehensive proposal for government-sponsored health insurance. It called for a federally sponsored health insurance program, along with permanent and temporary disability, maternity and death benefits, full federalization of the existing Federal-State unemployment insurance, expansion of old-age and survivors' insurance, and enlargement of public assistance.

The IWO officially endorsed the bill, launching a major "health and social security campaign" for 1945–46. Just as the IWO's leaders had regarded the passage of the Smith Act as an opportunity for anti-discrimination education within the IWO, during this campaign they issued a formal statement connecting the Order's special character as a multinational and interracial organization to its mission to expand social security legislation: "The forces who want to perpetuate discriminatory measures against the Negro people, the Jewish people, and the foreign-born, are the same elements striving to hamper every security measure, because misery, hunger, and insecurity are the means to perpetuate Jim-Crow, anti-Semitism, and other forms of discrimination," an internal IWO resolution in support of the bill stated. "The IWO, therefore, can play a special role in helping to put into motion the nationality group communities of America on the basis of the struggle for the Wagner-Murray-Dingell bill."[49] Although President Truman sanctioned the revised 1945 version of the bill, it never received wide support in Congress. Without the support of the American Medical Association, and after the first Republican Congress in over ten years was elected in 1946, it was clear that Truman could not carry the support for New Deal social programs that his predecessor had accomplished.

As Congressional support for New Deal programs waned, the New Deal's popular appeal reached its apex. As the IWO continued to harness this appeal, it attained a peak record of 181,000 members in March 1946. "Why has [the IWO] been so successful?" an editorial in the JPFO's periodical, the *Jewish Fraternalist*, rhetorically asked. The article concluded that loyalty with "the great American working class" and organized labor helped the IWO sustain the "core of American democracy . . . the greatest bulwark blocking the way of the fascist-minded money bags."[50] This focus on unity belied the obvious fact that the IWO's continuous and uncritical support for the Soviet Union created major divisions within the American public sphere. While fighting reactionary rhetoric on the right, the JPFO applied these same tactics to their own critics. Sam Pevzner, in a column for the *Jewish Fraternalist* in the summer of 1946, blasted charges of persecution against Jews in the Soviet Union by writing, "I wondered what gave birth to this gory canard . . . [even] the most conservative Jews . . . have to admit that the status of Jews in that land is one of full equality and opportunity."[51] The fact that anti-Semitism was a crime in the Soviet Union subject to harsh punishment, he argued, was a commonly known fact: "to be a Jew nowadays and to not know this, means you are either abysmally ignorant or a psychopathic hater of the land of Socialism."[52] As the Cold War began to gain purchase both at home and abroad, the divisive issue of the Soviet Union punctuated debates throughout the decade. However, in the immediate postwar years, the JPFO continued to garner support for its Jewish cultural work. As American Jews struggled to come to terms with the decimation of European Jewry, many sought to engage with Yiddish language and culture, and to educate themselves and their children within the JPFO's rubric.

Albert Kahn (1912–1979), nephew of the famed modernist architect of the same name, became president of the JPFO in 1945. Although widely known as a committed radical, Kahn did not come from the working class. Educated at Dartmouth, Kahn became radicalized as a volunteer in the Spanish Civil War and later ran for office as a member of the American Labor Party. Kahn publicly broadcast his growing interest in Jewish culture as a direct result of his involvement with the JPFO, and his growing recognition of American Jews' need for a deeper engagement with the past. In a Jewish History Week meeting in November 1945, Kahn announced, "Until recently, I could only say 'lechaim.' But I'm learning Yiddish now. Why? Because Yiddish is an integral part of the Jewish culture. I want to know about the Jewish culture; I want to be enriched by it. The better a Jew I become, the better an American I become . . ." he said.[53] The support for Yiddish language and culture grew across the JPFO's initiatives in the 1940s, forming the core of its mission.

While educated, assimilated outsiders like Kahn politicized their personal discovery of Yiddish culture, veterans like Itshe Goldberg continued to rally JPFO parents to the cause of Yiddish education. In the postwar years, he persisted in regarding assimilation, along with anti-Semitism, as one of the greatest threats facing American Jews. In "The Yiddish School and Yiddish Culture in America," a 1947 article compiled from a series of speeches he had given during the war years, Goldberg published a detailed manifesto outlining what he regarded as the role of Yiddish in American life. In the wake of World War II and the destruction of a thousand-year-old Jewish civilization, Goldberg wrote, American Jews now had a special mission to work on behalf of Jewish culture. "We cannot think calmly and with cool objectivity regarding the fate of Yiddish culture, or of its future development," he wrote. "In these current times, it is necessary to renew our dedication and responsibility to strengthening our national culture."[54] Although Goldberg acknowledged that Eastern European Jewish culture had been decimated, he focused on the act of rebuilding Jewish culture as a mission of quasi-religious import: In Jewish Europe today, it is a time of "cultural rebuilding, of *mayse bereyshis* [creation]," he wrote.[55] Yet American Jews needed to take seriously the responsibility for their national culture. "We believe in our culture, in its potential, power, and endurance," Goldberg said.[56] He excoriated the false promise of Jewish emancipation in Enlightenment Europe, when Jews had exchanged their group autonomy for individual freedom. Relating that circumstance directly to the contemporary context, he wrote, "We cast aside assimilation, and with it the so-called promise of liberation [inherent in] the Jewish Question. There is no liberation through assimilation—there is only imprisonment."[57] The rest of the essay built upon this theme: all assimilation is profound cultural loss, or outright theft. The mission of progressive Jews in America was to complete the unfulfilled project of American democracy by deepening their own cultural awareness, and by engaging in the struggle to allow others to do so as well.

Goldberg continued his essay by offering a definition of modern Jewish culture as distinctly secular, historic, multilingual, and left-wing. Goldberg then suggested that this latest "awakening" in the postwar U.S. toward national culture was especially, although not exclusively, important for American-born Jews, who had recently begun to reconnect with their own culture. As proof for this hypothesis, he stated that the IWO had made recent inroads in attracting members seeking greater cultural awareness, especially from American-born English-speakers. The heart of the issue, Goldberg concluded, and the reason that progressive American Jews might yet win the struggle against assimilation, was that, culturally and politically, "the melting pot has a scorched bottom." He wrote, "It is anti-democratic and anti-American to follow the jingoistic theory of complete cultural assimilation, because ultimately this cultural assimilation is . . . no more than a domination by one ruling culture at the expense of all other cultures. Our goal should be the attainment of a cultural as well as political democracy in the United States. . . ."[58] Goldberg believed that, in order not to lose any of the distinctive nature of American Jewish culture through the generations, American Jews must faithfully uphold the two main pillars of American Jewish culture: the continuity from past generations, and the creativity and innovations of the present. Making the case for the Yiddish language as a cornerstone of this foundation, Goldberg claimed that the bilingual nature of American Jewish culture was its greatest asset, and its most powerful symbol.

Goldberg's theoretical understanding of the role of Yiddish culture in the postwar era complemented the practical work of Jewish cultural activism being undertaken at the same time by the IWO's newest section, the Emma Lazarus Division of the JPFO (ELD). This women's organization emerged in 1944 as a direct outgrowth of women's wartime activism. The Emmas, as members of the ELD were known, proclaimed their organization to be a "cultural and civic organization for women . . . dedicated to advance the interests of the Jewish people and the country as a whole." They stood for the idea that the struggle for labor and the Jewish struggle were, in essence, inextricable: "We believe that the struggle for Jewish freedom everywhere—in the U.S.A., Europe and Palestine—can be won only if the Jewish people travel together with labor and all progressive forces."[59] The Emmas listed their objectives as protecting the freedom of Jews in all lands, promoting the "progressive currents in Jewish culture and traditions, fostering understanding and harmonious community life between Jews and non-Jews, Negro and white Americans," while working for democracy through the labor movement. The ELD sponsored essay contests where respondents answered the question, "Why I Joined the Division." One woman wrote, "I wanted to join a progressive Jewish organization . . . my activities are mainly outdoors since I have a baby. Many of our mothers do the same. They call us the 'Carriage Brigade.' We go into the shopping section with placards, leaflets, and set up tables. There hasn't been an important issue which we did not bring to our neighborhood—Jewish refugees, the Taft-Hartley Bill, discrimination, rent . . . ," she wrote. In addition to these social issues, there were cultural considerations as well, she said: "My child goes to *shule* because I want her to learn the Jewish language."[60] The ELD focused much of its energy on improving the JPFO's *shule* education and curriculum, especially for English-speaking children coming into Yiddish-speaking classrooms. The primary language in the shules continued to be Yiddish, because parents had made that demand, even if they themselves did not speak Yiddish in the home. This continuity between home and school, ELD leaders argued, would help to reinforce among both parents and students the idea of Yiddish as the national language of the Jewish people.[61]

During and after the war, the JPFO attempted to address the disjuncture between its historic opposition to Zionism, and its growing support for a Jewish settlement in Palestine. In 1948, JPFO leaders issued a document entitled, "Declaration of Principles of the Jewish Peoples Fraternal Order of the International Workers Order," in which they formulated their new approach to Zionism: "We consider the Yishuv [settlement] in Palestine an integral and important part of Jewish life, whose future is closely tied with the future of the Jewish people throughout the world . . . ," the document stated.[62] Underscoring their enduring commitment to progressive labor and anti-imperialism, JPFO leaders declared their intention to work with other Jewish organizations in the United States on behalf of the Jews of Palestine, so that the "Yishuv can develop into a free Jewish national democratic home, based on brotherly cooperation with the Arab peoples."[63] Yet internally, members worried that too much support for building Jewish Palestine would distract from the JPFO's primary responsibility of rebuilding Jewish institutions in the diaspora, especially in Eastern Europe. Itshe Goldberg argued, "to give up the relief campaign [in Europe] would be to recognize Israel as the only *yishuv* in the world, and to negate the importance of all others. We are facing a new kind of destruction of Jewish life, not in numbers exterminated but in an undermining of Jewish cultural life."[64] The Emma Lazarus Division approached the issue by stating that their work on behalf of the Jewish state did not necessarily mean that they were siding with the American Jewish establishment, but rather that the two sides shared a common goal, supporting Jewish peoplehood: "The ELD does not agree with Hadassah, or any of the Zionist organizations on the question of Zionism, but we ardently and energetically support the right of the Jewish people of Israel to develop their state as an instrument of a free and independent nation . . . ," one resolution stated.[65] As evidence of their public support for the new Jewish state, the JPFO staged a ceremony in Madison Square Park on July 16, 1948. Rubin Saltzman, Itshe Goldberg, ELD head June Gordon, and *Jewish Fraternalist* editor Sam Pevzner appeared in a large *New York Times* photo alongside five ambulances they were donating to the Red Mogen David, Israel's version of the Red Cross.[66]

As the JPFO received a measure of public recognition for its campaigns on behalf of Israel, it faced a new set of concerns at home, leading to anxiety over rising fascist forces in the United States. On the evening of September 4, 1949, 20,000 people gathered in Cortlandt, fifty miles north of New York City, to hear a concert by the prominent African-American artist, Paul Robeson. After the performance, the evening turned ugly. As the audience left the grounds, they faced a hostile crowd throwing rocks and yelling epithets. According to one account, snipers hid in the trees, hoping to assassinate Robeson. Protestors, assisted by police, lined the road and threw rocks into car windows as concertgoers attempted to make their way home. Bloody clashes went on through the night. Protestors shouted racial slurs against Jews and Blacks, yelling, among other things, "N--- loving Jews, down South we'd string you up. Go back to Moscow."[67] The protest was ostensibly organized to protest comments Robeson had recently made in solidarity with the Soviet Union. Popular resentment also targeted the audience members, many of whom were Jews, Blacks, and white ethnic trade union members from the New York metropolitan area. In its investigation of the event, the American Civil Liberties Union found that, while the demonstration against the concert had been organized to express hatred of communism, the resulting, "unprovoked" riot was fueled largely by anti-Semitism.[68]

As one author wrote in the *Jewish Fraternalist* in October 1949, "Peekskill revealed a new aspect of anti-Semitism in the United States"—a combination of elements, which historically existed separately now united in a menacing way. "This was an American pogrom," the article declared, encouraged by official propaganda and supported by local law enforcement.[69] At the JPFO's national board meeting in November 1949, Samson Milgrom warned that the JPFO needed to fight the isolation forced upon the organization by "reactionary attacks." "There is a fertile field for broad coalitions," he argued. It was the JPFO's duty to constantly fight any manifestation of white supremacy, especially when it came to racism against Blacks, since their treatment was a marker of larger political trends and currents in the United States. "The conditions of the Negro people are a barometer of the state of our democracy," he said. "This question must be the basis of all our work throughout the Order. We cannot fight against anti-Semitism without fighting for Negro rights, as well. We must have an integrated struggle in which our publications and our cultural work must become important instruments. We want the Negro people to regard us as a staunch ally in a common fight."[70]

Eddie Nelson, the executive secretary of the new Douglass-Lincoln Society, the IWO's national section for Blacks, also participated in the JPFO's discussion on race relations. "Negro people are not interested in theoretical democracy but in a living reality," he said. "We must find some medium to express our theoretical claim that culture is of the people and must serve the people. We must lay bare the super-profit motive for racism in America . . . and especially how racism is eating the heart of our Order."[71] In keeping with these concerns, and in light of the disintegration of the JPFO's working relationships with mainstream Jewish organizations, the IWO formulated an official declaration of its inherent support for the United States, and the Order's goals for greater equality and a fuller democracy:

> The interracial, multi-national composition of the Order makes it truly a representative American fraternal organization dedicated to the principles of brotherhood, security, and equality, with sole allegiance to the United States. The Order supports all efforts for the achievement of a better life for the workers and common people of our country through peaceful and democratic methods, and re-affirms its opposition to the use of force and violence against the government, the democratic institutions of our country, the people, racial and national groups, organizations or individuals.[72]

Such declarations did little to quell a rising tide of anti-communist sentiment outside of the IWO. Yet it did reorient its programs toward the postwar world, where support for civil rights and the peace movement began to take an increasingly prominent role among the American left. However, the "reactionary forces" the Order had always fought against now loomed closer, threatening to claim the movement entirely.

On Mother's Day, 1950, the Emma Lazarus Division issued an announcement declaring that the growing attacks on Blacks, Jews, the foreign-born, and all who dared to stand with them against the reactionary warmongers, signified an all-out war against civil rights and the welfare state: "Because the peace forces are rising, the reactionaries in Congress cannot afford to follow a step-by-step schedule as Hitler did: first Communists and Jews, then trade union and so on . . . in one short year, it has become clear that the objective is destruction of all Civil Rights," their announcement declared.[73] From within the movement, it certainly looked like a war of the worlds, and JPFO leaders knew they risked losing everything they had built over the past twenty years. To a certain extent, they did. In 1950, New York State's Department of Insurance began an investigation into the IWO, alleging that it "was and is dominated by the Communist Party," and that allowing it to continue transacting business would be hazardous to policyholders, creditors, and the public.[74] By 1953, the IWO was ordered dissolved by the New York courts, and was no longer allowed to recruit new members. After a protracted court battle that extended to the Supreme

Court of the United States, the IWO officially lost its charter. By 1954, the IWO, and almost $8 million of its assets, were liquidated.

As a precaution against forced dissolution, the JPFO had already officially removed the ELD and the JPFO's school network from its corporate structure, and these organizations were thus able to continue to run independently, as the Emma Lazarus Federation of Jewish Women's Clubs and the Jewish Service Bureau for Education, respectively. Much of the leadership of these organizations remained intact after the transfer. However, the JPFO lost its "crown jewel," a manor house in Connecticut that it had purchased as an old-age home for members. While older members turned to the Yiddish *Frayhayt* for institutional affiliation, younger members built a community around the English-language *Jewish Life* magazine (later *Jewish Currents*). These members also formed the Organization of Jewish Cultural Clubs and Societies, a direct descendent of the JPFO's fraternal lodges. Goldberg, June Gordon, Sam Pevzner, and other former JPFO leaders used this platform to campaign publicly for peace in the Middle East, support for Yiddish culture, and opposition to nuclear proliferation and the Vietnam War.[75]

Over a twenty-year period, the International Workers Order developed from a marginal, left-wing Jewish fraternal organization to a multi-ethnic, national political and cultural movement, while retaining a visible Jewish leadership and a sustained commitment to Jewish culture and communal defense. Its greatest successes came from its ability to create connections across racial and ethnic groups, building a larger political community. Outside of the strict structures of the Party, or at least one step removed from its discipline and hierarchy, the IWO created the opportunity for community-building on the left. The Order struggled with the question of how to take the issues of the immigrant working class and translate them into a wider movement, relatable to by the larger society. Although some American political movements in the 1960s and 1970s did focus on ethnic-political mobilization—most notably Cesar Chavez's organizing of farm workers—this did not become the norm within the labor movement. Sociologist Richard Flacks, himself a product of the IWO's *shules* and Camp *Kinderland*, has noted that the American left has been most successful when it functions as a cultural force rather than a political party.[76] In the case of the JPFO, the forging of enduring bonds within a close cohort of Jewish activists created a lifelong sense of purpose and community that long outlasted membership in, and loyalty to, the Communist Party. Out of a critique of the American "melting pot" ideology that failed to deliver prosperity, security, or equality, the men and women of the JPFO developed a comprehensive set of Jewish cultural institutions that, although largely unknown today, played a significant role in the lives of many thousands of American Jews at midcentury.

Notes

1. *Jewish Fraternalist*, June–July 1945, 3.

2. Ibid.

3. International Workers Order Records, 1927–1956, 5276. Kheel Center for Labor-Management Documentation and Archives, Cornell University Library. Box 42, Folder 4 [hereafter IWO Records, Kheel].

4. Quoted in Maurice Isserman, *Which Side Were You On? The American Communist Party During the Second World War* (Urbana, IL: University of Illinois Press, 1993), 174.

5. Reprinted in the *Jewish Fraternalist*, June–July 1945, 2. Also see testimony of Rubin Saltzman, Record on Appeal, vol. IV, p. 3288, *In re* International Workers Order, 305 N.Y. 258 (1953) [hereafter Testimony of Rubin Saltzman].

6. Reprinted in the *Jewish Fraternalist*, June–July 1945, 2.

7. Joyce Antler, "Justine Wise Polier and the Prophetic Tradition," in *Women and American Judaism: Historical Perspectives*, eds. Pamela Nadell and Jonathan Sarna (Waltham, MA: Brandeis University Press, 2001), 284. Also see *Jewish Polity and American Civil Society: Communal Agencies and Religious Movements in the American Public Square,* eds. Alan Mittleman, Jonathan Sarna and Robert Licht (Lanham, MD: Rowan & Littlefield, 2002). As an example of the rapid change in climate, in his Madison Square Garden speech on May 26, 1945, Rubin Saltzman had remarked, "Only a week ago, the President of the American Jewish Congress in Chicago said to us: 'Your Jewish Peoples Fraternal Order is a healthy, living limb of the Jewish People.'" *Jewish Fraternalist*, June–July 1945, 3.

8. Quoted in Shana Bernstein, *Bridges of Reform: Inter-racial Civil Rights Activism in 20th Century Los Angeles* (New York: Oxford University Press, 2011), 130–32.

9. Recent publications in American Jewish historiography that consider the JPFO briefly, and primarily in relation to its exclusion from major Jewish communal bodies, include Shana Bernstein's *Bridges of Reform*; Stuart Svonkin, *Jews Against Prejudice: American Jews and the Fight for Civil Liberties* (New York: Columbia University Press, 1997); Deborah Dash Moore, *To the Golden Cities: Pursuing the Jewish Dream in Miami and L.A.* (New York: Free Press, 1994); and Victor Navasky, *Naming Names* (1980; New York: Hill and Wang, 3rd ed., 2003). Publications that touch on the JPFO's cultural program include Stephen H. Norwood, *Antisemitism and the American Far Left* (New York: Cambridge University Press, 2013); and Paul C. Mishler, *Raising Reds: The Young Pioneers, Radical Summer Camps, and Communist Political Culture in the United States* (New York: Columbia University Press, 1999); Also see Joyce Antler's treatment of the JPFO's Jewish women's clubs, in *The Journey*

Home: Jewish Women and the American Century (New York: Simon and Schuster, 1997); and Gennady Estraikh's *Yiddish and the Cold War* (Oxford: Legenda, 2008).

10. Rubin Saltzman obituary by Morris Schappes, *Jewish Currents*, May 1959, 25–26.

11. Testimony of Rubin Saltzman, p. 3288.

12. Saltzman obituary, *Jewish Currents*, May 1959, 26.

13. "Resolution on Negro Work," IWO Records, Kheel, Box 1 Folder 10.

14. See, for example: "Reds Call on Police to Guard Their $15,000," *New York Times*, April 14, 1930, 19. This article identifies Max Bedacht as the executive secretary of the Communist Party, and William Weiner as the secretary of the National Bureau of the Jewish Faction of the Communist Party. See also "Radical Group Holds First Convention," *New York Times*, May 30, 1931, 2; "6 Officers in IWO Identified as Reds," *New York Times*, January 31, 1951, 7. FBI Information Matthew Cvetic testified extensively regarding the role of Communists, Milgrom in particular, within the IWO. See, for example: "Reports Reds Knew Draper and Adler," *New York Times*, May 18, 1950, 12, and Testimony of Matthew Cvetic, Record on Appeal, vol. IV, p. 2376, *In re* International Workers Order, 305 N.Y. 258 (1953).

15. See, for example: "International Workers Order Pledges $50,000 Fund to Aid C.P. Election Drive," *Daily Worker*, August 4, 1936; quoted in testimony of Rubin Saltzman, Record on Appeal vol. IV, p. 3315, *In re* International Workers Order, 305 N.Y. 258 (1953).

16. See, for example: "Fight on 'Reaction' Urged; Workers Order Asked to Elect 'Progressive' Candidates," *New York Times*, Sept. 11, 1938, 2.

17. Rubin Saltzman, *Tsu der Geshikte fun der Fraternaler Bavegung* [*Toward the History of the Fraternal Movement*] (New York: International Workers Order, 1936), 58.

18. Testimony of Irving Neugebauer in reference to Respondents' Exhibit KY, "For Freedom—Let's Build the J.P.F.O." *Bulletin of JPFO Lodge 489*. Record on Appeal, vol. VI, p. 3999, *In re* International Workers Order, 305 N.Y. 258 (1953).

19. Mary L. Heen, "Ending Jim Crow Life Insurance Rates," *Northwestern Journal of Law & Social Policy* 4, No. 2, (2009): 360–99. Metropolitan Life eliminated explicit race-based rates for some new policies in 1948, but race-integrated mortality tables did not become the industry standard until the 1960s.

20. Testimony of Peter Shipka, Record on Appeal, vol. IV, pp. 3486–87, *In re* International Workers Order, 305 N.Y. 258 (1953).

21. "Guiding Policy for the Communists in their leadership and work in the IWO," IWO Records, Kheel, Box 19, Folder 6. Undated.

22. "Protokol fun di zitsung fun der yidisher sektsiye bay der konvenshon fun internatsiyonaler arbeter ordn, opgehelt dem 19tn un 20stn yuni, 1933." ["Meeting notes of the Jewish Section of the International Workers Order, held June 19th and 20th, 1933"]; YIVO Institute for Jewish Research, New York [hereafter YIVO], RG 117, Box 80, Folder 80.6.

23. Ibid.

24. Interview with Itshe Goldberg, American Jewish Committee Oral History Project, Oct. 16, 1986. Collection of the New York Public Library. Also see interview with Itshe Goldberg by Paul Buhle, Oral History of the American Left, Collection of the Tamiment Library, New York University.

25. "Lenin vegn dertsiung," ["Lenin on Education"], in *Proletarishe Dertsiung* [*Proletarian Education*], January 1935: 4; YIVO.

26. Itshe Goldberg and A. Bergman, "Di program fun undzere shul," ["The Program of Our Schools"], *Proletarishe Dertsiung* [*Proletarian Education*], January 1935: 5–6; YIVO.

27. Ibid.

28. "Konspekt fun di yidishe kinder shuln baym internatsiyonaln arbeter ordn" ["Outline of the Yiddish Children's Schools of the International Workers Order"], United States Territorial Collection, RG 117, Box 80, File 79.4; YIVO.

29. Ibid.

30. *Heym un Dertsiung* [*Home and Education*], November 1939: 24; YIVO.

31. Testimony of Rubin Saltzman, p. 3433.

32. Pamphlet, RG 117 Box 80, Folder 79.4; United States Territorial Collection, YIVO. Also see Lucy Dawidowicz's discussion of this incident in her report, "Jewish People's Fraternal Order of the International Workers Order." Library of Jewish Information, American Jewish Committee, November 1950, 7.

33. *Almanakh: Baytrog fun Yidn tsu dem Oyfboy fun Amerika—Tsen Yoriker Yubiley fun Internatsiyonaler Arbeter Ordn.* [*Almanac: Contributions of Jews to the Building of America—Tenth Anniversary of the International Workers Order*] (New York: Kooperative Folks-Farlag, International Workers Order, 1940), 458. Also see Arthur Sabin's discussion of membership decline in 1940, in *Red Scare in Court: New York versus the International Workers Order* (Philadelphia: University of Pennsylvania Press, 1993), 20.

34. Testimony of Rubin Saltzman, p. 3434.

35. Testimony of Rubin Saltzman, p. 3438.

36. See discussion of the Nisei (second-generation) leftist response in Scott Kurashige, *The Shifting Grounds of Race: Black and Japanese Americans in the Making of Multiethnic Los Angeles* (Princeton, NJ: Princeton University Press, 2010), 124.

37. "Meeting notes from National Conference of General Lodges," IWO Records, Kheel, Box 9, Folder 1.

38. "This and That," Max Bedacht editorial column, *Fraternal Outlook*, April 1941: 3.

39. Ibid.

40. Herbert Benjamin, *Our Plan for Plenty* (New York: International Workers Order, 1941), unpaginated inside cover.

41. Benjamin, *Our Plan for Plenty*, 12.

42. International Workers Order Records, 1927–1956, 5276. Kheel Center for Labor-Management Documentation and Archives, Cornell University Library. Herbert Benjamin Correspondence, Box 5, Folder 10.

43. "Resolutions of the Anthracite Area, 1940." IWO Records, Kheel, Box 8, Folder 9.

44. Benjamin makes explicit reference to being assigned to this task by the Party. He later resigned because of internal conflicts over the re-structuring policy. "Executive Secretary—Herbert Benjamin, 1941–42," Box 5, Folder 6, IWO Records, Kheel. Also see a discussion of this conflict in Roger Keeran, "National Groups and the Popular Front: The Case of the International Workers Order," *Journal of American Ethnic History* 14, No. 3. (1995): 23–51.

45. Herbert Benjamin, "Uncle Sam's Nephews and Nieces," *Fraternal Outlook*, February 1941: 15.

46. Ibid.

47. Testimony of Rubin Saltzman, p. 3216.

48. M. Moran Weston, "How Poll Tax Engenders Fascism in the South and Helps Undermine Democracy in the North," *New York Age*, Aug. 15, 1941, 2.

49. IWO Records, Kheel, Minutes, 1944. Box 1, Folder 11.

50. *Jewish Fraternalist*, March 1946: 3.

51. *Jewish Fraternalist*, August 1946: 29.

52. Ibid.

53. IWO Records, Kheel, Box 16, Folder 2.

54. Itshe Goldberg, "Di Yidishe Kultur un di Yidishe Shuln in Amerike," in *In Dinst fun Folk* [*In the People's Service*], eds. I. Goldberg and R. Saltzman (New York: Yidishe-Folks Ordn, 1947), 67.

55. Goldberg, "Di Yidishe Kultur un di Yidishe Shuln in Amerike," 68.

56. Ibid.

57. Ibid.

58. Goldberg, "Di Yidishe Kultur un di Yidishe Shuln in Amerike," 70

59. "First National Convention of the Emma Lazarus Division," *Jewish Fraternalist*, October 1947: 6.

60. Ibid.

61. IWO Records, Kheel, JPFO board minutes, Box 27, Folder 3.

62. IWO Records, Kheel, Box 27, Folder 1.

63. IWO Records, Kheel, Box 27, Folder 3.

64. IWO Records, Kheel, Box 27, Folder 2.

65. IWO Records, Kheel, Box 28, Folder 1.

66. "Presenting Ambulances for Shipment to Israel," *New York Times*, July 17, 1948, 4.

67. Quoted in Howard Fast, *Peekskill USA: Inside the Infamous 1949 Riots* (Mineola, NY: Dover Publications, 2006), 115. Originally published as *Peekskill: USA* by the Civil Rights Congress, 1951.

68. Appendix I, "Summary Conclusion of the American Civil Liberties Union Investigation of the Two Peekskill Affairs," in Fast, *Peekskill USA*, 97.

69. *Jewish Fraternalist*, September–October 1949: 6.

70. IWO Records, Kheel, Box 27, Folder 1.

71. IWO Records, Kheel, Box 27, Folder 2.

72. Ibid.

73. IWO Records, Kheel, Box 27, Folder 1.

74. *In re* International Workers Order, 199 Misc. 941 (N.Y. Sup. Ct. 1951).

75. See, for example, "American Jewish Leftists Support Israel on Peace but Hit Dayan, Allon, Begin." Jewish Telegraphic Agency, Oct. 3, 1969.

76. Interview with Richard and Mickey Flacks, Santa Barbara, California, Aug. 7, 2012.

4

Paul Novick, a Standard-Bearer of Yiddish Communism

Gennady Estraikh

After one fails, one can go on and fail better.

—Samuel Beckett

The history of the daily *Frayhayt* (*Freedom*, 1922–1988) began when a group of journalists left one of the other New York-based Yiddish dailies, the socialist *Forverts* (*Forward*), in the fall of 1921. Among the rebels, who were unhappy with the *Forverts*'s editorial line of disapproving the Bolshevik, totalitarian form of socialism, the two former Bundists, Moissaye (Moyshe) Olgin (1878–1939) and Paul (Peysakh) Novick (1891–1989), were destined to hold prominent roles in the American Yiddish Communist press. Olgin became one of the first two co-editors of the *Frayhayt*, but in 1923 he left it, resuming his editorship of the newspaper in 1929.[1] Following Olgin's death, Novick replaced him at the helm of the newspaper and stayed in this capacity until its closure in 1988.

Novick was born on September 7, 1891, in the then-Russian town of Brest-Litovsk (Brisk in Yiddish; now Brest in Belarus) into the family of a shopkeeper, and was traditionally educated until the age of sixteen, when he left the yeshiva run by the prominent rabbi, Khaim Soloveitchik, also known as Khaim Brisker. Novick joined the Jewish Labor Bund in 1907 and devoted himself to acquiring a secular education. In 1913 he went to New York after a three-year stint in Zurich, where he worked in a cigarette-casing factory. He started his life in America as a garment worker, but soon became an official and secretary of the Jewish Socialist Federation (JSF), formed with the strong involvement of Bundist immigrants in 1912 as the Yiddish-language branch in the Socialist Party of America. In 1915, he began to write for the JSF's weekly organ *Di naye velt* (*The New World*). Like many other Jewish immigrants, notably socialists, Novick returned to Russia following the February Revolution in 1917. He lived in Petrograd, Minsk, Moscow, Vilna, and Warsaw, and worked as a journalist and editor in the Bundist press. Thus, he edited the Vilna *Unzer shtime* (*Our Voice*), where his predecessor was the future great Yiddish scholar Max Weinreich, and he was news editor of the Warsaw *Lebns-fragn* (*Current Issues*).

In October 1920, Novick resettled, this time permanently, in the United States. He rejoined the JSF and wrote for the *Forverts* in 1920–21until he sided with the left, and more numerous, wing of the JSF when it split from the Socialist Party in 1921. When the *Frayhayt* was founded, Novick became its first news editor, and later secretary of its editorial board and assistant editor. He left the communist paper in 1923 and for a couple of years worked as a staff member of the Chicago daily *Yidisher kuryer* (*Jewish Courier*), which spoke for Orthodox Jewish immigrants. It seems that Novick had problems with accepting, in his words, "the cursed 21 conditions" which determined admission to the Comintern.[2] Yet, ultimately he turned into a diehard communist and did not desert the paper during the two mass departures of its disillusioned readers and writers: the first in 1929, when all periodicals of the Communist Party USA (CPUSA) echoed the Comintern's interpretation of the anti-Jewish riots in Palestine as a commendable episode in the local Arabs' struggle against their British and Zionist colonizers, and, the second in 1939, after the Molotov-Ribbentrop Pact.[3]

A self-educated man, Novick did not come close to the skilled political journalist, literary critic, translator, and prose writer Olgin, who received his higher education in Kiev, Heidelberg, and New York, and obtained a doctorate at Columbia University. Nonetheless, in American pro-Soviet circles, Novick remained an influential Jewish communal leader, and as such he would often determine the political behavior of Yiddish-speaking left-wingers in the United States, whose numbers during and after World War II were low but not negligible: the *Morgn-Frayhayt*'s circulation of 21,000 in 1947 almost equaled the circulation of the CPUSA's English-language *Daily Worker*.[4] Both newspapers were published in the same nine-story building owned by the CPUSA at 35 East Twelfth Street, between University Place and Broadway.

The situation had become different in the 1950s, when the CPUSA had lost much of its membership and a number of institutions, including the International Workers Order (IWO), which used to define the Jewish landscape of communist life in America and had been suppressed or dissolved.[5] Many Yiddish-speakers left the communist movement during this period, when the presumptive affinity between Jews and communism (or, euphemistically, *un-Americanism*) "inspired fear in the hearts of the Jews."[6] In this political climate, communist ideologists, including *Morgn-Frayhayt* journalists, counteracted the anti-Semitic connotations of American Cold War rhetoric by striving to find something to praise in Soviet nationalities politics.

The whitewashing ability of communist journalism had dramatically decreased in strength after April 1956, when an article, entitled "Our Pain and Our Consolation," in the Warsaw Yiddish newspaper *Folks-Shtime* (*People's Voice*) provided revealing information about the tragic fate of Yiddish writers during the Stalinist period. The *Folks-Shtime* article confirmed the material published by the *Forverts* journalist, Leo Crystal, who went on a fact-finding trip to the Soviet Union at the beginning of 1956. In Moscow, the Israeli embassy helped Crystal to get access to some fragments of the truth about the destiny of the Jewish Anti-Fascist Committee (JAFC), thirteen of whose leading members, including the Yiddish writers David Bergelson, Itsik Fefer, David Hofshteyn, Leyb Kvitko, and Peretz Markish, were executed on August 12, 1952, accused of plotting on behalf of "Zionism" and "imperialism." The "evidence" of this included past contacts with Novick, who had visited the USSR from September 1946 through January 1947.[7]

During a stopover in Warsaw, Crystal shared his findings with the *Folks-Shtime* editor, Hersh Smolar, who decided, after obtaining consent of the top Polish functioneers, to reveal this information to his paper's readership. While the American Communists initially rejected Crystal's articles as malicious anti-Soviet slander, the publication in the newspaper of Polish Communists made it impossible to cling to the pretense that nothing extraordinary had happened to the JAFC and its milieu. The disclosure caused an uproar in the Jewish world and set off a firestorm in its pro-Soviet circles, bringing to an end the period that, in Novick's words, at first "seemed to be a misunderstanding, then a puzzle and later, as the years passed, an inexplicable nightmare."[8] In a stark turnaround, Novick acknowledged his paper's submissive relationship with the Soviet Union and promised that, from now on, Soviet life would be observed and analyzed through the prism of "constructive criticism."[9]

In the meantime, the *Morgn-Frayhayt* continued to be printed under the same name, though some activists suggested rebranding it (as did the journal, *Jewish Life*, which turned into *Jewish Currents*) in order to emphasize its "progressive" rather than communist character. The decision to become "progressive" was not simply a result of soul-searching in 1956. Beginning from the mid-1930s, American Communists had publicized themselves as disseminators of a "progressive secular Yiddish culture."[10] An interesting interpretation of "progressiveness" is contained in the unpublished memoirs, *Things I Have Learned*, written in the early 1960s by Alex Bittelman. This veteran of the American Communist movement revealed that in the late 1950s he came to "the idea of a progressive Jewish nationalism—a good nationalism—as the main condition for Jewish national survival and as an organic part of all progressive nationalisms in the world, including socialist nationalism."[11] In the words of Novick, his newspaper was "not only an instrument to build the people's organizations," it was "not only an instrument in the people's fight for a better life," but it was "of itself a progressive Jewish cultural institution."[12] He was clearly alluding to Lenin's words: "A newspaper is not only a collective propagandist and a collective agitator, it is also a collective organizer."[13]

The "progressive" nature of the *Morgn-Frayhayt* formed also a veneer, behind which Novick and his fellow editors sought to camouflage their communist links and thus shelter its journalists and activists in the caustic climate of the postwar years. Officially, the newspaper did not belong to the network of CPUSA institutions. According to a 1946 description, it avoided the status of a CPUSA organ through an arrangement by which the Party "support[ed] the Morgen Freiheit Association, in accord with its program, as a non-Party anti-fascist Jewish organization" and "as a unifying political center of the more consistent Jewish anti-fascist movements."[14] The publisher of the *Morgn-Frayhayt* and its sister journal *Jewish Life/Jewish Currents* claimed to be an independent association, while Novick and his like avoided publicizing their CPUSA membership (in 1948, as a security measure, Party membership cards were discontinued) and invoked the Fifth Amendment during official interrogations.[15] For all that, Novick continued to be prosecuted as a communist loyalist. One of the accusations raised against him was that he made false statements under oath in obtaining American citizenship in 1927, a charge that carried the threat, never materialized, of his denaturalization.[16]

In 1956, an additional reason emerged for muting the link between the newspaper and the Party: Novick and his colleagues sought to placate their readership by manifesting their ideological independence from any—Soviet or American—communist authorities. The *Morgn-Frayhayt*'s publicized moral revulsion against Stalinism and ritual commemorations of the murdered Soviet Yiddish writers helped reduce the fallout from the turmoil that followed de-Stalinization. Novick claimed later that he had "saved the progressive Jewish movement in America from the lot of the progressive Jewish movements in other countries."[17] In March 1996, I asked Itshe Goldberg, editor of the left-wing literary journal *Yidishe kultur* (*Yiddish Culture*), why Novick, his close friend, had not left the Party in the late 1950s and in the 1960s. Goldberg believed that it was a pragmatic posture: "He stayed as long as he could, trying to lead his followers away as an organized group." Indeed, the *Morgn-Frayhayt* succeeded in keeping a large number of its readers and supporters, and preserving some elements of the organizational structure created among them.

Novick's transformation into a critical observer of Soviet politics did not happen overnight. From the hindsight of the late 1980s, he mentioned Nikita Khrushchev's 1956 speech denouncing Stalin as a breaking point. "Then there was Howard Fast's [autobiography] *The Naked God* in 1957."[18] Indeed, condemnation of Soviet politics by the popular novelist and winner of a Stalin International Peace Prize in 1953, Howard Fast, had a strong impact on Novick and other members of the *Morgn-Frayhayt* staff, who knew Fast personally and respected him. In March 1956, when the Internal Revenue Service staged a politically motivated raid on the *Daily Worker* and padlocked its offices' doors, Fast and other writers and editors of the English-language paper used the offices of their Yiddish neighbor.[19]

Harry Schwartz, the *New York Times* specialist in Soviet affairs, reported Fast's departure from the CPUSA in a front-page article, entitled "Reds Renounced by Howard Fast."[20] Interestingly, on that same day, February 1, 1957, Novick wrote a friendly letter to Fast, asking his permission to run the *Folks-Shtime*'s translation of his novel *The Story of Lola Gregg* in the *Morgn-Frayhayt*.[21] In June, Fast's name again appeared in the *New York Times* when he decided to make known his correspondence with the Soviet novelist, Boris Polevoy. In 1955, Polevoy, a top functionary in the Soviet Writers' Union, and several other socialist realists visited New York, where they repudiated the leaked information about the executions of their Yiddish colleagues. In his letter, Fast related how Polevoy had deceived him by telling that the poet Leyb Kvitko "was alive and well and living" in his apartment house as Polevoy's neighbor, "when he was among those executed and long since dead."[22]

In the beginning of August 1957, the *Forverts* featured Simon Weber's article "Howard Fast Tells Why He Departed from the Communists," based on the Yiddish journalist's two-day-long conversations with the writer.[23] In the fiercely fissiparous world of the New York Yiddish press, Weber—who began his journalistic career at the *Morgn-Frayhayt,* but in 1939 joined the *Forverts*—and Novick were sworn enemies. In his conversation with Weber, Fast recalled that in April 1949 at the World Peace Congress in Paris, he learned from Alexander Fadeev, chairman of the Soviet Writers' Union, the following (dis)information: In 1943, when the poet Itsik Fefer visited America as a representative of the JAFC, the U.S. intelligence operatives recruited him to be a spy and, as such, he succeeded in luring many Jewish intellectuals into his underground anti-Soviet cell. Nonetheless, he failed to recruit Solomon Mikhoels, chairman of the JAFC, who threatened to denounce Fefer and his fellow conspirators. For that reason, according to "leaked" narrative, Fefer organized Mikhoels's liquidation in Minsk in January 1948. According to Fast, Novick—whom Weber kept calling the "twangy little Jew" (*fonfevater yidl*)—became one of the several American Communists privy to Fadeev's revelation. It was a serious accusation, especially as a former *Morgn-Frayhayt* writer had already accused Novick of suppressing any mention of the arrested Soviet Yiddish writers.[24]

On August 24, 1957, *Literaturnaia gazeta,* the central organ of the Soviet Writers' Union, informed its readers that Fast had broken with the Communist Party, becoming "a deserter under fire" and an author of "anti-Soviet slander."[25] It seems that this article signaled to Novick that he could address the accusations made against him, and he wrote Fast a long vituperative letter, categorically rejecting the assertion "that somebody—whoever it might be—'reported' to me about the 'conversation' with Fadeev in Paris." In his September 5 reply, however, Fast reiterated his accusation and added: "Have you no heart? No reason? No conscience? Neither you nor I even whispered when they murdered Bergelson—doesn't that bother you?" On October 16, 1957, Novick retorted: "There is bitter irony in your question whether I am not 'bothered' by the murder of Bergelson. For years we have been running after you to try to find out, to do something. . . . You were not so 'bothered' and were busy with other things. I don't condemn you so much for this, but certainly there is no truthfulness in equating my interest in the matter with your lack of interest at the same time."[26]

Fast revisited the events of the 1950s in his 1990 book, *Being Red,* which is full of striking inaccuracies. For example, Fefer, who during World War II lived and worked hundreds of miles from the frontline, in Kuibyshev (now Samara) and Moscow, appears as "an officer in the Red Army who had fought gallantly through the defense of Russia during the Nazi invasion and was a Hero of the Soviet Union."[27] The 1990 version does not mention the whole story of Fefer's alleged conspiracy, while the secret session with Fadeev is described as being set up because shortly before the trip Novick authorized Fast to deliver the message that the National Committee of the Communist Party "had decided to issue a charge of anti-Semitic practices against the Communist Party of the Soviet Union."[28] When *Being Red* came out, Novick was no longer alive to comment on this radically different record of events.

Fast's accusations certainly hurt Novick, but he continued to maintain that the Stalinist blot on communism had not undermined the integrity of communist ideology itself. In the 1950s, positive news from Poland brought some solace to him and his circle. In contrast to the Soviet Union, where Yiddish cultural activities had remained almost completely paralyzed since the late 1940s, Poland boasted a fairly vibrant, if small-scale Jewish communal life, with clubs, schools, and cooperative enterprises operating in several Polish towns. The Warsaw State Yiddish Theatre performed in Poland and abroad. A relatively strong group of Yiddish literati could print their writings in the semi-daily *Folks-Shtime*, the monthly journal *Yidishe Shriftn* (*Yiddish Writings*), and the publishing house, Yidish Bukh (Yiddish Book). The main social basis for Yiddish cultural life rested on the cooperatives' workers and their families, who accounted for almost a fifth of the country's Jewish population in the late 1950s and 1960s.

In 1946, Novick spent three months in Poland and took part in the establishment of the *Folks-Shtime*.[29] Western left-wingers lavished praise on Poland's Jewish life and nurtured illusions that they could incentivize Soviet decision makers to reproduce a similar model.[30] However, Soviet ideologists' vision of Jewish life remained focused on Birobidzhan, which despite its demographic insignificance provided the Kremlin ideologists with the missing link—national territory—and, therefore, made the Jews look, at least on paper, less of an anomaly in the territory-based ethnic structure of Soviet society. As Novick wrote following his 1936 trip to the Far Eastern Soviet Jewish autonomous region: "Birobidzhan. A word that is now on the lips of Jews all over the world. An expression of workers' strength for the full solution to the Jewish question."[31]

Meanwhile, strong international and domestic pressure forced the Kremlin to allow some "non-Birobidzhan-centered" forms of Jewish cultural life. In March 1959, Sholem Aleichem's centenary, widely marked in the

Soviet Union, helped create a precedent of Yiddish publishing in post-Stalinist Moscow. On March 4, 1959, the Jewish Telegraphic Agency reported that "Israeli bookstores were offered today by the Soviet State Publishing House, in Moscow, copies of a new edition of Sholem Aleichem's writings in Yiddish. This is the first time in ten years that Moscow has offered the book market any works in the Yiddish language. (In New York, a bookstore specializing in Soviet literature, announced it had received a cable from the publishing house Mezhdunarodnaia Kniga, of Moscow, offering the same book for sale in the United States. . . .)."[32] The main event of the jubilee celebration took place in the Moscow Hall of Trade Unions. Present also were American guests: Paul Novick, and the African-American singer, Paul Robeson who performed a couple of Yiddish songs.[33]

Two years later, the Soviet leadership allowed the Soviet Writers' Union to publish a Yiddish literary journal, *Sovetish Heymland* (*Soviet Homeland*). It was clear to everyone that Soviet decision makers permitted the journal's publication as a trade-off with foreign intercessors: we give you a journal and books, but you stop bothering us with your ideas about building an infrastructure for Jewish cultural and social life in the Soviet Union. Novick, like many other Yiddish activists on the political left, regarded *Sovetish Heymland* as a journal "obtained by [their] pleading and sobbing." Hundreds of *Morgn-Frayhayt* readers formed the most numerous contingent of the Moscow journal's subscribers in the United States. In November 1963, on his first transatlantic voyage, Aron Vergelis, editor of the Moscow Yiddish journal, found that the milieu of the *Morgn-Frayhayt* formed his only receptive audience in the United States.[34] Around the same time, in October 1963, a conference on the status of Soviet Jews led to the establishment of the American Jewish Conference on Soviet Jewry. "After that there was no longer pressure brought within any Jewish circles, except the tiny pro-Communist element, to stop American Jews from pleading the cause of Soviet Jewry."[35]

However, even the "pro-Communist element" had problems with Soviet propaganda. In 1963, an anti-Semitic lampoon, *Judaism without Embellishment* by Trofim Kichko, released in Kiev under the imprint of the Ukrainian Academy of Sciences, aroused outrage in the West, angering also the *Morgn-Frayhayt* editors. On March 22, 1964, the newspaper published an angry editorial stating that the cartoons in the book were "reminiscent of the well-known caricatures of Jews in anti-Semitic publications. . . . The blunders in the anti-religious drive as well as—or even more so—the serious errors in the restoration of the Jewish cultural institutions destroyed during the Stalin cult (more correctly, the non-restoration of these institutions) are matters that disturb many honest people, friends of the Soviet Union."[36] On April 12, at a convention in New York attended by a couple of thousand people, Novick demanded that the author be tried and punished. He became once again angry when the monthly magazine, *USSR*, of the Soviet Embassy in Washington published in its May 1964 issue an article by the Moscow Orientalist, Joseph Braginsky, who wrote about "natural assimilation" of Jews into Soviet civilization.[37] Novick rejected assimilation as a "natural" process in the United States as well, arguing that those American Communists who propagated this theory would end up isolated within the Jewish community.[38]

In November 1964, Novick came to the Soviet Union as a guest of the weekly *Literaturnaia gazeta* and spent two months in the country, visiting such cities as Kiev, Odessa, and Vilnius. It was his sixth Soviet sojourn, the previous ones being in 1929, 1932, 1936, 1946, and 1959. In a conversation with editors of *Sovetish Heymland* Novick underlined that the Moscow journal, which he considered as a publication of worldwide importance, was also his circle's journal.[39] He had numerous meetings with writers, academics, war veterans, rabbis, and officials, including Veniamin Dymshits, the highest-ranking Jew in the Soviet government. His hosts equipped him with numerous figures, which illustrated prominent Jewish presence in various of sectors of Soviet life. The fact that 46 percent of Moscow lawyers were Jewish displeased Novick, and rightly so, because it showed, indirectly, that Jews had serious problems with entering state legal institutions.[40]

In Kiev, he had a long conversation with functionaries of the Ukrainian Academy of Science, whose publishing house had produced Kichko's book. Novick continued to blame the overzealous antireligious propaganda, which linked Zionism with Jewish obscurantism. He drew a parallel with the militant antireligious campaigns, including Yom Kippur balls, organized by American Jewish left-wingers in the 1920s and 1930s.[41] The Novosti Press Agency, or APN, which acted as the main provider of Soviet material for such periodicals as *Morgn-Frayhayt*, organized Novick's meeting with a representative of the Office of the Chief Public Prosecutor to discuss the publication of Kichko's book. Novick found the conversation useful and agreeable, though by the end of it he stated: "It's necessary to fight against the existing remnants of anti-Semitism. I reckon, Lenin would have taken more strict measures."[42]

According to the historian Robert Gellately, "After Stalin's death in 1953, the 'good Lenin' was resurrected to chase out the 'bad Stalin' and his personality cult. [. . .] Khrushchev trotted out the myth of Lenin the noble and good to save the 'inner truths' of Communism from association with what were belatedly recognized as 'Stalinist evils.' Everything that had gone wrong in the country was now placed squarely on Stalin's shoulders."[43] Many Soviet and non-Soviet Communists shared the "back to Lenin" stance, clinging the comforting fable of the infallible Bolshevik leader. "Lenin," "Leninism" and "return to the Leninist norms" were invocations they reiterated in an attempt to assuage their anguish caused by the exposure of the real nature of Stalin's regime and, in the late 1960s, of the anti-Jewish campaign in Poland. In the wake of de-Stalinization, Novick promised his readers that his newspaper would seek an answer to the question: "Will the Soviet Union, coming back to Lenin's principles, also bring back Yiddish culture to the [level of the] 1920s?"[44]

The June 1967 war in the Middle East dramatically changed the climate in the Jewish sector of the international communist movement. In Poland, where anti-Israel and, generally, anti-Jewish rhetoric began to be regularly heard, a campaign against the "Zionist Fifth Column" became the authorities' reaction to the student demonstrations in March 1968. Novich lamented that in April 1968 "for the 25th Anniversary there were, with only insignificant exceptions, no foreign delegations present."[45] Many Polish Jewish Communists lost their jobs, were expelled from the Party, and forced to leave the country. The *Folks-Shtime*, previously published four times per week, underwent downgrading into a weekly, whereas the journal *Yidishe shriftn* and the publishing house Yidish Bukh ceased to exist.[46]

Shocked by this development, Novick wrote about the events in Poland as a tragic page in Jewish history and "also a tragedy for Socialism and for the world Socialist Movement." Nonetheless, he still hoped that Polish Communists would follow the example of the anti-Stalinist drive in the USSR, reacting "in the same way now to the violations which have occurred in Poland in the recent period." He argued that the blame for what had happened fell on "the anti-Jewish heritage of the pre-war chauvinist and capitalist Poland which reappeared in 1968 and must be eradicated."[47] It was his pet thesis that, in a socialist society, anti-Semitism was merely a "vestige" of the pre-socialist past, one of the remnants of capitalism, Hitlerism, and so on.[48] Therefore "[t]he supporters of Socialism among the Jewish people who fought for so many years against capitalism and its evils" should "not yield their belief in Socialism, the Socialism of Lenin which decisively fought against anti-Semitism."[49]

Not only did the *Morgn-Frayhayt* criticize the leadership of Poland, whose course was condoned by top communists in the Soviet Union and America, but it also disowned the Soviet line of condemning Israel as the aggressor and hailing the Arab states as strongholds of anti-imperialism. Novick saw Israel as a product of the successful struggle against British colonialism and proclaimed his allegiance to the young state (as *an important* rather than *the central* Jewish community), condemning Gamal Abdel Nasser's anti-Israeli rhetoric.[50] (In 1963, during his trip to the Soviet Union, he was happy to hear the rumors that members of the Presidium of the Communist Party's Central Committee objected to Nikita Khrushchev's decision to award Nasser the title Hero of the Soviet Union.)[51] Novick's position, which essentially mirrored the Soviet position of the late 1940s rather than the Soviet government's later escalating friendship with the Arab world, resulted in Novick's aligning himself with the splinter Israeli Communist Party, Maki, whose leaders, Shmuel Mikunis and Moshe Sneh, were critical of the pro-Arab stance of the Soviet Union. The Kremlin, however, recognized the other, predominantly Palestinian, Israeli Communist Party, Rakah, led by Meir Vilner and Tawfik Toubi.

On June 6, 1967, after the beginning of the war, the *Morgn-Frayhayt* editorial was entitled "Save Israel." Later in the same year, the two groups, Novick's and the Maki, brought out a joint pamphlet whose purpose was "to clarify an important and complex problem, specifically from the viewpoint of those progressives who maintain that the State of Israel conducted a defensive war during the six days between the 6th and 11th of June, 1967."[52] The Six-Day War turned many former anti-Zionists into devotees of Israel. Pro-Israel feelings were running high also among the communists. In a private letter to Sid Resnik, a regular contributor to *Morgn-Frayhayt*, Novick made plain his position:

> I am sure you don't think it's easy for us. It might be easy for those who think or even say openly (there are such people) that the establishment of Israel was a mistake and, therefore, this 'mistake' should be rectified. They don't spell it out openly, but their deeds speak for themselves. [. . .] For many years, we've been promoting the slogan: 'Israel came to stay'—and we meant it. So, when we saw the attempts to get rid of the 'mistake,' to liquidate Israel, we called to save Israel.[53]

The CPUSA leadership and, perhaps, their Moscow advisers could not remain sanguine about the Novick group's dissent. The press mentioned that Gus Hall, general secretary of the Party, and Harry Winston, executive secretary, included replacement of Novick in the plans for purges, discussed in Moscow during their visit in the summer of 1969.[54] In reality, a campaign against Novick began before the two leaders' Moscow trip. In March 1969, the *New York Times* learned about a circular letter that the CPUSA central apparatus had distributed among all local organizations, accusing the *Morgn-Frayhayt* (whose circulation then was 6,000 copies a day) and *Jewish Currents* (4,200 copies a month) in "increasingly abandoning their past." At issue were the editors' deviations from the Party line, most notably their "obsession with the false issue of 'black anti-Semitism,'" their support of Israel and the Communist Party led by Mikunis and Sneh, "anti-Soviet opposition to the military action of the Warsaw Pact countries in Czechoslovakia," and their criticism of the anti-Semitic campaign in Poland.[55]

Aron Vergelis did not have direct access to the *New York Times* (and he did not know any English), but, judging by his letters preserved in Novick's YIVO archival collection, he was briefed in detail about Novick's confrontation with the CPUSA leadership. On April 3, 1969, Vergelis wrote to his New York colleague, expressing his hope that "the cohort of courageous fighters of progressive Jewish America" would follow the right ideological line. He advised Novick to be patient. "Please, don't do any negative steps, [. . .] don't let, so to speak, the emotional stream to pull out logs from the raft, on which the *Morgn-Frayhayt* conveys its readers from [formulating] a question to [finding] an answer to it." In a letter dated from April 11, 1969, Novick reassured Vergelis that his criticism of the Soviet Union was "a friendly one" and that his paper had always remained devoted to its "Olgin line." (Olgin's picture adorned the masthead of the newspaper.) Novick mentioned that his generally strained relations with the Party leadership worsened even more when the *Morgn-Frayhayt* began to express an independent view on the events in Poland. In addition, Novick was annoyed that his Party leaders saw the YKUF, the World Jewish Cultural Union (established in the aftermath of the left-dominated Yiddish Cultural Congress in Paris, September 1937), as a nationalist organization.[56] Also, they would under no circumstances admit cases of anti-Semitism among the African-American population. Novick referred to a "Jewish expert" in the Party leadership whose "fossilized dogmatism" could ruin everything. He clearly meant Hyman Lumer, one of the Party's national secretaries and editor of the Party's journal *Political Affairs*, who as early as 1965 criticized Novick for "seek[ing] Jewish survival as an end in itself."[57]

Novick's position in the Party became particularly vulnerable in 1970, when Moscow launched an all-out anti-Zionist campaign. In January of that year, the Soviet Communist Party's Department of Propaganda suggested "to organize, with the participation of the editorial board of the journal *Sovetish Heymland*, protests of Soviet citizens of Jewish nationality against the provocative campaign carried out by Zionist organizations." On March 4 of that year, Vergelis appeared among a group of well-known Soviet Jews in a televised press conference concerning "problems associated with the situation in the Middle East." An editorial article in the *Morgn-Frayhayt*, published on March 15, 1970, wrote that "Such words as 'Hitlerism' and 'Nazism' which were used at the press conference are an insult not only to the members of the Israel army but also to the Jews in Israel who still carry numbers of the Nazi concentration camps on their arms; all Jews are hurt by such expressions."[58]

In February 1971, the first international conference in defense of Soviet Jews was convened in Brussels as a reaction to Soviet restrictions and repressions, notably the trial in Leningrad in 1970 of a group of unsuccessful hijackers who attempted to flee the country and settle in Israel. On December 27, 1970, Novick wrote that the "atmosphere created by anti-Zionist, anti-Semitic hysteria" of some Soviet propagandists might have contributed to the severity of the sentences given the hijackers. Yet on January 1, 1971, he was happy to inform his readers that the "last days of the past year brought significant gains for justice and humanism. The death sentences imposed on two Jews in the Leningrad trial were removed." Two days later, he emphasized that his paper had "taken in the Leningrad case—as it has in all other important matters—a balanced view, seeing the complete picture."[59]

In July 1971, the *Morgn-Frayhayt* was among the few non-Soviet Jewish publications and groups that congratulated *Sovetish Heymland* on its tenth anniversary.[60] Soon, however, the conflict between the two periodicals reached a point of no return. It happened after the appearance of the November 1971 issue of *Sovetish Heymland* with an editorial criticizing the New York newspaper for its policy of "conciliation" with non-communist Yiddish journalists. From then on, over the years, the ideological gap between Novick's "progressivism" and Soviet Communism mouth-pieced by Vergelis widened, dragging an increasing number of people and organizations into the quarrel. After 1971, Novick's name disappeared from new editions of Vergelis's travel log "Twenty Days in America," which chronicled his 1963 foreign trip. In the later editions such phrases were also cut, such as the one mentioning that "on the seventh floor, in a modest building at 35 East Twelfth Street has been pounding the courageous heart of Winchevsky's and Olgin's newspaper."[61] In 1977, Vergelis contended that the *Morgn-Frayhayt* had lost its credentials of being a "battle forum" of Olgin, and other legendary founders of the newspaper.[62]

On June 1, 1971, a letter was sent to Novick, signed by three leading communists: Hyman Lumer, Claude Lightfoot, and José Ristorucci. They informed Novick that the Political Committee had designated them "as a sub-committee to look into the matter of your status as a member of the Communist Party. In view of your continuing opposition to important aspects of Party policy, as reflected in your speeches and writings and in the editorial policies of the Morning Freiheit, the Political Committee has reached the conclusion that the present state of affairs cannot be permitted to continue." The troika suggested to Novick that they meet and discuss these issues. They met, indeed, on June 7, and on June 22; Novick mailed to several addressees, most notably to Gus Hall, a statement he "promised the committee of three." In the covering letter he underlined that the statement "was drafted and finalized in consultation with comrades of the Morning Freiheit and the leadership of the Jewish mass organizations." He listed his constituency: "the Clubs and Societies, with around 12,000 members, the Women's [Emma Lazarus] organization, the YKUF and reading circles, the choruses and mandolin orchestras, the progressive children's schools and other institutions embrace a mass movement reaching into *scores of thousands*. . . ."[63]

Novick could not understand the "inexplicable and even maddening reasons" for branding his newspaper "as racist, white chauvinist." Yet, he explained in his statement, that the Middle East was "*the* issue which prompted your committee to place before me on June 7 the alternative of either resigning from the Communist Party, or be expelled." Therefore, he decided to draw the Party leadership's attention to a lesson he had learned from his communist circle's history:

> In the months of August-September 1929 the M[orgn-]F[rayhayt] as well as the progressive Jewish organizations were in a crisis in connection with the unrest in Palestine at that time. We came into a head-on collision with the Jewish community. Although we were much stronger numerically at that time and the crisis was much milder than the present one and of short duration, we paid dearly for our stand, having lost a great many of our

> readers and having weakened our mass base. Years later we *were criticized for our lack of flexibility*, for our failure to avoid this head-on collision with the community (from which we were ostracized). That crisis was child's play compared to the present one in the Middle East, both in intensity and duration, when there is a Jewish State and after the Jewish people lost six million men, women and children during World War II. There can be no question that were we to apply now in relation to the Middle East the tactics of 1929 the MF would long ago have ceased to exist and the progressive mass organizations would have been shattered, if not totally destroyed. [. . .]
>
> As of now we are still a force among the Jewish workers, as well as in the Jewish community generally to a certain extent. [. . .] Were we to change our position we would be ostracized as in 1929 and years following, practically until June 1941 [when Germany attacked the Soviet Union].[64]

Why, he wondered, was he suddenly censured in 1971, after four years of "understanding and tolerance," rather than to be attacked in 1967, when he had clearly formulated his position toward Israel-Arab relations? In conclusion, he defiantly stated: "Since I believe in the importance of the role of a Marxist party, the CP, in the USA, of which I have been a member for over 50 years, I cannot and will not bring myself to resign from it, as suggested by your committee."[65]

In the following months, Lumer and several other top communists, including Mortimer Daniel Rubin, national organizational secretary, continued waging the anti-Novick campaign. They issued a statement against him that included charges of "racism," focusing on the Party's fight to free African-American activist, Angela Davis. Novick's opponents argued that this important issue had been downplayed in the *Morgn-Frayhayt*, which "gave it little more than lip service" in its pages. Novick admitted that his newspaper had few articles defending Angela Davis and that he began campaigning only after a meeting with Party officials.[66] At the same time, he could not agree that the *Morgn-Frayhayt* supported Jewish emigration from the Soviet Union. In reality, Soviet Jewish emigration devastatingly disappointed Novick, who saw it as "a tragic development for socialism." Although he could not stand the anti-Zionist hysteria of the Soviet authorities and media, he naively predicted that many of the emigrants would soon flee Israel, "where the worker face[d] a difficult struggle," and return to the Soviet Union.[67] He repeatedly stressed that the Jewish state, however important it was, had to play a secondary role in the life of Soviet, American, and other Jews.[68]

Still, in the eyes of his dogmatic communist critics, Lumer et al., Novick had done an unforgivable thing by aligning himself with "the renegade Mikunis-Sneh group in Israel, which has abandoned the path of Marxism-Leninism and has become little more than an appendage to the [Golda] Meir regime and its reactionary foreign policy. In line with this, he has repudiated the Communist Party of Israel led by Vilner and Toubi, which our Party has recognized as the only true Marxist-Leninist party in Israel."[69] The CPUSA leadership could not condone Novick's " 'balanced' position," which "placed an increasing share of the burden of responsibility on the Soviet Union itself." Moreover, "At the time of the Leningrad hijacking trial he signed his name, along with others, to a telegram calling on the Soviet government to free all the defendants." The *Daily Worker* called upon loyal Communist Yiddish readers to replace Novick as editor, but the CPUSA had no more control over the newspaper.[70]

While in 1957 the party was in a crisis, with a membership shrunk to less than 4,000 members, its ranks had more than quadrupled by the end of 1972.[71] The disproportionate influence of the Jewish membership also was a thing of the past.[72] Therefore, the small group of Yiddish-speaking veterans, whose obstinacy became a political burden, could be sacrificed in order to solidify the Party and to please the Kremlin. On February 16, 1972, the National Committee decided to expel Novick from the CPUSA, charging him with "opportunistic capitulation to the pressures of Jewish nationalism and Zionism."[73] According to other sources, he at that time "was not expelled from the CPUSA—as had been proposed . . . Instead, the CPUSA decided to avoid a possibly devastating internal fight over this issue and delayed acting on the ouster of the long-time communist."[74] Novick's expulsion was made public in *Der Veg* (*The Way*), the Yiddish newspaper of Israeli Communists, on May 9, 1973.[75]

For a year or so after the public break of relations, Novick continued to write detailed and essentially friendly letters to Vergelis. Fear of being isolated can explain Novick's desperate attempts to preserve some links with Moscow, his erstwhile center of ideological gravity. On July 11, 1972, he shared his thoughts with Vergelis on the Soviet Jewish emigration, arguing that deviations from the "Leninist norms" were at the heart of the problem. In his one-sided analysis, Novick surmised that Soviet Jews voted with their feet, protesting against the lack of Jewish cultural institutions and the proliferation of anti-Semitic publications. On another note, Novick derided the quality of Birobidzhan-related propaganda fiction that the *Morgn-Frayhayt* received from the Soviet Union, most notably from APN. The articles describing Jewish life in Birobidzhan sounded so shaky that he simply could not use them. On October 12, 1972, he sent to Vergelis a seven-page, single-spaced letter, signed with the words "for friendship and understanding."[76] However, it was preposterous to expect friendship or understanding from Vergelis, a seasoned and disciplined ideological warrior.[77]

Even after Novick's expulsion from the CPUSA, the Party's ideologists continued to attack him, accusing him of serving the interests of imperialism and Zionism. Novick, in his turn, charged the CPUSA leaders with hatred for Israel that bordered on anti-Semitism and advised them to "sit down and have a series of self-criticism to find out why you are so isolated in this country, whereas the Communist Parties of Italy, France and Spain are so strong."[78] In all, Novick's links to the communist world had been cut loose and he had to navigate the dwindling circle of his followers, coordinating his movements within the triangle of periodicals of the American Jewish ex-Communist left: *Morgn-Frayhayt*; *Yidishe kultur*, edited by Itshe Goldberg (1904–2006); and *Jewish Currents*, edited by Morris U. Schappes (1907–2004). Novick's minuscule international contacts included the Canadian sister circle, grouped around the journal *Outlook*, and a similar group in Argentina.[79] In the beginning of the 1970s, the Maki group had almost disappeared from the Israeli political landscape. Nonetheless, Novick's paper braved all these turbulences and survived longer than, for example, *Der Tog* (*The Day*), one of the most important New York Yiddish dailies.[80]

Still, the crisis of 1956 played a very significant role, determining the morals of the Yiddish Communist circles in the final three decades of its withering. The post-1956 transformation of the group of believers in the Soviet system into an independent "progressive" movement of Jewish socialists had two components: on the one hand, it was a pragmatic decision of such people as Novick, who saw it as the only way to preserve at least some parts of the left-wing Yiddishist circles; on the other hand, many "progressives" sincerely sought to find a new compromise between their socialist and nationalist aspirations. While pragmatism initially dominated the steps and pronouncements of Novick and his ilk, the component of "sincerity" gradually began to determine their ideological tribulations.

Despite Novick's ouster from the CPUSA, he remained an irreparably awkward figure in the American Jewish world, widely remembered for his past practice of glorifying Stalin. After 1956, his devotion to Leninism invited skepticism and ridicule. Samuel Margoshes, one-time editor of *Der Tog*, wrote that Novick's ideological concessions were "too weak and too late."[81] Simon Weber was even sharper in his assessment of *Morgn-Frayhayt*. He admitted that such "progressive" periodicals as the *Morgn-Frayhayt* had "been trying latterly to distance themselves from Moscow, being under the influence of the Italian, Spanish, and other more independent Communists." Yet he considered their political stance as an affront to Jewish values and interests and therefore was not ready to accept them in the Jewish press community.[82] Surely, many of the ideological accusations were, in fact, motivated by personal animosity.

In its post-communist iteration, the *Morgn-Frayhayt* endured as an outlier in American Jewish life. The paper continued to appear thanks to annual fundraising appeals, which would bring money for printing expenses, while the editorial staff received minimal remunerations. In the last seven years, the newspaper had to reduce its periodicity, coming out three times a week and then turning into a weekly. Finally, in September 1988, it became clear that the small circle of readers and writers, almost exclusively octogenarians or older, could no longer maintain the existence of their periodical. Thus, although the *Morgn-Frayhayt* circle became collateral damage in the communist movement's struggle with its Stalinist legacy, natural causes rather than the trauma of 1956 ultimately brought about its decline. Emblematically, the very last issue marked the beginning of the Jewish New Year, Rosh Hashanah.[83]

While Soviet and pro-Soviet ideologists considered Novick's stand as a communist heresy, Novick, like many other Jewish and non-Jewish veterans of the international communist movement, talked himself into believing that he was a custodian of *real* Leninism, whose ideas had been distorted by Soviet, American, and other Stalinist-style pseudo-communists, but could become attainable at some future time, when circumstances improved. Until the end of his life, Novick perceived himself as a custodian of the ultimate truth concerning "progressive" Yiddish culture in the United States. Sid Resnik, who was Novick's main English translator for many years, described him as "an extraordinary man—a Jewish Marxist, left-wing leader, and . . . a very competent journalist," whose life's tragedy was "that he wanted to die first, and the paper would continue. Instead, the paper died first, and he had to live a year with the knowledge that he survived the paper rather than the opposite."[84]

Notes

1. Tony Michels, "Communism and the Problem of Ethnicity in the 1920s: The Case of Moissaye Olgin," in *Studies in Contemporary Jewry* 25 (2011): 38, 42. On June 17, 1929, the *Frayhayt* got a double-barreled name, *Morgn-Frayhayt*, or *Morning-Freedom*, when it started appearing as a morning rather than an afternoon newspaper.

2. Novick's letter to the Yiddish writer David Einhorn, on Oct. 10, 1921; in David Einhorn Papers, RG 277, folder 27. YIVO Archives, New York. See also Gennady Estraikh, "Di shpaltung in 1921: der krizis in der yidisher sotsyalistisher bavegung," *Forverts*, Oct. 13, 2006.

3. In fact, "no mass departure of Jewish members (as opposed to fellow-travelers) occurred" in 1939; see James G. Ryan, *Earl Browder: The Failure of American Communism* (Tuscaloosa, AL: University of Alabama Press, 1997), 186. See also Henry F. Srebrnik, " 'The Jews Do Not Want War!': American Jewish Communists Defend the Hitler-Stalin Pact, 1919–1941," *American Communist History* 8, No. 1 (2009): 49–71.

4. David A. Shannon, *The Decline of American Communism: A History of the Communist Party of the United States since 1945* (London: Stevens and Sons, 1960), 90.

5. Paul C. Mishler, *Raising Reds: The Young Pioneers, Radical Summer Camps, and Communist Political Culture in the United States* (New York: Columbia University Press, 1999), 131–32.

6. Hasia Diner, *The Jews of the United States: 1654 to 2000* (Berkeley and Los Angeles: University of California Press, 2004), 277.

7. The full transcript of the trials, translated into English, has been made available in *Stalin's Secret Pogrom: The Postwar Inquisition of the Jewish Anti-Fascist Committee*, eds. Joshua Rubenstein and Vladimir P. Naumov (New Haven, CT: Yale University Press, 2001).

8. Paul Novick, *Jewish Life in the United States and the Role of the "Morning Freiheit"* (New York: Morgen Freiheit, 1957), 24. See also Gennady Estraikh, "Metamorphoses of *Morgn-frayhayt*," in *Yiddish and the Left*, eds. Gennady Estraikh and Mikhail Krutikov (Oxford: Legenda, 2001), 144–66.

9. Paul Novick, "Di shtelung tsum sovetn-farband," *Morgn-Frayhayt*, Jan. 27, 1957; idem, "Vos far a tsaytung iz di Morgn-frayhayt?" *Morgn-Frayhayt*, Jan. 28, 1957.

10. Moyshe Olgin, *Folk un kultur* (New York, 1939), 30–49, 58. See also Bat-Ami Zucker, "American Jewish Communists and Jewish Culture in the 1930s," *Modern Judaism* 14, No. 2 (1994): 180–81.

11. Alex Bittelman, "Things I Have Learned" (Autobiographical typescript, 1963). Collection 62, box 1, page 691; Tamiment Library/Robert F. Wagner Labor Archives, New York University.

12. Paul Novick, *Role of the Jewish Press* (New York: Morning Freiheit, 1962), 52.

13. Vladimir Lenin, *The Birth of Bolshevism: Lenin's Struggle against Economism* (Chippendale, NSW: Resistance Books, 2005), 76.

14. "Communist Work among the American Jewish Masses: Resolution of the National Groups Commission of the CPUSA, October 1946," *Political Affairs* (November 1946): 1035.

15. See, for example, "Foreign Press Editors Silent at Quiz," *Washington Post,* Jan. 18, 1955; *John Lennon: The FBI Files* (Minneapolis, MN: Filiquardian Publishing, 2009), 299.

16. "Faces Denaturalization," *New York Times,* Aug. 26, 1953; "Acts to Denaturalize Editor," *New York Times,* Aug. 28, 1953; "U.S. Merges Suits against Six Reds," *New York Times,* Dec. 24, 1954; "The Inquisition of Paul Novick," *Jewish Life* 9, No. 10 (1955): 14–15; "Transcript of Proceedings. Passport Hearing in the Matter of Paul Novick. April 6, 1956," Department of State, Washington, DC, 9, 14, 15.

17. Paul Novick, *Amerikanishe yidn, der tsionism, medines yisroel* (New York: Morgen Freiheit, 1972), 39.

18. Arthur J. Sabin, "A Voice of the Jewish Left," *Response* 15, No. 3 (1987): 54.

19. Gerald Sorin, *Howard Fast: Life and Literature in the Left Lane* (Bloomington: Indiana University Press, 2012), 303.

20. Harry Schwartz, "Reds Renounced by Howard Fast," *New York Times,* Feb. 1, 1957; "Howard Fast Balks at Queries on Reds," *New York Times,* Feb. 22, 1957.

21. Gennady Estraikh, "Professing Leninist Yiddishkayt: The Decline of American Yiddish Communism," *American Jewish History* 96, No. 1 (2010): 41.

22. Harrison E. Salisbury, "Writers in the Shadow of Communism," *New York Times,* June 9, 1957.

23. Simon Weber, "Hauard Fest dertseylt farvos er iz avek fun di komunistn," *Forverts,* Aug. 2, 1957; Aug. 4, 1957.

24. Borukh Fenster, "Redaktor fun komunistisher Frayhayt iz a biterer soyne fun yidishn folk," *Forverts,* Feb. 16, 1956.

25. "Howard Fast Assailed by Soviet as a 'Deserter' and Slanderer," *New York Times,* Aug. 25, 1957. Ironically, articles disowning Fast for his "traitorous activities" would appear as part of the Soviet anti-Zionist campaign, though Fast did not reveal himself as a supporter of Zionism. *Evreiskaia emigratsiia v svete novykh dokumentov,* ed. Boris Morozov (Tel Aviv: Ivrus, 1998), 29.

26. Estraikh, "Professing Leninist Yiddishkayt," 43–44.

27. Howard Fast, *Being Red* (Boston: Houghton Mifflin, 1990), 330.

28. Ibid., 206. See also Maurice Isserman, "It Seemed a Good Idea at the Time," *New York Times,* Nov. 4, 1990. Still, some historians cite *Being Red* as a document; see, for example, Albert D. Chernin, "Making Soviet Jews an Issue," in *A Second Exodus: The American Movement to Free Soviet Jews,* eds. Murray Fried-

man and Albert D. Chernin (Hanover, NH: University Press of New England, 1999), 18–19.

29. Paul Novick, *The Jewish Problem in Poland* (New York: Morgen Freiheit, 1969), 2.

30. Eleonora Bergman, "Yiddish in Poland after 1945," in *Yiddish and the Left*, eds. Gennady Estraikh and Mikhail Krutikov (Oxford: Legenda, 2001), 167–77; Nathan Cohen, "The Renewed Association of Yiddish Writers and Journalists in Poland, 1945–48," in *Yiddish after the Holocaust*, ed. Joseph Sherman (Oxford: Boulevard Books, 2004), 15–36; Gennady Estraikh, "The Warsaw Outlets for Soviet Yiddish Writers," in *Under the Red Banner: Yiddish Culture in the Communist Countries in the Postwar Era*, eds. Elvira Grözinger and Magdalena Ruta (Wiesbaden: Otto Harrassowitz, 2008), 217–30.

31. Quoted in Joshua S. Rubenstein, "Night of the Murdered Poets," in *Stalin's Secret Pogrom: The Postwar Inquisition of the Jewish Anti-Fascist Committee,* eds. Joshua S. Rubenstein and Vladimir P. Naumov (New Haven, CT: Yale University Press, 2001), 30.

32. "Moscow Publishers Sholem Aleichem in Yiddish; Offers Book Abroad," *Jewish Telegraphic Agency Daily News Bulletin*, March 4, 1959, 4.

33. Paul Novick, "Correspondence from Moscow: On the Life of Jews and Jewish Life in the Soviet Union," *Jewish Currents* 13, No. 6 (June 1959): 14–15; Jonathan Karp, "Performing Black-Jewish Symbiosis: The 'Hassidic Chant' of Paul Robeson," *American Jewish History* 91, No. 1 (2003): 53–81.

34. See Paul Novick, "Getseylte teg mit Arn Vergelis," *Yidishe kultur* 10 (1963): 41–43.

35. Andhil Fineberg. Transcript of interview. William E. Wiener Oral History Library of the American Jewish Committee. New York Public Library Oral Histories, box 24, no. 1 (1974): 5-208, 5-210.

36. "World Reaction—Soviet Confusion: Western Communists Join in Protests," *Jews in Eastern Europe* 2, No. 5 (1964): 25.

37. Isi Leibler, *Soviet Jewry and Human Rights* (Melbourne: Human Rights Publications, 1965), 52, 55, 58–60.

38. "Russia's Jewish Policies under Debate," *Jewish Advocate*, Boston, Feb. 18, 1965.

39. Paul Novick, "S'iz do a velt mit arbet," *Sovetish Heymland*, No. 2 (1965): 130–32.

40. Paul Novick, *Yidn in Sovetn-Farband: a rayze fun tsvey khadoshim in dem sovetishn land* (New York: Morning Freiheit, 1965), 12. See also Simona Pipka and Roman Pipka, "Inside the Soviet Bar: A View from the Outside," *The International Lawyer* 21, No. 3 (1987): 855.

41. Novick, *Yidn in Sovetn-Farband*, 12–13.

42. Estraikh, "Professing Leninist Yiddishkayt," 48. Kichko's anti-Zionist publications continued to appear in the 1960s and 1970s. See, e.g., Vladimir V. Bol'shakov, "Kritika sionizma v sovetskoi istoriografii," *Voprosy istorii*, No. 9 (1973):

78–88; Richard Brookhiser, "A Look at Soviet Antisemitism," *National Review*, Dec. 22, 1978, p. 1576.

43. Robert Gelatelly, *Lenin, Stalin, and Hitler: The Age of Social Catastrophe* (New York: Alfred A. Knopf, 2007), 10. See also Gennady Estraikh, "Les gardiens yiddish du léninisme: Des vétérans du communisme polonais règlent leurs comptes avec le passé," *Bulletin du Centre de recherche français à Jérusalem*; http://bcrfj.revues.org/6567.

44. Paul Novick, "Der dokument vegn yidisher kultur in sovetn-farband," *Morgn-Frayhayt*, April 13, 1956.

45. Novick, *The Jewish Problem in Poland*, 4.

46. Novick, *The Jewish Problem in Poland*, 5; See also *The End of a Thousand Years: The Recent Exodus of the Jews from Poland*, eds. Itshe Goldberg and Yuri Suhl (New York: Committee for Jews of Poland, 1971) and Dariusz Stola, *Kampania antysyjonistyczna w Polsce, 1967–1968* (Warsaw: Instytut Studiow Politycznych PAN, 2000).

47. Novick, *The Jewish Problem in Poland*, 7.

48. See Paul Novick, "The New Jew in the Soviet Union," in Paul Novick and J. M. Budish, *Jews in the Soviet Union: Citizens and Builders* (New York: Morgen Freiheit, 1948), 21.

49. Novick, *The Jewish Problem in Poland*, 7.

50. Paul Novick, *Yisroel, tsionizm, un amerikaner yidn* (New York, 1961).

51. Novick, *Yidn in Sovetn-Farband*, 17.

52. *War and Peace in the Middle East* (New York, 1967), 1.

53. Sid Resnik, "Peysekh Novik, redaktor fun der Morgn-Frayhayt," *Di Pen* 30 (1997): 6.

54. Ronald Koziol, "Top Leaders of U.S. Reds are Purged," *Chicago Tribune*, Oct. 2, 1969.

55. Peter Kihss, "U.S. Reds Assail 2 Jewish Papers," *New York Times*, March 30, 1969.

56. See Matthew Hoffman, "From Czernowitz to Paris: The International Yiddish Culture Congress of 1937," in *Czernowitz at 100: The First Yiddish Language Conference in Historical Perspective*, eds. Kalman Weiser and Joshua A. Fogel (Toronto: Lexington Books, 2010), 151–64.

57. Estraikh, "Professing Leninist Yiddishkayt," 51.

58. Gennady Estraikh, "An Opportunist Anti-Zionism: Sovetish Heymland, 1961–1991," in *Rebels Against Zion: Studies on the Jewish Left Anti-Zionism*, ed. August Grabski (Warsaw: Żydowski Instytut Historyczny, 2011), 157.

59. See Joseph Levy, "The Morning Freiheit's 'Balanced' Approach," *Jewish Affairs* 2, Nos. 2–3 (1971): 6–9. For the "Leningrad case," see, for example, Yaacov Ro'i, "Strategy and Tactics," in *The Jewish Movement in the Soviet Union*, ed. Yaacov Ro'i (Baltimore: The Johns Hopkins University Press, 2012), 54–60.

60. "Bagrisungen tsum zhurnal 'Sovetish heymland,'" *Sovetish Heymland* 7 (1971): 10–15.

61. See further the following two editions: *Azoy lebn mir: dokumentale noveln, fartseykhenungen, reportazhn*, ed. Aron Vergelis (Moscow: Sovetskii Pisatel, 1964), 431 and Aron Vergelis, *Rayzes* (Moscow: Sovetskii Pisatel, 1976), 32. The pioneer Jewish proletarian poet and journalist Morris Winchevsky (1856–1932) was one of the founders of the *Frayhayt.*

62. "Di 'Morgn-Frayhayt' af fremde vegn fun antisovetizm un protsienizm," *Sovetish Heymland* 5 (1977): 140–41.

63. Estraikh, "Professing Leninist Yiddishkayt," 55.

64. Ibid.

65. Ibid., 55–56.

66. *The Theory and Practice of Communism: The Communist Party, USA* (Washington, DC: U.S. Government Printing Office, 1973), 2005, 2012.

67. Novick, *Amerikanishe yidn, der tsionizm, medines yisroel*, 41.

68. Paul Novick, *Di natsionale un yidishe frage in itstikn moment* (New York: Morgen Freiheit, 1970), 30; idem, "Tsienizm un anti-tsienizm," *Zamlungen* 59 (1976): 16–17.

69. Estraikh, "Professing Leninist Yiddishkayt," 57.

70. Harvey Klehr, *Far Left of Center: The American Radical Left Today* (New Brunswick, NJ: Transaction Publishers, 1991), 44.

71. Guenter Lewy, *The Cause that Failed: Communism in American Political Life* (New York: Oxford University Press, 1990), 308.

72. By 1989, the CPUSA had only around 300 Jewish members. See Herbert Romerstein and Eric Breindel, *The Venona Secrets: Exposing Soviet Espionage and America's Traitors* (Washington, DC: Regnery Publishing, 2000), 391.

73. "U.S. Communists Say Yiddish Paper Serves 'Imperialism,'" *New York Times*, May 15, 1977.

74. *John Lennon*, 299.

75. See Resnik, "Peysakh Novik, redactor fun der Morgn-Frayhayt," 6.

76. Estraikh, "Professing Leninist Yiddishkayt," 58.

77. Gennady Estraikh, "Aron Vergelis: The Perfect Jewish *Homo Sovieticus*," *East European Jewish Affairs* 27, No. 2 (1997): 3–20.

78. Peter Kihss, "Freiheit Editor Respond to Attack from U.S. Communist Newspaper," *New York Times*, May 22, 1977.

79. See, in particular, Leonardo Senkman, "Repercussions of the Six-Day War in the Leftist Jewish Argentine Camp: The Rise of Fraie Schtime, 1967–1969," in *The Six-Day War and World Jewry*, ed. Eli Lederhendler (Bethesda, MD: University Press of Maryland, 2000), 175–76.

80. *Der Tog* merged in 1953 with the conservative newspaper *Morgn-Zhurnal*; the *Tog-Morgn-Zhurnal* endured until 1973. See Charles A. Madison, *Jewish Publishing in America: The Impact of Jewish Writing on American Culture* (New York: Sanhedrin Press, 1976), 127.

81. *A briv fun Dr. Sh. Margoshes un an entfer fun P. Novik* (New York: Morgen Freiheit, 1967), 4.

82. *Velt-konferents far yidish un yidisher kultur* (Tel Aviv: Velt-byuro far yidish un yidisher kultur, 1977), 161–62.

83. "Freiheit Editor's 75th Birthday Party Is in a Class by Itself," *New York Times*, Feb. 15, 1978; "Morning Freiheit Folds," *Jewish Advocate*, Sep. 22, 1988.

84. Sidney Resnik, "It Was an Episode, a Long and Good Episode in History, and it is Ending," in *Aging Political Activists: Personal Narratives from the Old Left*, ed. David Philip Shuldiner (Westport, CT: Praeger Publishers, 1995), 205, 207.

5

Chasing an Illusion

The Jewish Communist Movement in Canada

Henry F. Srebrnik

Following the 1917 Bolshevik Revolution in Russia, many Jews in Canada gave uncritical support to the Soviet Union, and some even moved to the USSR to take part in the building of a socialist society. One Canadian Jewish woman, Suzanne Rosenberg, who grew up in Montreal, recalls in her memoirs that she was sixteen years old when her mother, a fervent Communist, organized a group of forty people and their children to emigrate to the USSR in 1931. She would remain in the Soviet Union, a prisoner of her mother's misplaced idealism, for more than a half-century.[1] For those remaining in Canada, many became involved, either as members or sympathizers, with the Communist Party of Canada (CP). Founded in 1921, by 1927 the CP had formed a national Jewish Bureau, a subcommittee of the party's central committee, with members in Montreal, Toronto, and Winnipeg.[2] Historian David Rome asserted that the Jewish group was the most vital faction in the Canadian Communist movement: "It was a total society with its own political and cultural institutes."[3] The Jewish Communists, in particular, felt duty-bound to "counteract the nationalist, imperialist Zionist movement" by demonstrating that the Soviet Union had "the only true and sensible solution" to the "national question." Winnipeg's North End, home to most of the city's 15,000 or so Jews, was a hotbed of radical politics, and among the Jews, its cultural life was dominated by secular Yiddishists, to the extent that "the strongest of Winnipeg's Jewish political organizations . . . were leftist."[4] As the Winnipeg district bureau of the CP stated in a resolution passed at a meeting in January 1930, it was necessary to rally Jewish support for the USSR "upon the basis of the national aspirations of the Jewish people."[5] Indeed, the struggle between Jewish Communists and their opponents for leadership of the Jewish working class was "a hallmark of the immigrant community in the inter-war period."[6]

Communists active in the Jewish community encouraged the formation of organizations that would appeal to Jews interested in preserving their Jewish culture in non-Zionist ways. They would combat ethnic nationalism while harnessing feelings of Jewish identity to the class struggle. A variety of "front" organizations operated in the Jewish community, especially among its large urban working class. Yiddish-language pro-Soviet groups, comprised mainly of east European working-class immigrants were, in particular, concerned with Soviet treatment of its Jewish population. Organizations such as the Friends of the Soviet Union (FSU), formed in 1930, grew in numbers and influence in the Jewish community. Specifically Jewish groups were also created, as tension between anti-Soviet social democrats and pro-Soviet radicals grew, particularly in the Workmen's Circle (*Arbayter Ring*), which had in 1922, at its Toronto national conference, condemned Soviet-style Communism. In 1923 the Jewish Communists in Toronto opened a *Frayhayt* Club and organized the Jewish Women's Labour League (*Yidishe Arbayter Froyen Farayn*), which organized a children's camp, *Kindervelt*, on Lake Ontario in 1925. One year later, the Communists broke away from the Workmen's Circle altogether and formed the Labour League.[7] In Winnipeg, radical Jewish women formed the *Muter Farayn*, or Mother's League in 1919.[8] The Jewish Communists also founded a weekly newspaper, *Der Kamf*, in November 1924. Joshua ("Joe") Gershman assumed the editorship in 1935 and would remain at the helm of *Der Kamf* and its successor, the *Vochenblat-Canadian Jewish Weekly*, until it ceased publication in 1978.[9]

While a part of the Communist "family," the extensive network of groups fashioned by the Jewish Communists enabled them to remain somewhat independent of the Communist Party. (One could belong to the Jewish movement without formal adherence to the Party.) Among these groups were two left-of-center organizations whose specific aim was to provide support for the Soviet project to establish a Jewish socialist republic in the Birobidzhan region in the far east of the USSR. One was the Association for Jewish Colonization in the Soviet Union (*Gezelshaft far Yidishe Kolonizatsye in Ratn-Farband*), known by its Yiddish acronym, ICOR, founded in the United States in 1924 and active within the immigrant working-class milieu.

Its Canadian branches became a separate Canadian organization in 1935. The second was the American Committee for the Settlement of Jews in Birobidjan (Ambijan), a popular front group for English-speaking, middle-class Jews. Ambijan was founded in 1934 during a period when the Communists were seeking alliances against the increasing menace of Nazism and fascism. Its Canadian counterpart, the Canadian Birobidjan Committee, did not operate in Canada to any extent until after World War II.

Given the close proximity, geographic and cultural, of Canadian Jews to American Jews, the Canadian ICOR at first functioned as a section of the American organization. Sam Lapedes of Toronto, chair of the Jewish Bureau of the Communist Party of Canada, spoke at a March 1932 national plenum of the American ICOR and told delegates that the ICOR in Canada had recently gathered much strength.[10] By then, the Canadian ICOR had begun to establish its independence from the American center. At a conference held in Toronto on February 11–12, 1933, delegates from ICOR branches in Montreal, Toronto, Hamilton, Windsor, and Cornwall decided that the eastern Canadian section should formally incorporate the newly formed western Canadian branches into a national organization with headquarters in Toronto.[11] A conference in Toronto the next year brought together fifty-six delegates from five eastern Canadian cities; they vowed to make the ICOR a "mass organization" that could defend the Soviet Union and fight fascism and Zionism.[12] The delegates decided to begin publishing a periodical, the *Kanader "Icor,"* with Harry Guralnick as editor; the first issue, not surprisingly, carried as its lead story the decision of the Soviet government the month before to transform Birobidzhan into a Jewish Autonomous Region.[13]

By October 1934, there were 5,000 ICOR members in Canada,[14] and the next year the Canadians became independent of the American ICOR. The first Canadian national ICOR convention was held in Toronto on March 24–25, 1935. War and fascism were condemned and the delegates called for the "Jewish masses" in Canada to mobilize for the defense of the Soviet Union, which had "eliminated the bleak lack of rights which the Jews had experienced in tsarist Russia, abolished pogroms, anti-Semitism and in general every form of national oppression." The Soviet Union had spared no effort to rejuvenate the life of the Jewish masses by drawing them into industrial and agricultural work; encouraging Jewish culture, "national in form and socialist in content"; developing autonomous Jewish districts in the Crimea, Ukraine, and Belarus; and finally designating Birobidzhan as an area of concentrated Jewish settlement, which would become a Soviet

Republic. The ICOR called upon its members to organize celebrations in Jewish communities throughout the country and to defend the "only homeland of all the oppressed and the exploited, the country that had liberated all national minorities, including the Jewish masses—the Soviet Union!"[15] Abraham Shek, the national secretary, observed that the previous year had seen the proclamation of a Jewish Autonomous Region (JAR) in Birobidzhan and elections to its Soviet. People who had hitherto not paid much attention "have now realized that only in the Soviet Union has the national question been solved and only in the Soviet Union have the Jewish masses become prosperous."[16]

Throughout the 1930s, the Jewish Communists saw Zionism as their main enemy, and they spared no effort in contrasting Jewish colonization efforts in Soviet Russia to the creation of a Jewish homeland in Palestine. Unlike Palestine, *Der Kamf* stated, Birobidzhan was "not soaked in the blood of race hatred."[17] In 1934, Moishe Katz reported in the *ICOR Bulletin* that, despite the "fantasies" of the Zionists, the reality in Palestine was one of mass unemployment. Instead of siding with the Arab workers, he wrote, the Zionists were in league with British imperialism and encouraged British troops to suppress Arab demonstrations.[18] On other occasions the *Bulletin* asserted that the Histadrut, the labor federation in Palestine, was collaborating with Hitler by selling oranges to Nazi Germany instead of joining a worldwide boycott of German goods. By themselves practicing "the darkest chauvinism," the Zionists were doing the Nazis' work.[19] The creation of Birobidzhan was said to be a "catastrophe" for the Zionist servants of British imperialism and would serve as a "death blow" to their "adventure" in the so-called "Jewish homeland."[20]

At a meeting held in Toronto May 17, 1935, the national executive decided to take an active role in a national conference to deal with matters concerning the development of a mass people's movement for friendship with the Soviet Union, to be held under the auspices of the Friends of the Soviet Union (FSU), in Toronto, on June 29–30. The ICOR appealed to all Jewish workers and popular organizations to participate in the conference, which was intended to pressure the Canadian government into establishing normal relations, including trade, with the USSR, and into refusing to aid Germany or Japan. At present, the Canadian government was anti-Soviet in its policies, and supported those countries eager for war against the USSR.[21]

Given this situation, asked Sam Lipshitz, should the ICOR concern itself with the forthcoming federal election? The 1935 national convention had called upon the ICOR to reach out to other labor and progressive organizations. "We here in Canada wish to deliver the strongest death-blow against international fascism" and "we want to halt the spread of the fascist blaze in this country." Hence, contended Lipshitz, it would be a mistake to remain passive bystanders. In the coming campaign, therefore, the ICOR would endorse Communists plus any other candidates "who declared themselves ready to fight for our demands." Lipshitz made it clear that the ICOR would be tacitly supporting William Lyon Mackenzie King's Liberal Party.[22]

In October 1935 the Liberals defeated R. B. Bennett's Conservatives. In July 1936 the new Liberal government repealed Section 98 of the Criminal Code, which had effectively made the Communist Party and groups such as the ICOR illegal; those Communists who had been jailed under its provisions were released. The movement had now begun to benefit from the rightward shift in the world Communist movement that followed the change of political line agreed to at the seventh congress of the Communist International (Comintern) held in the summer of 1935. At this congress, it was decided to abandon the "class against class" approach, which castigated all non-Communists as political enemies or collaborators, and to embark upon a popular front anti-fascist strategy by allying with non-Communist socialists, liberals, "progressives," and other democrats. The CP central committee followed suit by endorsing the "Canadian People's Front" in November 1935.

CP leaders such as Tim Buck, Stewart Smith, and Joseph Baruch (J. B.) Salsberg, a Jewish member of the national executive of the ICOR, now toured the country and spoke regularly on the radio, presenting the Communist viewpoint on numerous issues. Buck was not Jewish nor were matters of Jewish concern uppermost on his agenda. Still, he frequently addressed Jewish supporters and in the 1935 election ran for a seat in Parliament in Winnipeg North, a hotbed of Jewish radicalism, where the prominent Communist Sam Carr campaigned for him in Yiddish.[23] At one meeting held on March 20, 1936, in Montreal, before an audience of 500, Buck contended that Zionism offered no solution to Jewish problems and "eulogized the efforts made by the Soviet Union with a view to establishing a Jewish autonomous state in Eastern Siberia known as Biro-Bidjan, which, he said, was given to the Jews as a home."[24] The Party now had "greater social, political, moral and cultural force than at any time in its history."[25]

Given the increased awareness that Hitler posed a terrible danger to European Jewry, many Canadian Jews saw in the USSR a potential bulwark against the spread of fascism, which in turn made some more receptive to the politics of the Jewish pro-Soviet organizations. Herman Abramovitch of the national executive reminded ICOR activists of the growing strength of anti-Semitic and fascist movements in Canada. In Quebec, in particular, anti-Semitism had spread "like wildfire." There had been some anti-Semitic rallies there, staged by fascists such as Adrien Arcand, "that would not be put to shame even by Hitler's bandits."[26]

So Montreal remained a hotbed of ICOR activity. By early 1936 there were 150 ICOR members in Montreal and a new English-language branch was about to be created; in July the Montreal ICOR also created a Birobidjan Committee. The city was the site of the second national convention of the Canadian ICOR, held May 8–10, 1936, to coincide with the second anniversary of the declaration of autonomy for Birobidzhan. The convention was attended by seventy-eight delegates from ten ICOR branches and sixty-four organizations. Abraham Shek reported on the campaign on behalf of Birobidzhan, which had made "great strides" in the two years since it had been declared a Jewish Autonomous Territory. Sholem Shtern, described as a "proletarian poet from Montreal," contrasted the situation of the Jews in Poland to those in the Soviet Union. "Birobidzhan showed the way for the Jewish masses everywhere," he declared. "We will live to see the day when every country will have a Birobidzhan which will create heroes from among the Jewish masses." During the previous year the ICOR had provided support to the FSU, the League Against War and Fascism, and had supported Jewish anti-fascist conferences in Montreal, Toronto, and elsewhere. The convention expressed its desire to see closer contact between the ICOR and the FSU, at both the national and local levels.[27]

International Communist "stars" were aware that Montreal had a large and supportive Jewish left and tailored their message accordingly. When British Communist MP William Gallacher arrived in Montreal on August 8, 1936, for the start of a cross-Canada speaking tour, he spoke before 3,500 people at the Mount Royal Arena on the subject of Communism and the "Jewish question." He lashed out at the Zionists for their "collaboration" with "British imperialism" and pointed to the USSR and in particular to Birobidzhan as an indication of how Jews would live in a workers' state. "The Jews must align themselves with the working class and the progressive movement as the solution of the Jewish problem cannot be found under the imperialist control," he declared.[28]

By 1937 the Spanish Civil War had taken center stage in the Communist movement, "The branches across the country have taken a very lively part in the work of raising aid for the Spanish people's government," reported Herman Abramovitch at a December 19, 1937 ICOR conference in Toronto. It was decided to mount a special campaign to help the Mackenzie-Papineau Battalion, formed in July 1937 as a unit of the International Brigades. The fourteen Toronto branches of the Labour League also resolved to support the ICOR's campaign on behalf of the Spanish Republicans. In Montreal, the ICOR had already taken the initiative in organizing a committee to raise money for Dr. Norman Bethune's medical unit in Spain.[29] The final defeat of the Spanish Loyalists by Franco's Nationalists in the spring of 1939 dampened the spirits of the Jewish Communists.

The Canadian Jewish Congress (CJC) had been reconstituted as the "umbrella" organization for Canadian Jewry in 1933. The ICOR was not admitted and would continue a running battle with the "bourgeois" CJC throughout the decade. The general secretary of the Congress, Hananiah Meyer Caiserman, was all too familiar with the tactics of the Communists. He cautioned against cooperation in any anti-fascist "united front" with the Communists. "Various elements are endeavouring to create the impression that the Jewish people and Communism are one and the same thing," he wrote on December 6, 1936, to Rabbi Solomon Frank of Winnipeg, president of the Western Division of Congress. Some community leaders were cooperating with the Communist-dominated League Against Fascism and Anti-Semitism and thereby weakening the Congress.[30]

In spite of opposition from Rabbi Frank, the Communists in western Canada did succeed in penetrating the CJC. On April 2, 1938, Ben Sheps, a Zionist and Congress activist in Winnipeg, informed Caiserman that "We have had many problems with J. A. Cherniak, our vice-president and his Anti-Fascist Committee." A meeting of the CJC held in Saskatoon July 17–18, 1938, to counter anti-Jewish propaganda in the west was attended by Harry Guralnick as an official delegate representing a Winnipeg society, and other participants cited his presence as proof that the Jewish Communists were willing to cooperate in the achievement of Jewish unity. Sheps wrote Caiserman again on October 25: "We still have trouble with the League Against Fascism and Anti-Semitism. Cherniak insists we accept them and cooperate with them, and admit two of their people into our committee on refugees. . . . I am afraid that sooner or later we will have to fight them openly." To augment their work in the League, in early 1938 the Communists had formed their own People's Committee Against Anti-Semitism and Fascism, with Dr. Simon Gold of Montreal as president, and Charles Rosen as secretary. Cherniak became its Winnipeg representative and would remain so until the signing of the German-Soviet Non-Aggression Treaty, or Hitler-Stalin Pact, in August 1939.[31]

The period following the signing of the pact was a difficult one for Jewish Communists and the ICOR fell silent. Since the Communists opposed Canada's declaration of war against Germany, the CP and many of its fronts were declared illegal in May 1940 under the War Measures Act, which gave the government the authority to intern political dissidents without trial, ban political organizations, seize property, and abridge freedom of the press (*Der Kamf* was shut down, though it was succeeded in October 1940 by a new publication, the *Kanader Yidishe Vochenblat*). Eventually 133 Communist officials would be interned, while others, such as Fred Rose and Sam Carr, fled to the United States. They would not return to Canada until after the Nazi invasion of the USSR.[32]

Meanwhile, those who chose to remain within the fold began to reassure themselves that, after all, the Communists had been in the forefront of the battle against fascism for decades, whereas others had been less militant, even appeasers. Clearly, argued the Jewish Communists, it was best to place one's trust in those who had always been proved right in the past. The pact was therefore praised as a brilliant move by Stalin which would strengthen the Soviet Union and weaken Hitler. The Communist movement had now jettisoned the popular front politics of the late 1930s and resumed its earlier ultra-left-wing sectarianism. Even though the war had begun and Jews in Europe were trapped in Hitler's inferno, the *Vochenblat* published negative stories concerning the Zionist *yishuv* in Palestine: it noted in late 1940, for example, that 25 percent of the Jews in Palestine were unemployed and suffering from demoralization.[33]

When the USSR did come under attack on June 22, 1941, the Jewish Communists quickly dropped their anti-war stance and called on all Jews to give unqualified support to the Soviet Union. The *Vochenblat* argued that the Western allies were the real villains of the story: had the allies not spurned the Soviet Union before 1939, Stalin would not have been forced to come to terms with Germany.[34] In what was either an example of wishful thinking or deliberate misinformation, the paper began printing stories that described a rising tide of revolutionary anti-fascist fervor in Nazi-occupied Europe and even in Germany itself. It was confidently asserted that the Germans were receiving "death blows" on the eastern front, and would soon be brought to account for their "horrific deeds" in occupied Poland and elsewhere.[35]

In August 1941 the Jewish Anti-Fascist Committee (JAFC), headed by prominent Soviet Jewish personalities, had been formed in Moscow to seek aid from the Jews in the West; soon its appeals would become a regular feature in the *Vochenblat*.[36] The future of the world and of the Jewish people now hung in the balance, editorialized the *Vochenblat*, and "we must do all we can for victory over bloody Hitlerism."[37] The Communists quickly went into action. The paper announced that a mass meeting would be held at Maple Leaf Gardens in Toronto on July 8. Calls were made for Canada to establish diplomatic and trade relations with the USSR.[38] A similar gathering was held in the Montreal Forum on July 22.[39] On September 28 the New York journalist and pro-Soviet activist B. Z. Goldberg addressed a large meeting in Montreal organized by the Quebec Committee for Allied Victory. On November 3, Goldberg spoke in Toronto on behalf of the Toronto Labour League, alongside Sol Shek, secretary of the League (and brother of Abraham).[40] The League, unlike many other CP-led groups, had managed to survive the hiatus of 1939–1941 almost undiminished.[41] Now, as Morris Biderman, a member of the Labour League since 1937 and its president after 1942, would eventually recall in his autobiography, the League "benefited and became acceptable in the community" as "Toronto's outspoken Jewish pro-Soviet organization."[42]

In Winnipeg, a meeting was held at the home of Dr. Benjamin Victor on October 24 to plan for ways to help the USSR. When the newly created Winnipeg Council for Allied Victory held its first big meeting on November 9, Victor, as chair of the event, read out the appeal made by the JAFC for help. Other speakers included lawyer Joe Zuken and Labl Basman, who had become secretary of the Jewish Committee for Medical Aid to the Soviet Union, an affiliate of the Council. Monies collected would be sent to Russia via the Canadian Red Cross.[43] Joe Zuken would be elected a Winnipeg school board trustee for Ward 3, where the overwhelming majority of Winnipeg Jews lived, in late November 1941.[44]

By the end of 1941, with the United States in the war as well, mainstream Jewish organizations such as the CJC had joined the pro-Soviet effort, and notables such as Allan and Samuel Bronfman, president of the CJC, were also becoming involved. In Montreal, a mass rally of 12,000 people, organized by the Montreal Committee for Medical Aid to the Soviet Union, gathered in the Forum on December 18. The meeting, which raised $20,000, was addressed by two prominent speakers: Joseph E. Davies, the former U.S. ambassador to the USSR, whose influential book, *Mission to Moscow*, had recently been published; and Liberal MP Peter Bercovitch, the city's only Jewish member of Parliament. Davies told his audience that "Stalin is a great man. . . . Everything he has done has been the result of his fervent idealism." At the rally, Allan Bronfman called on Canadian Jews to raise $1 million for Soviet war relief. By year's end $48,000 had been raised in Toronto and $10,000 in Winnipeg, where the CJC had joined with the Jewish pro-Soviet groups such as the Jewish People's Committee in order to raise money.[45] Such gatherings, with their resolutions calling for solidarity with the USSR and Jewish unity at home, would become commonplace for the duration of the war.

While the ICOR had become dormant with the onset of war, another Yiddish-language CP front, the World Jewish Cultural Union, or *Alveltlekher Yidisher Kultur Farband* (YKUF), founded in Paris in September 1937, gained strength. ICOR activists, such as Labl Basman and Dr. Victor in Winnipeg and Herman Abramovitch in Toronto, transferred their political energies into YKUF work. Dr. Victor had become chair of the Winnipeg YKUF and by early 1941 there were three YKUF reading circles in Winnipeg. Much of this pro-Soviet cultural ferment had occurred as a result of the arrival in Winnipeg, in 1940, of Basman, the new principal of the Sholem Aleichem School, formerly the Liberty Temple School. Founded in 1921, the school had become a pro-Soviet institution, separated from the *Arbayter Ring*, and changed its name, in 1932. Basman had taught at the school for two years after coming to Canada in 1928, and now once again brought "fire and dynamism [and] energetic liveliness" to the institution, while he "inspired others to work above and beyond their strength," remarked Boris Noznitsky, the vice-chair of the school committee.[46]

Sholem Shtern, in 1941, applauded the high literary standards of the YKUF journal *Yidishe Kultur*. With its articles on history and science, "*Yidishe Kultur* binds us to other countries," wrote Shtern. "It brings to our attention life in the Soviet Union, including the work of its Jewish writers."[47] In late 1941, the YKUF branches in Montreal, Toronto, Hamilton, Windsor, Winnipeg, Calgary, and Vancouver were organized into a unified Canadian organization, with a central committee in Toronto, under the direction of Moishe Feldman and Rose Bronstein, who became, respectively, the national chair and national secretary.[48] In January 1942, the YKUF held its first major Canadian conference in Montreal. Nakhman Mayzel, literary critic and editor of *Yidishe Kultur*, traveled from New York to lecture on the novelists Sholem Asch and David Bergelson. The delegates called upon Canada to do its utmost to help the war effort and sent a resolution to that effect to Prime Minister Mackenzie King.[49]

The honorary president of the YKUF, Khaim Zhitlovsky, was already the grand old man of socialist Yidishkayt; during the war years, he became a Communist icon as well. When Hitler invaded the USSR, Zhitlovsky insisted that for Jews, this war was literally "a matter of life and death":

therefore all Jews, no matter what their political sympathies, must support the Soviets "*with all their heart*."[50] Zhitlovsky's 75th birthday in the autumn of 1941was celebrated by YKUF branches across the country. His sudden death in Calgary on May 6, 1943, while on a cross-Canada tour, "hit us like a thunderbolt," reported the *Vochenblat*.[51] Zhitlovsky had been an icon of the Yiddishist movement, particularly in western Canada, and he had inspired the founding of a strong secular Yiddish school system in the country.

As news of the Holocaust began to emerge, many Canadian Jews saw in the Soviets the only chance to save what little was left of European Jewry. As Ben Lappin, then a CJC officer, noted in later years, "The summer of 1943 was no time to cast aspersions on the Soviet Union."[52] This widespread conviction provided the Canadian Jewish Communists with an unprecedented, if historically short-lived, series of electoral victories in the closing years of World War II. The stage was set with the visit of two illustrious Soviet Jewish emissaries to the Canadian Jewish community in September of 1943.The *Vochenblat* had already run many stories about the JAFC, in particular of its leading members, the actor Shloime Mikhoels and the poet Itzik Fefer.[53] When these two Soviet envoys, accompanied by the American Yiddish novelist Sholem Asch, visited Canada as part of a tour that included the Jewish communities of Britain, Mexico, and the United States, they were greeted at mass meetings of 25,000 people in both Montreal and Toronto.[54] Both the Canadian Jewish Congress and B'nai Brith held receptions for them in Montreal. Fefer said that Hitler had begun to realize that Jews were able to give as well as to receive blows. "Hitler was strongly mistaken about Russian Jewry," added Mikhoels. "It never occurred to him that Jews would fight back."[55] Fefer told a crowd at Maple Leaf Gardens roaring with approval that Stalin himself had seen the two emissaries off and had wished them good luck, while Mikhoels once again "spoke as witness to the Holocaust."[56]

In the 1940s, some 30 percent of the CP membership in Toronto was Jewish, according to Sam Lipshitz. In Montreal, related Harry Binder, then a leading Quebec Communist, the figure may have been as high as 70 percent.[57] Communists were becoming ever more accepted in the community; no longer ostracized, but often lionized. Though the Communist Party had been banned in 1940, it reemerged in 1943 as the Labor-Progressive Party (LPP).[58] With the Soviets having turned the tide at Stalingrad, it would ride the pro-Soviet wave to electoral victories in heavily Jewish constituencies. Particularly in Montreal, fears of domestic anti-Semitism meshed with concern over the fate of the Jews of Europe. In December 1942, a well-known

Communist, Michael Buhay, was elected to the Montreal city council as one of three councillors from District 5, whose municipal boundaries to a large extent coincided with the federal riding of Cartier, where the majority of Montreal's Jews lived.[59]

The Communists now set their sights on a bigger prize. The city's predominantly Jewish neighborhoods, all within the federal riding of Cartier, would go the polls in August 1943 in a by-election made necessary by the death in 1942 of their Liberal MP, Peter Bercovitch. The 18,000 Jewish electors in Cartier constituted almost half the total number of voters and had made the riding a Liberal stronghold: both Bercovitch and his predecessor, Sam Jacobs, had been Jewish Liberals. The Communists selected as their candidate in the by-election the long-time Communist leader and pamphleteer Fred Rose. Rose was already well-regarded for his work in exposing fascism in Canada and had written articles and pamphlets on the subject. He had run as a candidate in the Cartier riding in 1935, winning 16 percent of the vote.[60] Rose had been arrested and interned in September 1942, but had been released after signing a memo agreeing to support the war effort.

Michael Buhay, in a profile of the candidate, emphasized that Rose was an energetic advocate for workers and a proud Jew.[61] The Jewish community of Cartier "have duties and obligations to the tortured Jews of Europe," declared Max Bailey, another prominent Montreal Jewish Communist. A Jew should definitely represent the riding, but, he added, in an allusion to the Liberal candidate, Lazarus Phillips, the representative of Montreal's Jewish establishment, the new MP need not be "a rich Jewish lawyer with connections in the multi-millionaire world." Rose's campaign literature described him as "A Friend of the U.S.S.R." and a supporter of "Soviet-Canadian Unity."[62] Rose's platform called for a "quick victory over Hitler," opposition to anti-Semitism, and Soviet-Canadian friendship," alongside such standard left-wing domestic items as slum clearance, a minimum wage, and postwar jobs.[63]

On August 9 Rose, with 5,789 votes, narrowly edged out the French Canadian nationalist candidate, Paul Massé, who received 5,639 votes running for the anti-war Bloc Populaire Canadien. Rose received few French Canadian votes, while Massé got almost no Jewish votes. Phillips came in third, with 4,180 votes.[64] Following his election, Rose played a prominent role in the Jewish Communists' pro-war efforts.[65] He also continued to battle against right-wing anti-Semites in Quebec. The coming defeat of Hitler by "the glorious Red Army" would be "the funeral march" of those who still hoped that anti-Semitism and fascism might survive in some form in Canada after the war, he told a rally on April 12, 1944.[66] In a speech to the House of Commons on July 4, Rose called for an inquiry into anti-Semitism in Quebec.[67] Thanks to his work as an MP, and the reflected glory of the Red Army's triumph over Hitler, Rose would retain his seat in the June 11, 1945 federal election, nearly doubling his vote, to beat a Liberal, Samuel Schwisberg, who ran second, and Massé. "Fred Rose knows Cartier. He knows the people and the countries from which they come," stated one of his election pamphlets. "Let us re-elect the courageous fighter, the defender of the Jewish people, as our representative," proclaimed another.[68]

The pro-Soviet sentiment that had swept the Jewish community, casting the USSR in the role of saviour of the Jewish people, had enabled the LPP to mobilize a mass base of support. The Communists had also been able to tap into the insecurity of Montreal Jews, who feared hostility and anti-Semitism on the part of so many French Canadians, ranging from intellectuals to street thugs.

In the August 8, 1944 Quebec provincial election, Michael Buhay of the LPP ran a respectable second to the Liberal candidate, Maurice Hartt, in the largely Jewish St. Louis riding, winning 6,512 votes to Hartt's 9,439. The Communists called for Jews to vote LPP in order to defeat the "dark dreams" of the Bloc Populaire and of Quebec Premier Maurice Duplessis's Union Nationale.[69] As a municipal councillor Buhay had introduced a resolution in March 1943 calling for the Montreal city council to formally protest Hitler's genocidal policies towards the Jews of Europe. Buhay's resolution failed. In contrast, the Toronto City Council passed a similar motion unanimously.[70]

In Ontario, J. B. Salsberg had been elected a Toronto alderman for Ward 4 in 1937 but despite support from the liberal *Toronto Star*, which approved of his "humanitarianism," he was defeated just a year later.[71] No assimilationist, Salsberg emphasized his Jewishness in his political and trade union activities. The Communist Party was, for him, "a vehicle for celebrating secular Judaism and cultural nationalism expressed through the medium of Yiddish."[72] He regained the seat at the beginning of 1943 and later that year became a member of the provincial parliament, winning the predominantly Jewish constituency of St. Andrew in August 1943; he would be re-elected in June 1945 with a comfortable majority and again in 1948 and 1951.[73] (Bellwoods, a neighboring riding with many Jewish voters, also elected a Communist, A. A. MacLeod.)[74] Aldermen such as Norman Freed, Sam Carr's uncle, elected to the Toronto city council from Ward 4 in 1944 despite having been interned between 1940 and 1942, also provided the

LPP with a visible profile in the Jewish community.[75] In the 1945 federal election, Tim Buck and Sam Carr, though losing to Liberals, both received substantial support in Toronto-Trinity and Toronto-Spadina, seats with large Jewish populations, while in Winnipeg Joe Zuken ran second in Winnipeg North to a candidate of the social democratic CCF. The Communists were certainly making their presence felt in the Jewish community.

At the end of 1944, the Jewish Communists organized the United Jewish People's Order (UJPO) to supersede the Labour League in Toronto and similar front organizations elsewhere in the country. The formation of the UJPO was to some extent an acknowledgment that the Jewish movement was a legitimate yet separate component of the Canadian Communist world. The UJPO also gained recognition within the larger Jewish community: the organization was admitted without difficulty as a member in good standing to the Canadian Jewish Congress.

The UJPO's leadership included well-known Jewish Communists and pro-Soviet fellow travelers. The national secretary, Morris Biderman, had been a member of the CP since 1927, manager of *Der Kamf* between 1937 and 1939, a member of the Labour League since 1937, and its president after 1942. Dr. Sam Sniderman of Hamilton was the national president. Others in the leadership were Sam Lipshitz, Sol Shek, Charles Starkman, Sholem Shtern, J. B. Salsberg, Alfred Rosenberg, Abraham Nisnevitz, Joseph Zuken, Sam Carr, Fred Rose, and A. B. (Archie) Bennett. With its network of schools, cultural centers, choirs, and camps, the UJPO hoped to become a major presence in the Canadian Jewish community, with branches in most major Canadian cities. It sponsored fund-raising dinners that included guests such as Toronto alderman Nathan Phillips, a future mayor of Toronto, and Abraham Feinberg, rabbi of Toronto's then preeminent synagogue, the Reform denomination Holy Blossom Temple.[76] By January 1948 the UJPO counted 1,368 members in Toronto alone. The *Vochenblat* became its *de facto* organ: In 1945, J. B. Salsberg was the president, Joshua Gershman general secretary, and Harry Guralnick, executive secretary, of the Canadian Jewish Weekly Association, the paper's publisher.

Now that Nazi Germany had been defeated, Jewish Communists were again hopeful that the construction of Birobidzhan might recommence. On June 28, 1945, the *Vochenblat* published an article, datelined New York, announcing the creation by Ambijan of an "Einstein Fund" to resettle. in Birobidzhan, 30,000 Jewish war orphans from Poland, Hungary, and Czechoslovakia. Ambijan had already helped resettle 3,500 children.[77]

During the second half of 1945 Canadian supporters of Ambijan made efforts to develop a Canadian-wide organization to support this work and organized the Birobidjan Appeal to Aid Jewish War Orphans in the USSR. On October 4, 1945, Gershman wrote to Dr. Victor in Winnipeg, advising him that "we have resolved to organize in Canada a movement for Birobidzhan" that would not be content merely to collect "pennies and dimes"; rather, it would undertake to send major items to Birobidzhan. As well, the new movement would undertake to create friendship between Canada and the Soviet Union, and between Canadian and Soviet Jews. Remarked Gershman, "we must make certain not to leave the impression that Birobidzhan is in competition with Palestine." Gershman told Victor that Ambijan would help to organize the new group[78]

In Montreal, a local Birobidjan Committee had already been formed in 1936 but it had ceased operations. It was not surprising, then, that Ambijan had the support of many active members of the Jewish community in Montreal. On November 19–20, 1945, representatives of various Jewish organizations agreed to form a provisional Canadian Birobidjan Committee; on February 17, 1946, the Committee held its first citywide meeting. Over 200 delegates, including MP Fred Rose, attended the conference, presided over by Max Bailey and Joseph Yass. J. M. Budish, chair of Ambijan's administrative committee and its executive vice-president, traveled to Montreal from New York to report to the conference on recent developments in Birobidzhan and on the activities of the American Birobidjan Committee on behalf of the war orphans. The delegates also heard a message from Albert Einstein, a long-time supporter of Ambijan. Declared Fred Rose, "I would like to see in Birobidzhan a monument from Canadian Jewry."[79]

Gershman wrote to Joe Zuken that "we shall strengthen the Montreal Birobidjan Committee and plan together with the Jewish People's Committee of Winnipeg and the various Russian-Ukrainian Farbands in the east, a national conference for the official inauguration of a Canadian Birobidjan Committee." Gershman suggested Charles Rosen as national director, and Winnipeg UJPO activist Louie (Vasil) Guberman as organizer for Winnipeg and points west.[80]

The formation of the Canadian Birobidjan Committees now almost complete, the Communists began a Dominion-wide fund-raising campaign to help in the building of Birobidzhan and, in particular, to raise money for the resettlement of 1,000 orphans there. In early May, the 106-member Toronto Jewish Folk Choir, under the direction of Emil Gartner, gave a performance at Massey Hall, Toronto, of the oratorio "Biro Bidjan," which was, in the words of Sam Carr, "a rhapsody of gratitude by Jacob Schaefer to the Jewish Autonomous Region of the Soviet Union." The Birobidjan Committee held its first Dominion-wide conference on May 26, 1946, at the B'nai Jacob Shul in Montreal. The following day, a "mass meeting" and concert took place at the *Folks Shule*. The Montreal Jewish Folk Choir, accompanied by a mandolin orchestra, sang Birobidzhaner songs and the cantata "Der mogen dovid bagrist dem roytn shtern" ("The Shield of David Salutes the Red Star"). The two keynote speakers were Dr. Victor of Winnipeg, and Rabbi Abraham J. Bick of the Warsaw Center, New York, president of the Union of American Jews of Ukrainian Descent and a member of Ambijan's National Committee.

Irving J. Myers, who was elected executive director, praised Montreal for being the first community to engage in pro-Birobidzhan work once the war had ended. Montreal activists had sent a transport of clothing for 3,500 orphans and had also been involved in many other activities, he stated. Dr. Victor gave a speech in which he drew on his personal experiences in Birobidzhan, which he had visited in 1936. Gershman, national organizer for the recently formed National Jewish Committee of the LPP, also spoke; he underscored the great significance of the new organization. A message of greetings from the Soviet embassy was read out, praising the committee for its efforts.

A manifesto describing the tragic conditions in which European Jews found themselves following the Holocaust was issued. "In the present gloomy circumstances in which our people find themselves," stated the manifesto, "the Jewish Autonomous Region in Birobidzhan shines like a bright beam. . . . We do not see a conflict between Biro-Bidzhan and Palestine," declared the manifesto. "There is room for [both] Zionists and non-Zionists in the aid work on behalf of Biro-Bidzhan. Just as all Jews are interested in helping with the construction of Palestine, and in aiding those Jews who wish to settle there, so too should the work on behalf of Biro-Birobidzhan and the Soviet solution of the Jewish question be evaluated by all Jews, without regard to party affiliation." The manifesto urged all Jewish organizations to help set up aid committees for Birobidzhan, and pleaded with them to not be misled by anti-Soviet groups.[81]

"Ever since the Canadian Biro-Bidjan Committee was organized, all the branches and sections of the Order have taken an active interest in the work of the Committee," national secretary Morris Biderman told the second national convention of the UJPO in Montreal on June 20–22, 1947.

"The Order last year made a considerable contribution to the financial campaign of the committee. We regard the financial campaign as not only a question of providing concrete help to the Jews of Biro-Bidjan but as a means of binding the friendship of the Jews of Canada and the Jews of the Soviet Union. It brings closer the day when world Jewish unity will be attained." The convention resolved "to give our full moral and financial help to the Jews of Biro-Bidjan and to the new immigrants who help to hasten the day when the Jewish Autonomous Region will be transformed into a Soviet Jewish Republic."[82]

The LPP had formed a National Jewish Committee during the war and the Communist attitude toward a Jewish homeland in Palestine had begun to change. Already, in April and in September 1945, the Committee had recommended support for the right of the Jewish population in Palestine to self-government. This, it declared, would help, rather than hinder, the economic and political progress of all of the Semitic peoples in the Middle East. Soon afterwards, Gershman wrote a thirteen-page report on "The Attitude of the Communists to the *Erets Yisroel* Problem," explaining that the party's position on Palestine had altered "due to the tremendous changes in the political world." (It is interesting to observe that he now used the term *Erets Yisroel*, or Land of Israel.) Gershman quoted statements made by the American and British Communist Parties and by the JAFC in Moscow in support of Jewish immigration to Palestine and Jewish aspirations to achieve statehood. In his conclusion, however, Gershman remarked that, although the Jewish *yishuv* had earned the right to nationhood in Palestine, "the final solution to the Jewish question will come about only through socialism."[83]

Indeed, as early as March 24, 1945, Fred Rose had said, in a speech in the House of Commons, that he hoped "the Arab leaders will understand that mass migration of Jewish people into Palestine is essential and is not a menace to a prosperous future of the Arab people." A Jewish state would be "a constructive factor in the development of the Near East."[84] In a letter to Gershman dated November 5, 1945, Joe Zuken reported that Rose had spoken that autumn at a Zionist mass meeting in Winnipeg, where "his talk made a good impression on those responsible for arranging the meeting and on the audience generally." Zuken also mentioned that Tim Buck had spoken to a Jewish meeting in Winnipeg on October 14 denouncing the 1939 British "White Paper" that limited Jewish immigration to Palestine.[85]

In 1947–1948, the attitude of the Canadian Communists toward Zionism underwent a further shift, made necessary by the Soviet Union's decision to support a Jewish state in Palestine. In order to clarify the new

Soviet line, Morris Biderman was sent, at the end of 1947, on a six-week voyage across western Canada. Biderman emphasized that the Soviet position had not been "a reversal from a pro-Arab to a pro-Jewish role"; rather, it was "based on the consistent Soviet policy on the national question and the self-determination of minorities" as practiced in the USSR itself.[86] Salsberg spent part of January 1948 in Tel Aviv and found himself "very excited" by what he saw.[87] Gershman declared in February 1948 that the *yishuv* in *Erets Yisroel* was entitled to "the most complete moral, financial and political help."[88] His comments were echoed by the national executive of the UJPO, which, at a special session, called on Canadian Jews to provide support for the Jewish community in Palestine.[89] "The Jewish Nation Must and Can Be Saved!" screamed a front-page headline in the *Vochenblat* of April 8. "The Canadian Jewish community must not remain silent in this critical time! Quick and drastic action is needed!"[90] The paper's pages were now devoted almost exclusively to the two Jewish states—the new one, about to be proclaimed in Tel Aviv, and the old one in the USSR, now twenty years old. Alfred Rosenberg took note of "two historic dates in the evolution of Biro-Bidzhan": March 28, 1928, when the Soviet government proclaimed Birobidzhan a site for Jewish colonization, and May 7, 1934, when Birobidzhan attained the status of an autonomous region." Since the end of the war, the Soviet Jews had thrown themselves "with the greatest enthusiasm" into the task of building their socialist republic in Birobidzhan, wrote Rosenberg. But in no way was Birobidzhan a competitor to *Erets Yisroel*. "Indeed, with the growth of democracy and freedom in the east European countries, it is now possible to solve the Jewish problem on an entirely new basis. The establishment of a Jewish state in *Erets Yisroel* is one aspect of the determination to solve the problem of the Jews overseas and is in compliance with the national feelings and interests of the Jewish masses in other parts of the world. No sincere Jew can see a contradiction between Biro-bidzhan and *Erets Yisroel*," Rosenberg concluded.[91]

However, by early 1949 disquieting reports about Soviet anti-Semitism were circulating in the general and Jewish press, putting the Communists on the defensive. Birobidzhan was trotted out as proof that "Anti-Semitism has literally been eliminated in the USSR" and that "[t]he new Soviet generation does not know what race hatred is."[92] The Jewish Communists could also still play the pro-Israel card. After all, had not the Soviets proved themselves the best friends of the Jewish people by fighting for a Jewish state in Palestine? The USSR and the new "people's democracies" in eastern Europe remained "in the vanguard of the fight for a secure and free state of

Israel," asserted Joshua Gershman, and Communists were waging "the most constructive struggle of all on Israel's behalf."[93] Soon even these appeals to the Jewish community would become untenable, as Soviet attitudes toward Israel began to shift. Still, in November 1949 the Jewish Communists duly celebrated the 32nd anniversary of the Bolshevik Revolution and Birobidzhan was, as usual, included in the list of reasons why the Jewish people owed the Soviet Union such a debt of gratitude.[94]

As the second half of the twentieth century dawned, the *Vochenblat* could still editorialize, in its "Balance Sheet" of the previous half-century, that among the greatest achievements of the previous fifty years had been the outlawing of anti-Semitism in the USSR and the creation of two Jewish states, Birobidzhan and Israel.[95] Joshua Gershman was typical of most Jewish Communists at the time in maintaining that anyone who read Article 123 of the Soviet constitution, which made discrimination a severely punishable crime, "would grasp at once the absurdity of the allegation of 'anti-Semitism' in the USSR."[96] So, despite the setbacks suffered by the Canadian Communist movement after 1945, with the onset of the Cold War and the sensational disclosure of domestic Communist complicity in Soviet espionage in the country, the Jewish Communist groups at first managed to retain much of their following within the community. The Soviet Union had, according to the Communists, fathered one Jewish state, Birobidzhan, which was celebrating its second decade, and had been midwife, by its support of the *yishuv* in the United Nations, to the birth of a second Jewish state, Israel. The new "people's democracies" had provided the military arms that had enabled the Jewish state to fend off the invading Arab armies. All of this had followed upon the Soviet role in defeating Hitler and liberating the remnant of European Jewry, and, by establishing socialist governments in eastern European nations such as Czechoslovakia, Hungary, Poland, and Romania, presumably putting an end to the underlying economic and social causes of the anti-Semitism and reaction that had been rife in that region for centuries.

And this was reflected in the Communists' continued base of support, particularly in Montreal. In the spring of 1947, the Cartier seat came open following the arrest of incumbent Fred Rose for espionage a year earlier (as noted below). The riding at the time comprised some 18,000 French Canadians, 16,000 Jews, 2,000 Anglo-Saxons, and 4,000 people of other ancestries. Michael Buhay had now replaced Rose as standard-bearer for the LPP. Maurice Hartt jumped into the federal arena on behalf of the Liberals, while Paul Massé again ran for the Bloc Populaire. Hartt won the by-election with 9,493 votes, followed by Massé with 6,739 and Buhay with 6,419.[97] Considering that elsewhere in Canada, Cold War politics had almost completely marginalized Communists, this was no mean feat. In December 1947 another stalwart of the Jewish Communist movement, Max Bailey, won election to the Montreal city council from the heavily Jewish District 5, situated within the federal Cartier riding, following Buhay's death in August.[98]

In the federal election of June 1949, the LPP candidate Harry Binder, Montreal organizer for the party, ran second behind Hartt in Cartier; elsewhere in the country, Communists fared far worse. As late as June of 1950, in a by-election held in the riding following the death of Hartt, Binder again ran second to the Liberal's Leon Crestohl, with 3,913 votes against 9,701.[99] Binder managed to win election to the Montreal city council from District 5 in December 1950, succeeding Bailey, and served for two years.[100]

Still, the Canadian Jewish Communist organizations did begin to collapse with the intensification of the Cold War. Following the disclosure in September 1945 by Igor Gouzenko, a clerk in the Soviet embassy in Ottawa, of a Soviet spy ring operating in Canada during the war, a Royal Commission on Espionage was struck in early February 1946, headed by two Supreme Court justices, Robert Taschereau and R. L. Kellock. Ten days later, the RCMP detained thirteen people, who were held without charges and were not allowed to see their families or have access to lawyers; the detainees were forced to testify against themselves.[101] Following the publication of several of the Commission's interim reports in March 1946, Fred Rose, Sam Carr, and other Jewish Communists were charged with various crimes. Rose was convicted of espionage in June and was sentenced to six years in jail. His Cartier seat was declared vacant by a unanimous vote of the House of Commons on January 30, 1947; Prime Minister Mackenzie King himself introduced the resolution.[102] Carr had fled to the United States after Rose's arrest, but was caught by the FBI in 1949 and deported to Canada; charged with passport violations, he served six years in prison.[103]

By now only the most committed of Communists "remained willing to defend an ideology that the Canadian state was clearly prepared to fight and vilify with all means at its disposal."[104] A Fred Rose Defence Committee was formed in Montreal in 1946, after Rose had been refused bail while appealing his verdict, with Alex Gauld as chair and Michael Buhay as secretary-treasurer.[105] But even handing out its literature proved dangerous work: a McGill University student distributing a pamphlet entitled "The Defence of Fred Rose," which included a petition requesting the release of

Rose on bail, was arrested by the anti-Communist squad of the Montreal police on charges of seditious libel and was himself refused bail. The plant where the pamphlets were printed was raided and several thousands of the circulars were seized, along with the plates. Private homes were also searched and literature seized.[106]

Given this climate of opinion, even people on the fringes of the movement saw their livelihoods threatened and their mobility circumscribed. When Sam Lipshitz returned from a Yiddish cultural conference in Poland in 1949, and went on a speaking tour and solicited contributions for the *Vochenblat*, he was told by a shopkeeper in Edmonton, "a very loyal supporter for many years," to leave his shop immediately. Lipshitz was told by another merchant that the RCMP "had come into a number of stores and warned them about me."[107] Biderman wrote Gershman about disarray in the Winnipeg UJPO, where "the situation is getting not better but worse," with much infighting, animosity and pressures from without.[108]

In Montreal, on January 27, 1950, the "anti-subversive" squad of Maurice Duplessis's Quebec provincial police, using the Quebec "Padlock Law," shut down the Morris Winchevsky Cultural Centre, which had opened in November 1947, and the Morris Winchevsky School.[109] In June of 1950, the Korean War began, and the Communists found themselves accused of supporting Canada's enemies. In the November 1951 Ontario provincial election, J. B. Salsberg hung on to his seat, although the other LPP member of the legislature, A. A. MacLeod, was defeated.[110] By the time the Canadian Jewish Congress met at its ninth plenary session in October of 1951, the UJPO had been expelled from the organization.[111]

It was not until 1956, however, that the Jewish Communist movement received its mortal blow, in the form of the "secret speech" by Nikita Khrushchev at the 20th congress of the Communist Party of the Soviet Union, in which Khrushchev exposed the murderous deeds of Stalin and his henchmen. The report of Stalin's crimes against the Jews of Russia, with detailed revelations of anti-Semitic repression in the Soviet Union after 1948, including the murder of the cream of Yiddish writers and intellectuals in August 1952 and the so-called "Doctors' Plot" in early 1953, were published in the Polish press and elsewhere. Nowhere was the crisis of faith more profound than among the Jewish Communists. For most, it became painfully clear that the Soviet Union was in fact a despotism and that its espoused ideals, which had inspired so many, were nothing more than cynical camouflage and window dressing. They now realized that, in their aspirations to build a democratic future without war and oppression, they had committed themselves to a social system that proved, in every sense, the negation of that vision.

Although the UJPO, at conferences in Toronto and Montreal at the end of December 1956, defined itself as an independent organization unaffiliated with any political party, most of the membership knew better.[112] Several prominent members, including Biderman, Lipshitz, and Salsberg, struggled for a few years to save the organization by freeing it from Communist domination. But by 1959, they were gone. Biderman, in his statement of resignation, spoke of the "strife and inner struggle," the "long and bitter debates," that had wracked the organization. By October 1959 the total UJPO membership had declined to 872.[113] Those who left formed the New Fraternal Jewish Association in 1960. Sam Carr took over the presidency of the UJPO and steered it once again in a pro-Soviet direction. The organization's new national executive in April 1960 declared that it did not want to be a "base for political struggles against the Soviet Union and the Communist Party of Canada."[114] Those who remained were mainly Communists like Labl Basman, Rose Bronstein, and Joshua Gershman.

After three decades as an organizer, trade unionist, and elected official, J. B. Salsberg left the Communist Party in 1957, denounced and vilified by Tim Buck and the leadership for daring to question Soviet policies. "The Jewish question had broken Salsberg's faith." Now referring to the party as a "straightjacket," he would eventually re-engage with the mainstream Jewish community.[115] Sam Lipshitz, who also left the CP in 1957, after being a member of its central committee from 1943 to 1956, acknowledged that "the political line" of the ICOR had been "dominated by the Communist Party." By virtue of his position as a high-ranking CP official, he said, "I was involved in the ICOR. I made it my business to in some way supervise their activities. At one point in the early 1930s, during the very deep economic crisis, when a lot of people were leaning towards the left-wing movement, and out of sympathy for the Soviet Union, the ICOR had a good following. A lot of Jews who were not left wing but nationalist, for them the idea of a Jewish state even under the Soviet regime, was very attractive."[116] Morris Biderman, who also quit the CP in 1957, remarked, "We in the Labour League and the UJPO believed that Jewish colonization in the Soviet Union, and the idea of a Jewish homeland, was a good thing. We had doubts before 1956, but we held our doubts until we realized what had happened. The whole idea of Birobidzhan, in retrospect, I don't think it was a genuine attempt to provide a homeland for Jews. The idea was more to get rid of the Jews who thought of settling in the Crimea. The political leaders of the Soviet Union must have known that it wouldn't work."[117]

Biderman, however, differentiated between "two kinds of Communists among Jews—Communist Jews and Jewish Communists. The former happened to be born to Jewish parents but had nothing in common with Jewish consciousness." The latter, however, were involved in movements such as the ICOR because they were "genuinely interested and concerned with the creation of a Jewish territory in the Soviet Union with its own language, culture and economy: In other words, a Jewish homeland."[118]

Yet some of the Jewish Communists would continue their pro-Soviet activities. They "belonged to a party that was stronger than any religion," explained Biderman. "To betray it was a sin."[119] Joshua Gershman was one example. Though he acknowledged "the monstrous crimes committed against Jewish cultural workers and institutions in the Soviet Union," the pain of which had "grown and intensified,"[120] he refused to follow people such as Biderman, Lipshitz, and Salsberg out of the CP. "The Party is my life, without it I am nothing," he told Morris Biderman. "What will I do, where can I be active?" Gershman finally left, due to his differences with Soviet policy toward Israel and toward its own Soviet Jewish population, in 1977.[121] The *Vochenblat* expired in 1978. Gershman died a decade later, on April 30, 1988.[122]

Notes

1. Suzanne Rosenberg, *Soviet Odyssey* (Toronto: Penguin Canada, 1991), 31–33.

2. Norman Penner, *Canadian Communism: The Stalin Years and Beyond* (Toronto: Methuen, 1988), 273; Gerald Tulchinsky, *Branching Out: The Transformation of the Canadian Jewish Community* (Toronto: Stoddart, 1998), 119–22.

3. Rome was interviewed January 22, 1983, by Lewis Levendel; see *A Century of the Canadian Jewish Press: 1880s–1980s* (Ottawa: Borealis Press, 1989), 151. Erna Paris quotes a CP official as stating that in 1929, some 20 percent of the members were Jewish. Erna Paris, *Jews: An Account of Their Experience in Canada* (Toronto: Macmillian Canada, 1980), 145.

4. Tulchinsky, *Branching Out*, 9.

5. Quoted in Lita-Rose Betcherman, *The Little Band: The Clashes Between the Communists and the Political and Legal Establishment in Canada, 1928–1932* (Ottawa: Deneau, [1982]), 98.

6. Irving Abella, *A Coat of Many Colours: Two Centuries of Jewish Life in Canada* (Toronto: Key Porter Books, 1999), 177.

7. Ruth A. Frager, "Politicized Housewives in the Jewish Communist Movement of Toronto 1923–1933," in *Beyond the Vote: Canadian Women and Politics*, eds. Linda Kealey and Joan Sangster (Toronto: University of Toronto Press, 1989), 267–68; Michelle Cohen and Ester Reiter, "Women, Culture, Politics, *Yiddishkayt* and the Yiddish *Arbeiter Froyen Farein*," *Outlook* 33, No. 2 (1995): 9–11; Stephen A. Speisman, *The Jews of Toronto: A History to 1937* (Toronto: McClelland and Stewart, 1979), 316–17. Both the Jewish Women's Labour League and the Labour League would become part of the pro-Communist United Jewish People's Order (UJPO) in 1944.

8. Roz Usiskin, "Winnipeg's Jewish Women of the Left: Radical and Traditional," in *Jewish Radicalism in Winnipeg, 1905–1960* (*Jewish Life and Times*, Vol. 8) ed. Daniel Stone (Winnipeg: Jewish Heritage Centre of Western Canada, 2003), 112.

9. Michael Buhay of Montreal was editor for the first two years. He was succeeded in 1926 by Philip Halperin, who died in 1932. Ber Green of New York in turn temporarily succeeded him, followed by Harry Guralnick, until 1935. In the mid-1930s, *Der Kamf* had a circulation of about 3,000. During World War II, the *Vochenblat-Canadian Jewish Weekly* had a print run of 4,000–5,000 copies. Levendel, *A Century of the Canadian Jewish Press*, 130–35.

10. "Protokol fun plenum," *ICOR* 5, May 1932, 8–9.

11. "ICOR optaylung," *Der Kamf*, April 14, 1933, 3.

12. Abe Victor, "Oyfn 3tn tsuzamenkumpft fun alkanader Icor sektsye in Toronto 10tn un 11tn marts, 1934," *ICOR Biro-Bidzhan Souvenir-Zhurnal* (New York: ICOR, June 1934), 40.

13. "Biro-bidzhan farvandlt in yidisher autonomer sovyetisher teritorye," *Kanader "Icor"* 1, June 1934, 1.

14. "In der Icor baveygung," *ICOR* 8, January 1935, 19.

15. "Editoryals: Grayt zikh tsu di november-fayerung!," *Kanader "Icor"* 2, October 1935, 1.

16. *Der ershter natsyonaler tsuzamenfor fun dem kanader "icor"* (Toronto: National Executive of the Canadian "Icor," 1935), 2–32; "Deklaratsye fun dem ershtn natsyonaln tsuzamenfor fun dem 'icor' in kanada," *ICOR* 8, 4 (April 1935): 10–11.

17. Y. G., "Fun yordn biz amur," *Der Kamf*, December 9, 1932, 3.

18. Moishe Katz, "Di letste antviklungen in Palestina," *"Icor" Bulletin* 5, January 1934, 6, 8.

19. "1 milyon mark Hitler-gelt far der Histadrut," *"Icor" Bulletin* 5, January 1934, 7.

20. A. Hamer, "Biro-bidzhan—an umglik far di tsyionistn," *Kanader "Icor"* 1, June 1934, 11.

21. "Di baveygung fur frayntshaft mit dem sovyetn-farband," *Kanader "icor"* 2, No. 8 (June 1935): 1; "'Icor'-taytikayt iber kanada," *Kanader "icor"* 2, No. 8 (June 1935): 4; Jack Cowan, "'Icor' Participates in National Conference of Friend-

ship with the U.S.S.R.," *Kanader "icor"* 2, 8 (June 1935): [16]. Cowan visited the USSR in 1934 and then became national secretary of the FSU.

22. Sh. Lipshitz, "Darft der 'icor' zikh batayliken in kumende federale valn?" *Kanader "icor"* 2, No. 8 (June 1935): 2, 7.

23. Henry Trachtenberg, "The Winnipeg Jewish Community in the Inter-war Period, 1919–1939: Anti-Semitism and Politics," *Canadian Jewish Historical Society Journal* 4, No. 1 (1980): 58–59.

24. "No. 800: Weekly Summary Report on Revolutionary Organizations and Agitators in Canada, 1st April, 1936," in *R.C.M.P. Security Bulletins: The Depression Years, Part III, 1936*, eds. Gregory S. Kealey and Reg Whitaker (St. John's, NL: Canadian Committee on Labour History, 1996), 146.

25. John Manley, "'Communists Love Canada!: The Communist Party of Canada, the 'People' and the Popular Front, 1933–1939,"*Journal of Canadian Studies/Revue d'études canadiennes* 36, No. 4 (2001–2002), 60–63, 68–69, 72–75, 79, 82.

26. H. Abramovitch, "Antisemitism in kanada," *Kanader "icor"* 2, No. 11 (February 1936): 6–7. Anti-Semitism in Quebec was a recurring theme in ICOR literature and was the subject of the lead editorial in the English section of *Nailebn-New Life*, the publication of the American ICOR, in the summer of 1939. "Anti-Semitism in Canada," *Nailebn-New Life* 13, No. 8 (1939): 3 [English section].

27. A. Shek, "Foroys, tsu a brayter folks-organizatsye fun dem 'icor' in kanada!" *Kanader "icor"* 3, No. 1 (May 1936): 5–7; *Far der yid. autonomye gegnt* (Toronto: National Executive of the Canadian "Icor," 1936), 3–30.

28. "Gallacher Says British Labor is Observing Spain," *Daily Clarion*, Toronto, August 13, 1936, 1, 3; "No. 820: Weekly Summary Report on Revolutionary Organizations and Agitators in Canada, 19th August, 1936," in *R.C.M.P. Security Bulletins: The Depression Years, Part III, 1936*, 350–51. See also John Manley, "A British Communist MP in Canada: Willie Gallacher Builds the Popular Front," *Communist History Network Newsletter* 6 (1998), 6–11.

29. "In kanader 'icor,'" *Nailebn-New Life* 12, No. 3 (1938): 35 [Yiddish section]; F. Golfman, "Montreal 'icor'-taytikayt in 1937," *Nailebn-New Life* 12, No. 3 (1938): 36 [Yiddish section]; Minutes of Hamilton ICOR meeting of February 7, 1937, "Minute Book of Hamilton Chapter of ICOR," Goldie Vine papers, 1930–1948, Multicultural History Society of Ontario, Series 85, Jewish Canadian papers, F1405, File 085-015, MU 90042.01, Archives of Ontario, Toronto [hereafter AO]; typewritten undated ms of a December 19, 1937 speech by Herman Abramovitch, 25–26; in Jewish Canadiana, Institutions—ICOR; Jewish Public Library, Montreal [hereafter JPL].

30. See *Canadian Jewish Archives: The Jewish Congress Archival Record of 1936*, New Series, 8, ed. David Rome (Montreal: Canadian Jewish Congress, 1978), 68–69, 74.

31. David Rome, *Clouds in the Thirties: On Antisemitism in Canada. 1929–1939. A Chapter on Canadian Jewish History*, Section 11 (Montreal: National Archives, Canadian Jewish Congress, 1980) 541–42, 548–51, 554–58; *Ershter*

alveltlekher yidisher kultur-kongres, pariz, 17–21 Sept. 1937: Stenografisher barikht (Paris: Tsentral-farveltung fun alveltlekher yidish kultur-farband [YKUF], 1937), 346, 364; "No. 883: Weekly Summary Report on Revolutionary Organizations and Agitation in Canada, Feb. 9, 1938," in *R.C.M.P. Security Bulletins: The Depression Years, Part V, 1938–1939*, eds. Gregory S. Kealey and Reg Whitaker (St. John's, NL: Canadian Committee on Labour History, 1997), 63–64; "No. 899: Weekly Summary Report on Communist and Fascist Organizations and Agitation in Canada," *R.C.M.P. Security Bulletins: The Depression Years, Part V, 1938–1939*, 261–62; Saul Cherniak, "Personal Perspective," in *Jewish Radicalism in Winnipeg, 1905–1960*, ed. Daniel Stone, 206.

32. See Reg Whitaker, "Official Repression of Communism During World War II," *Labour/Le Travail* 17 (1986): 135–66.

33. "Di lage fun di yidn in farsheydene lender," *Kanader yidishe vochenblat*, November 28, 1940, 4.

34. Moishe Kasoff, "Di diplomatishe tragedye fun yor 1939," *Kanader yidishe vochenblat*, July 3, 1941, 4, 6.

35. "Oyf di nazis in poylen tsitert di hoyt" [literally: "The Skin is Trembling on the Nazis in Poland"], *Kanader yidishe vochenblat*, February 26, 1942, 4.

36. See "Radio-ruf fun sovyet-yidishe shrayber tsint on a fayer in hartsen fun yedn yidn [sic] iber der gorer velt," *Kanader yidishe vochenblat*, September 4, 1941, 1, 6. For the history of this important wartime organization, see Shimon Redlich, *Propaganda and Nationalism in Wartime Russia: The Jewish Antifascist Committee in the USSR, 1941–1948* (Boulder, CO: East European Quarterly, 1982) and Shimon Redlich, *War, Holocaust and Stalinism: A Documented History of the Jewish Anti-Fascist Committee in the USSR* (Luxembourg: Harwood Academic Publishers, 1995). For its demise, see *Stalin's Secret Pogrom: The Postwar Inquisition of the Jewish Anti-Fascist Committee*, eds. Joshua Rubenstein and Vladimir P. Naumov (New Haven, CT: Yale University Press, 2001).

37. "Shnele un baldike aktsye—a lebns noytvendikayt tsu farnikhten hitlerism," *Kanader yidishe vochenblat*, July 10, 1941, 1.

38. "Anti-hitler masn-miting in maple leaf gardens," *Kanader yidishe vochenblat*, July 3, 1941, 8; S. Laserson, "Masn-miting in toronto ruft tsu-hilf di sovyetn kegn hitlerism," *Kanader yidishe vochenblat*, July 10, 1941, 2–3.

39. A. Kravitz, "Montrealer masn fodern hilf tsum sov. farband," *Kanader yidishe vochenblat*, July 31, 1941, 5.

40. "Labor lig nemt unter aktsyeh far alirteh armeyen," *Kanader yidishe vochenblat*, October 30, 1941, 1; "Farzamlung in viktori teater—a rizikeh demonstratsyeh far faraynikteh milkhomeh-aktsyes," *Kanader yidishe vochenblat*, November 6, 1941, 1, 8. Sol Shek had become secretary in 1937 and continued in the post when it was transformed into the United Jewish People's Order in 1944. Shek was born in Lokacz, Ukraine in 1901 and, after a period during which he lived in Palestine, came to Canada in 1934. For a brief biography, see Roz Usiskin, "Unzer Chaver Sol Shek 1901–1989," *Outlook* 27, No. 4 (1989), 21.

41. M. Feldman, "Der labor lig hot zikh derhoyben tsu di foderungen fun der tsayt," *Kanader yidishe vochenblat,* January 8, 1942, 5.

42. Morris Biderman, *A Life on the Jewish Left: An Immigrant's Experience* (Toronto: Onward Publishing, 2000), 60.

43. L. Basman, "Lomir helfn leshn dem fayer—itst iz di tsayt," *Kanader Yidishe Vochenblat,* November 6, 1941, 4; "Komitayt tsu hilf sovyetn gegrundet in vinipeg," *Kanader yidishe vochenblat,* November 6, 1941, 5; "Yidishe masn ibern land gibn mitn gantsen hertsn far miditsinisher hilf tsu alierteh," *Kanader yidishe vochenblat,* November 13, 1941, 1, 8.

44. After serving twenty years on the board, Zuken would be elected a member of city council for another twenty-two. His brother Bill Ross (born Cecil Zuken), who would lead the Manitoba CP from 1948 to 1981, had already served as a school board trustee for the ward from 1936 until he was forced underground in 1940 and was stripped of his position. The two brothers had come to Canada with their mother in 1914, having been preceded by their father two years earlier. Ross joined the CP in 1929, but Zuken was not formally a member until 1943, when the banned Communist Party reemerged as the Labor-Progressive Party (LPP). Doug Smith, *Joe Zuken, Citizen and Socialist* (Toronto: James Lorimer, 1990), 8, 36, 82, 97, 103–5.

45. "Royter-krayz kampanye farn sovyetn-farband krigt brayten opruf tsvishn ale shikhten," *Kanader yidishe vochenblat,* December 25, 1941, 2, 5; A. Kravitz, "A historisher farzamlung," *Kanader yidishe vochenblat,* January 1,1942, 2; P. Nayer, "S'iz gekumen der tog ven di velt hot zikh ongehoybn dervisn dem emes vegn dem sovyetish-daytshen opmakh," *Kanader yidishe vochenblat,* February 19, 1942, 5.

46. "Der ykuf in kanada in iber di velt," *Kanader yidishe vochenblat,* January 23, 1941, 2; Boris Noznitsky, "Zikhroynes," in *Unzer shule: Sholem aleichem shule. 25 yor yubl-bukh 1921–1946,* eds. Labl Basman et al. (Winnipeg: Sholem Aleichem Institute, 1946), 20–21.

47. Sholem Shtern, "Der yidisher layener un der zhurnal 'yidishe kultur,'" *Kanader yidishe vochenblat,* January 23, 1941, 5–6. Born in Tishevitz, Poland, in 1906, Shtern came to Montreal in 1927. He died in 1990. On Shtern's background, see Rebecca Margolis, *Jewish Roots, Canadian Soil: Yiddish Culture in Montreal, 1905–1945* (Montreal: McGill-Queen's University Press, 2011), 33, 81–84.

48. M. F., "Tsentraler ykuf-komiteyt gegrunden in kanada," *Kanader yidishe vochenblat,* October 30, 1941, 7.

49. "Al-kanadishe ykuf konferents fraytik, shabes un zuntik in montreal," *Kanader yidishe vochenblat,* January 15, 1942, 1; "A grus der kanader ykuf konferents," *Kanader yidishe vochenblat,* January 15, 1942, 4; Sholem Shtern, "A vikhtiker kultur tsuzumenfor," *Kanader yidishe vochenblat,* January 15, 1942, 4–5; "Der ershte alkanadishe ykuf-konferents," *Kanader yidishe vochenblat,* January 29, 1942, 6; "Premier king entfert oyf milkhome-rezolutsye fun kanader-ykuf konferents," *Kanader yidishe vochenblat,* February 26, 1942, 6.

50. Khaim Zhitlovsky, "Der gebot fun der tsayt," *Kanader yidishe vochenblat*, August 28, 1941, 5 (emphasis in original).

51. "Zhitlovsky memorial-miting, zuntik, 23-tn may, in viktori teater, b. z. goldberg, redner," *Kanader yidishe vochenblat*, May 13, 1943, 1.

52. Ben Lappin, "When Michoels and Feffer Came to Toronto," *Viewpoints* 7, No. 2 (1972), 45.

53. See for example, I. K. Baylin, "Itzik fefer—royt-armayer un dikhter," *Vochenblat*, August 19, 1943, 3.

54. H. Abramovitch, "25 toyznt yidn giben entuziastishe oyfname sovyetish-yidisher delegatsye bay rizike mitingen in montreal un toronto," *Vochenblat*, September 9, 1943, 1.

55. "A. Reporter," "Kaboles-ponem diner fun yidishn kongres far sovyetish-yidisher delegatsye," *Vochenblat*, September 9, 1943, 6.

56. Ben Lappin, "When Michoels and Feffer Came to Toronto," 53–55.

57. Paris, *Jews*, 145–46.

58. "Manifesto of Labor-Progressive Party," *Canadian Tribune*, Toronto, August 26, 1943, 16. The name was restored in 1959.

59. Buhay was born in London, England in 1890 and came to Canada in 1909. He and his sister Becky Buhay became charter members of the Canadian Communist Party in 1920. Michael had run as the Communist candidate for the federal parliament in the Cartier riding in 1922 and 1926. He was the first editor of *Der Kamf*, from 1924 to 1926, and had visited the USSR in 1928. Sidney Sarkin, *An emes'ter folks mentsh: Michael buhay* (Montreal: Old Rose Printing Co. [1944]), 3–11.

60. For example, *Fashizm iber kanada*, also published in English as *Fascism Over Canada: An Exposé*; and *Hitler's 5th Column in Quebec*, both published by the Communist-Labor Total War Committee in 1942 and updated in a second edition put out by Progress Publishers in 1943.

61. Michael Buhay, "Fred rose—der mutiker arbayter-kemfer un shtoltser yid," *Vochenblat*, August 5, 1943, 5–6.

62. Max S. Bailey, "The Jewish Seat is Not in Danger!" *Kartier nayes—Cartier News*, August 6, 1943, 1–2; "Elect a Friend of the U.S.S.R. Rose Stands for Soviet-Canadian Unity," *Kartier nayes—Cartier News*, August 6, 1943, 2–3. This pamphlet was published by the Fred Rose Election Committee; in the Joshua Gershman papers, F1412-6-3, Box 60, "Yiddish Pamphlets," AO.

63. "10 Poonktn fun mayn program," pamphlet in the Joshua Gershman papers, F1412-6-3, Box 60, "Yiddish Pamphlets," AO. See also "Fred Rose's program in di kartier bay-valn," *Vochenblat*, July 15, 1943, 5.

64. Abel Vineberg, "More than Half of Cartier Voters Failed to Cast Ballots on Monday," *Montreal Gazette*, August 11, 1943, 11, 17.

65. See, for instance, a notice for a Victory Loan rally held at the Jewish Communists' headquarters on October 27, 1944, under the auspices of the *Yidisher Hilfs Farayn*, with Rose as the featured speaker; in the Joshua Gershman papers, F1412-1, Box 1, File 4, AO.

66. "Attack Anti-Semitism," *Montreal Gazette*, April 13, 1944, 17. The meeting, held under the auspices of the LPP, also heard from J. B. Salsberg, Michael Buhay, and Joshua Gershman. Salsberg, who had been elected to the Ontario legislature the previous August, called anti-Semitism "an evil which not only offends the Jews and Negroes, but whites and many others."

67. "Ask Royal Commission Inquiry Into Antisemitism in Quebec," *Der Yidisher zhurnal—Daily Hebrew Journal*, Toronto, July 5, 1944, 1.

68. "Dem 11-tn yuni vidervaylt fred rose," [13]; pamphlet in the Joshua Gershman papers, F1412-6-3, Box 60, "Yiddish pamphlets," AO; notice from the "People's Committee for the Re-election of Fred Rose," in the program booklet for the *Nineteenth Annual Concert of the Montreal Jewish Choir*, presenting "Memories of the Past," at the Monument National Theatre, Montreal, 21 and 22 April 1945. Canadian Jewish Congress Collection, Series ZB, Box 1, "Fred Rose," file 7, "Varia," National Archives and Reference Centre, Canadian Jewish Congress, Montreal [hereafter NARC].

69. "Tsu ale mitglider fun yidishn hilfs farayn," pamphlet issued by the Jewish Assistance and Social Organization (emphasis in original), in the Joshua Gershman papers, F1412-6-3, Box 60, "Yiddish pamphlets," AO; "Vi Azoy kenen mir shtarken di hant fun godbout in st. louis divizyeh?" LPP advertisement in the *Kanader Adler*, Montreal, August 4, 1944, 8; election results in *Montreal Daily Star*, August 9, 1944, 1.

70. "Montrealer city council hert vegn farfolgungen oyf yidn," *Kanader yidishe vochenblat*, March 11, 1943, 8; "Comments by the Editor," *Canadian Jewish Weekly*, April 1, 1943, English page (8) of the *Vochenblat*. This was the first time the paper introduced a section in English.

71. Gerald Tulchinsky, *Joe Salsberg: A Life of Commitment* (Toronto: University of Toronto Press, 2013), 59–60.

72. Tulchinsky, *Joe Salsberg*, 25.

73. His victory "was very much an ethnic phenomenon," Tulchinsky writes, because most of the city's Jews lived in "the Spadina-College nexus" and Salsberg won some 90 percent of their votes. Tulchinsky, *Joe Salsberg*, 68.

74. Salsberg had narrowly lost in St. Andrew in the 1937 provincial election. Born in Lagev, Poland in 1903, he came to Canada with his family in 1911. By the 1920s he had become a Toronto union organizer, joined the CP in 1926, and was by the 1930s a leading member of the CP and the leader of its trade union section. After leaving the CP in 1957, he went into the insurance business. He died in 1998. Cynthia Gasner, "J. B. Salsberg 'a Unique Personality,' " *Canadian Jewish* News, Toronto, February 19, 1998, 3; Ron Csillag, "Lives Lived: Joseph Baruch Salsberg," *Globe and* Mail, Toronto, March 6, 1998, A22.

75. "Banket tsu fayern dervaylung fun ald. norman freed," *Vochenblat*, January 13, 1944, 1.

76. Tulchinsky, *Branching Out*, 129–32; Levendel, *A Century of the Canadian Jewish Press*, 137; Irving Abella, "Portrait of a Professional Revolutionary: The Recollections of Joshua Gershman," *Labour/Le Travailleur* 2 (1977), 208.

77. "'Ambidzhan' vet shafn an 'einstein-fond' tsu bazetsn 30,000 yidishe yesoymim in biro-bidzhan," *Vochenblat*, June 28, 1945, 4. The *Toronto Daily Star* had already carried an Associated Press story from New York reporting that Ambijan would settle 30,000 orphans in Birobidzhan. "Russia Shelters 30,000," *Toronto Daily Star*, May 30, 1945, Section 2, 1.

78. Letter from Joshua Gershman to B. A. Victor, Toronto, October 4, 1945, in the Joshua Gershman papers, F1412-1, Box 1, File 7, AO.

79. "Alef Raysh" [Alfred Rosenberg?], "Biro-bidzhan konferents bashlist oys-shtaten a fakh-shul far yidishe yesoymim in biro-bidzhan," *Vochenblat*, February 21, 1946, 1–2; "Canadian Birobidjan Committee," *Ambijan Bulletin* 5, 1 (1946): 7–8.

80. Letter from Joshua Gershman to Joseph Zuken, Toronto, March 8, 1946; in the Joshua Gershman papers, F1412-1, Box 2, File 9, AO.

81. S. C., "Classic, Say Critics Hailing New Concert by Jewish Folk Choir," *Canadian Jewish Weekly*, May 9, 1946, English page (8) of the *Vochenblat*; "Groyse delegatsye kumt tsu birobidzhan konferents, zuntik, may 26-tn in montreal," *Vochenblat*, May 16, 1946, 1; H. Abramovitch, "Kanader biro-bidzhan komitayt bashlist ayntsuordinen toyzent yidishe yesoymim," *Vochenblat*, May 30, 1946, 1; "Ruf fun biro-bidzhan komitayt tsu di yidn fun kanada," *Vochenblat*, June 6, 1946, 3.

82. *20 Years Progressive Fraternalism in Canada. Main Reports and Resolutions of the 2nd National Convention of the United Jewish Peoples Order, Held in Montreal, June 20th, 21st and 22nd, 1947* (Toronto: National Executive, U.J.P.O., 1947), 7, 22–23, 52–53.

83. J. Gershman, "Di shtelung fun di komunistn tsu der erets yisroel problem," typewritten undated ms [probably October 1945]; in the Joshua Gershman papers, F1412-7-3-1, Box 67, AO.

84. "Palestine Jewish State Can be Achieved in New World Order F. Rose M.P. Tells Parliament," *Der yidisher zhurnal—Daily Hebrew Journal*, Toronto, March 25, 1945, 1.

85. Letter from Joseph Zuken to Joshua Gershman, Winnipeg, November 5, 1945; in the Joshua Gershman papers, F1412-1, Box 1, File 7, AO.

86. "Palestine Plan Not Fully Understood," *Canadian Jewish Weekly*, January 1, 1948, English page (8) of the *Vochenblat*.

87. Tulchinsky, *Joe Salsberg*, 97–98.

88. J. Gershman, "Mir muzn gebn dem yishuv in erets-yisroel fulshtendike moralishe, finantsyele un politishe hilf," *Vochenblat*, February 12, 1948, 4.

89. "Natsoyonale ekzekutive fun yid. folks ordn ruft shtitsen kampanye far yishuv in erets-yisroel," *Vochenblat*, February 26, 1948, 1.

90. "Di yidishe melikhe muz un ken geratevet vern!" *Vochenblat*, April 8, 1948, 1.

91. A. Rosenberg, "Tsvay historishe dates in der antviklung fun biro-bidzhan," *Vochenblat*, May 13, 1948, 7.

92. Aaron Maxwell, "No Bigotry in the USSR," *Canadian Jewish Weekly*, April 7, 1949, English page (8) of the *Vochenblat*.

93. J. Gershman, "Jews in Eastern Europe Reveal Healthy Progress," *Canadian Jewish Weekly*, February 3, 1949, English page (8) of the *Vochenblat.*

94. A. Nisnevitz, "Yidn hobn bloys dankbarkayt tsu dem sovyetn-regirung," *Vochenblat*, November 10, 1949, 5, 8.

95. "Balance Sheet—And Survey," *Canadian Jewish Weekly*, January 5, 1950, English page (8) of the *Vochenblat.*

96. J. Gershman, "Facts Easily Debunk Vicious Slander of Soviet Anti-Semitism," *Canadian Jewish Weekly*, March 16, 1950, English page (8) of the *Vochenblat.*

97. "Cartier Needs a United Voice," *Montreal Gazette*, March 5, 1947, 8; "Democratic Principles Backed by Cartier Against Dictatorship Groups," *Montreal Daily Star*, April 1, 1947, 4.

98. "R. Alef," "Dervaylung fun max bailey tsu dem montrealer shtot-kounsil iz a vikhtiker zig far demokratsye," *Vochenblat*, January 1, 1948, 3; "Max bailey efent ofis in montreal," *Vochenblat*, January 22, 1948, 2.

99. "4,000 Cartier Electors Vote For Peace Program," *Canadian Jewish Weekly*, June 22, 1950, English page (8) of the *Vochenblat.*

100. "Harry binder vert dervaylt koynsilor," *Vochenblat*, December 14, 1950, 1; A. Rosenberg, "Dervaylung fun harry binder—a zig far yidishe masn," *Vochenblat*, December 21, 1950, 4. Binder quit the CP in 1957.

101. For an overview of its draconian powers and methods, see Dominique Clément, "Spies, Lies and a Commission: A Case Study in the Mobilization of the Canadian Civil Liberties Movement," *Left History* 7, No. 2 (2000): 53–79; and "The Royal Commission on Espionage and the Spy Trials of 1946–9: A Case Study in Parliamentary Supremacy," *Journal of the Canadian Historical Association New Series, Vol. 11* (2000): 151–72.

102. Rose, born in Lublin, Poland in 1907, came to Montreal in 1920. He joined the CP in 1927. After being released from prison in 1951, Rose and his wife Fanny moved first to Czechoslovakia, then to Poland, where he worked as an editor in Warsaw for an English-language publication, *Poland.* He died in 1983 at the age of 76. "MP Jailed as Spy Fred Rose Dies," *Montreal Gazette*, March 17, 1983, A7; "Former Member of House Convicted as Soviet Spy," *Globe and Mail*, Toronto, March 17, 1983, 8.

103. Carr, born Shloime Kogan in 1906 in Kharkov, Ukraine, came to Canada in 1924. In 1927 he joined the CP and studied at the Comintern's Lenin School in Moscow for two years. He was by 1930 the party's national organizer. He helped recruit volunteers for the Loyalists in the Spanish Civil War in the 1930s. Carr became head of the UJPO in 1960. He died in 1989. For more on this committed Communist and, according to some, the "real brains" of the party, see "Sam Carr Remembered," *Outlook* 27, No. 6 (1989: 10–11; Paris, *Jews*, 167–74, 176.

104. Alvin Finkel, "The Decline of Jewish Radicalism in Winnipeg After 1945," in *Jewish Radicalism in Winnipeg, 1905–1960*, Vol. 8, ed. Daniel Stone, 198.

105. See the circular letter from the committee, signed by Alex Gauld and dated November 11, 1946 soliciting funds *and* urging readers to protest "the

persecution exemplified in this refusal." Canadian Jewish Congress Collection, Series ZB, Box 1, "Fred Rose," file 7, "Varia," NARC.

106. "Reds Here Raided, Student Held, as Fred Rose Leaflet Distributed," *Montreal Gazette*, December 9, 1946, 13. For more on this period, see *The Gouzenko Affair: Canada and the Beginnings of Cold War Counter-Espionage*, eds. J. L. Black and Martin Rudner (Ottawa: Penumbra Press, 2006); J. L. Granatstein and David Stafford, *Spy Wars: Espionage and Canada from Gouzenko to Glasnost* (Toronto: Key Porter Books, 1990); Amy Knight, *How the Cold War Began: The Gouzenko Affair and the Hunt for Soviet Spies* (Toronto: McClelland and Stewart, 2005); Ross Lambertson, *Repression and Resistance: Canadian Human Rights Activists, 1930–1960* (Toronto: University of Toronto Press, 2005); David Levy, *Stalin's Man in Canada: Fred Rose and Soviet Espionage* (New York: Enigma Books, 2011); Merrily Weisbord, *The Strangest Dream: Canadian Communists, the Spy Trials, and the Cold War* (Montreal: Véhicule Press,1994); and Reg Whitaker and Gary Marcuse, *Cold War Canada: The Making of a National Insecurity State, 1945–1957* (Toronto: University of Toronto Press,1994). See also John Earl Haynes and Harvey Klehr, *Early Cold War Spies: The Espionage Trials that Shaped American Politics* (New York: Cambridge University Press, 2006), 48–59. These books contain much information on the arrest and trials of Carr, Rose, and others.

107. Sam Lipshitz, "Followed by the RCMP," in *The Un-Canadians: True Stories of the Blacklist Era*, ed. Len Scher (Toronto: Lester Publishing, 1992), 123–24.

108. Letter from Morris Biderman to Joshua Gershman, Winnipeg, November 7, 1949; in the Joshua Gershman papers, F1412-1, Box 2, File 19, AO.

109. "Masn-oyfbroyz kegn fashistishn akt fun premier duplessis nemt arum dos land," *Vochenblat*, February 2, 1950, 1–2; "Demand Reopening of Cultural Centre," *Canadian Jewish Weekly*, February 2, 1950, English page (8) of the *Vochenblat*. The anti-Communist legislation, officially entitled "An Act to Protect the Province Against Communistic Propaganda," which gave the provincial *government* the authority to raid and shut down any institution, and imprison any person, accused of disseminating Bolshevik propaganda, had been passed in 1937.

110. S. Lipshitz, "Ontario Election—Some Lessons," *Canadian Jewish Weekly*, December 6, 1951, 2. Salsberg lost his seat in 1955, in no small part due to the ill-advised eulogy he delivered in the Ontario legislature two years earlier when Stalin had died. Sam Lipshitz, who ran his campaigns, later would claim that Salsberg was pressured by the CP to make the speech. Interview, Sam Lipshitz, Toronto, June 9, 1998.

111. For details, see Ester Reiter and Roz Usiskin, "Jewish Dissent in Canada: The United Jewish People's Order," *Outlook* 42, No. 5 (2004): 20–22, 41.

112. "The UJPO Redefines its Aims and Purposes," *Canadian Jewish Weekly*, December 20, 1956, English pages (1–2) of the *Vochenblat*.

113. "Report to the Annual Conference December 5–6, 1959, by the Executive Director, M. Biderman," 1–2, 15 (tss.); in the Joshua Gershman papers, F1412-7-4, Box 72, file 11, AO.

114. "Report to the 5th National Convention of the U.J.P.O.—April 1960," 3 (tss.); in the Joshua Gershman papers, F1412-7-4, Box 72, file 11, AO.

115. Tulchinsky, *Joe Salsberg*, 113–14, 121.

116. Interview, Sam Lipshitz, Toronto, June 9, 1998. For more on Lipshitz, who was born in Radom, Poland, in 1910, came to Canada at age 17, and sat on the LPP's central committee from 1943 until 1956, see Levendel, *A Century of the Canadian Jewish Press*, 130–43, and Paris, *Jews*, 154-7, 193–98. After leaving the Communist movement, he opened a typesetting business. He died in Toronto at age 90 in 2000. Ben Rose, "Sam Lipshitz: Champion of the Yiddish Language," *Canadian Jewish News*, Toronto, September 28, 2000, 35.

117. Interview, Morris Biderman, Toronto, June 9, 1998.

118. Letter from Morris Biderman to the author, Toronto, January 27, 1999.

119. Biderman, *A Life on the Jewish Left*, 230.

120. J. Gershman, "We Cannot Agree With You, Madame Furtseva!" *Canadian Jewish Weekly*, June 28, 1956, English page (3) of the *Vochenblat*.

121. Interview with Joshua Gershman, Toronto, September 5, 1978; Biderman, *A Life on the Jewish Left*, 163; Abella, "Portrait of a Professional Revolutionary," 212–13. "A Letter From Joshua Gershman to the C. C. of the Communist Party of Canada," in which he announced he was withdrawing from the party, was published in the *Canadian Jewish Outlook* 15, No. 10 (1977): 10. See also the tribute to him by Sholem Shtern, "Y. Gershman—tsu zayne 75 yor," *Vochenblat*, September 13, 1978, 5.

122. "UJPO Activist Dead at 84," *Canadian Jewish News*, Toronto, May 19, 1988, 29.

6

The Canadian Jewish Left

Culture, Community, and the Soviet Union

Ester Reiter

The leftist Jewish community in Canada consisted of East European secular Jews arriving in the country in the first decades of the twentieth century, whose identity as Jews and socialists was linked to an internationalism that identified racism and the exploitation of all working peoples as central. In this chapter I will focus on several key aspects of this community, such as women's activism, particularly in the 1920s, and its emphasis on culture. I will also discuss two moments in Canadian history that give examples of the left's difficulties with the government and the organized Jewish community. The first is the Padlock law in Quebec and the reaction of the Canadian Jewish Congress when the newly built Winchevsky cultural center in Montreal was closed; and the second is the events that led to the 1951 expulsion of the United Jewish People's Order (UJPO) from the Canadian Jewish Congress.

Jews of the pro-Soviet left in Canada were mainly Eastern European immigrants, who with virtually no resources managed to create vibrant cultural, educational, self-help, and political activities that enriched their lives and made important contributions to the union movement, the peace movement, and cultural life in Canada. This was done in the face of a virulent anti-Semitism, a hostile state, and a history of anti-communism that goes back to the Winnipeg General Strike of 1919. The leadership of the Canadian Jewish Congress attempted to marginalize this left-wing, pro-Soviet community for ideological reasons as well as for their desire to be seen as "good Canadians." Critics referred to this as the "*sha shtil*" (hush-hush) policy of the Canadian Jewish Congress.

So while Jewish leftists sympathetic to the Communist Party played important roles as union activists, holders of political office, and contributors to the cultural life of the Jewish community, with some important exceptions, many of the historians of Jews in Canada writing in English either omitted mention of this community or marginalized its significance. Indeed, Stephen Speisman described the Labour League as "an embarrassment to the community."[1] "Who's Who" books listing prominent citizens from the Jewish community omitted leftists such as J. B. (Joe) Salsberg, the Communist member of the Ontario legislature from a Toronto seat, and Joe Zuken, the Winnipeg Communist alderman, both of whom held office for many years.[2]

In the past, anti-communism typically dominated scholarship about the communist-led left. Approaching all those holding pro-Soviet sentiments as "dupes" and mindless followers of "Moscow" obscures a much more variegated history. Fortunately, this is changing, at least in Canadian historical scholarship. Ian McKay, in a paper presented to a Canadian Jewish studies seminar in honor of Gerald Tulchinsky, maintained that even in the 1930s, when narrow dogmatism was at its height in the Communist Party of the "class against class" period, Communist Party members were hardly "soldiers of the international." The reality, he argues, was far more dynamic, complicated, and interesting.[3] Gerald Tulchinsky's biography of Joe Salsberg, a labor activist and member of the Ontario Legislature from 1943 to 1955 who remained in the leadership of the Communist Party throughout his career from 1926 to when he left in the late 1950s, presents a view of Salsberg as responsive to the needs of the Jewish community with an egalitarian vision that encompassed all people.[4]

Current research by young scholars such as Dennis Molinaro, examining Communist International material, found that key communist-led efforts, such as the activities of the Canadian Labour Defense League in mobilizing support against Section 98 of the criminal code that was used to deport or imprison radicals, and organizing the unemployed, were done despite, not because of, Moscow's directives. The gap between Comintern policy and the on-the-ground activities of the ethnic organizations is most evident in the responses to Communist Party attempts to Bolshevize and anglicize the Canadian Party. Jim Mochoruk documents the resistance of the Ukrainian left to this reorganization. When the party attempted to minimize the activities of the ethnic organizations, they lost almost half of their membership. The ethnic organizations not only survived, but flourished, quite in opposition to Moscow's plans.[5] Contributions of the Jewish left to union organizing have also in recent years received more attention from labor and feminist historians such as Joan Sangster, Ruth Frager, and Mercedes Steedman.[6]

It was a terrible disillusionment when pro-Soviet Jews learned that the Soviet Union did not embody the kind of society that they worked to create in Canada. However, I maintain that it is necessary to distinguish between the Soviet regime and what communists and the pro-communist Jewish left accomplished on Canadian soil. Left-wing Jews worked to build a "*shenere un besere velt*" ("a more beautiful, better world") in Canada in accordance with deeply felt ideals. Gramsci's concept of hegemony is useful for understanding how social movements such as the Jewish left are organized. Winning hearts and minds occurs not just through ideas but through participation, as people are mobilized in cultural institutions. Cultural practices are then articulated into a way of life, a conception of the universe, and an alternative hegemony develops, one quite at variance with that of the dominant classes.[7]

The notion of culture and of "conscientization," a term later used by Paulo Freire, goes back to early Marxist notions that we are not just "in" the world but "with" the world. Freire, the Brazilian educator known for his work in critical pedagogy, maintained that our humanity is defined by our ability to understand that we can act in the world. In the process of transforming the world, it is possible to humanize the world, and ourselves.[8] Stuart Hall describes the production of identity as a fluid process, the retelling of the past. Individuals position themselves in the narratives of the past through memory, fantasy, and myth.[9] The Jewish left's notion of ethnicity encompassed a universal vision of social justice, one of human mutuality. Issues such as the striking Irish silk workers in Paterson, New Jersey; the execution of Sacco and Vanzetti; the coal miners in Sydney, Nova Scotia; the violence of lynching; and the effects of colonization in Africa, were all deeply felt in the Canadian Jewish left. For them, class was the unifying factor for solidarity. This was a community of Jewish internationalists.

So these left Jews reshaped Jewish identity, defining it through culture rather than religion. The Jewish left was the equivalent of a university for working-class women and men. It was also a way of life, reinforced by being neighbors and friends as well as comrades. Singing in the choir or attending meetings also involved participating in picket lines, as well as dances, concerts, dinners, lectures, romances, and so on. The Jewish left provided a place where the values of respect for learning, for culture, and opportunities for personal growth merged with the political struggles of union support, and endless "bazaars"—fundraising events to support left-wing causes such as the camp, the *shule*, the Yiddish newspaper *Der Kamf*, and labor struggles that went beyond the Jewish community.

The life stories of many of the founders and activists bridge the old countries of Eastern Europe in the early twentieth century with their lives and involvements in Canada. Many Jews who arrived in Canada after the turn of the last century arrived with the conviction that society needed to change. They fled poverty and pogroms in Eastern Europe, having rejected the limitations of an increasingly narrow, insular, and corrupt theocratic world ruled by rabbis and the few rich Jews who instructed people to passively wait for God to fix things. It was a generational revolt, of young people thirsty for knowledge.

The anti-Semitism new immigrants found in Canada had a class component, which only served to strengthen the radical beliefs they had forged in Eastern Europe. Following the Bolshevik Revolution, the *Arbeter Ring* (Workmen's Circle)—a fraternal organization of left-leaning Jewish immigrants who were opposed to the exploitative capitalist system—split into two. After bitter internal battles *di linke* (the left), supporting the Bolsheviks, formed their own organizations. In the 1920s and 1930s, the Montreal left organization was called the *Kanader Arbeter Ring* (the Canadian Workmen's Circle), while in Toronto they called themselves the Labour League, and in Winnipeg the Frayhayt Temple or Liberty Temple Association. They were fraternal organizations and, like the *Arbeter Ring* they had once been part of, offered mutual aid in the form of life insurance, health, credit benefits and funeral facilities. The men's branches were organized by either *landsmanshaftn* based on the town of origin (Ostrovster, Chmelniker, Radomer, etc.) or by trade, including branches of tailors, cloak makers, furriers, and the like. These left organizations supported the establishment of Jewish Workers' Cultural Centres as well as groups such as the ICOR (*Gezelshaft far Yidishe Kolonizatye in Ratn-farband*), supporting colonization in Russia, and the YKUF, the *Alveltlekher Yidisher Kultur Farband* (World Jewish Cultural Union). The organization also supported choirs, sports leagues, mandolin orchestras, Jewish schools, and summer camps. In 1945, the Canadian groups in Montreal, Toronto, Winnipeg, Calgary, Windsor, Hamilton, and Vancouver came together to form the United Jewish People's Order (UJPO). There were many cross-border connections with their sister organization, the Jewish People's Fraternal Order, the Jewish section of the International Workers Order in the United States, organized in 1930.

While many participants in the activities of the left organizations were also members, not everyone was. Some came to dance or sing, or play sports, or enjoy the beautiful camps. Even fewer were Communist Party members. Although the pro-Bolshevik Jewish left is often referred to as the Jewish Communist left, Morris Biderman, the president of the Labour League and then the UJPO from 1942 to 1960, when he left both the Communist Party and the organization, estimated that perhaps 5 percent of the UJPO were actually Communist Party members. They referred to themselves as "progressive."

The Women Activists of the *Yidishe Arbayter Froyen Farayn*

The Bolshevik Revolution had caused great excitement on "the Jewish street." The new Soviet regime was the first to officially recognize Yiddish as a national language. In the 1920s a public educational system entirely based on the Yiddish language was established and comprised kindergartens, schools, and higher educational institutions. Two of the most well-respected teachers in the Canadian *shules*, Manya Lipshitz and Labl Basman, received their education in Yiddish pedagogical institutes in the 1920s in Eastern Europe. The Soviet Union in the early years had put in place laws that held particular promise for Jewish women. Equality before the law, civil marriage, legalization of abortions and the abolition of the category of "illegitimate children," and divorce, were some of the changes in the aftermath of the revolution.[10] Canadian women were particularly inspired by the writings of Alexandra Kollontai, appointed as head of the *Zhenotdel* (Women's Department) in the new regime. She advocated nothing less than a complete transformation of daily life in describing the material conditions necessary for women's equality.

While the pro-Bolshevik faction was fighting a losing battle for control of the *Arbeter Ring* in 1923, the women in Toronto withdrew to form their own organization, the *Yidishe Arbayter Froyen Farayn* (Jewish Women's Labour League). At first, they were part of a Jewish help committee, which worked to provide relief to those orphans left destitute by the chaos of the civil war following the Russian Revolution. However, they soon wanted to be more than an auxiliary of the men, and to have a broader scope for their activities. In the early years, the leading activists were called "*farbrente communistn*"—burning or fervent "reds."

Der Kamf and *Di Arbeter Froy*

The new Soviet regime's emphasis on women's issues was reflected in the Canadian Yiddish newspaper *Der Kamf* (*the Struggle*), which began publication in 1924. During the 1920s, "*Di Arbeter Froy*" (*the Working Woman*) was a regular feature in the newspaper. While addressing the challenges facing women in Canada, the articles expressed admiration for what they believed was a reality in the Soviet Union. These women considered feminism a bourgeois indulgence whereas what was needed was a proletarian revolution.

Influenced by Alexandra Kollontai, writers in *Der Kamf* looked to reorganizing family life as a way of improving women's conditions. They thought that technology along with collective effort would solve the problem of the housewife. Rachel Haltman advocated the industrialization of housework so that the home would be a place of rest, relaxation, and comfort for women as well as men. She argued that "when weaving, spinning, sewing, baking and brewing were removed from the home, it did not destroy the soul of the home." What remained was cooking, cleaning, washing, and ironing.[11]

Reproductive rights were another topic of discussion in 1926. In a *Kamf* article, F. Frumet declared: "It is an illusion that we live in a civilized society, removed from the dark days. Women have political equality, are in all the professions, even women ship captains—who could ask for more?" In Toronto a doctor was jailed for six years, his assistant for four, for performing an abortion where the woman died. "Whose business is it that a woman doesn't want children? Who cares that a woman wants a certain number of children and not be a child bearing machine her entire life? The hypocrisy of a system which prohibits the dispensation of birth control information and allows thousands of women to die each year is contemptible." In the author's view, the rich, who don't need this information as much as the poor, get what they need because they can pay.[12]

Rachel Watson put forward critiques of the family that foreshadow some radical feminist thinking of the 1960s. She argued that women's economic dependence on men leads to quarrels, exacerbated with the constant stress of making ends meet. "The man by nature is a bigger egoist and will, at every opportunity mak[ing] the woman feel that he puts her on her feet, she is lucky that he supports her and the children (of course)!"

Watson and the Jewish women's labor leagues were involved in mobilizing housewives' boycotts against rising food prices in the 1920s and 1930s, activities that the author argues are examples of housewives making linkages between production and consumption. However, Watson herself did not see the connection in this way. She expressed a very literal interpretation of Marx where only waged labor counts as productive. Reproductive work and household maintenance in Watson's view were not productive or visible "so the housewife is simply put, a parasite."[13]

Terrible working conditions were a constant concern, not just in the disproportionately Jewish "shmate" industry (garment industry), but in all wage labor. Becky Buhay, writing in 1925, declared that women made up 22 percent of the workforce in Canada, not including home workers or agricultural workers, who are not counted. In 1919, a prosperous year, she stated that women's wages were not more than 55 percent of men's, at about nine dollars a week. In Woolworth's and other department stores, women were often earning between five and six dollars a week.

One letter to *Der Kamf* by a woman described her slave-like situation.

> We work 52 hours a week, from 8:30 in the morning to 6 at night we must stand on our feet. . . . Whether it is busy or slow, the saleslady is always at fault. When business is slow, the manager says 'you have to be able to sell when everyone doesn't want to buy' . . . And you are never secure with this wretched job . . . In the firm where I work, it happened that salesladies who have worked 10–15 years, were fired without any prior notice. It is time to organize these slaves for a struggle for humanitarian working conditions.[14]

Buhay, along with her friend Annie Buller, were the only two women, both Jews, who were in the Central Committee of the Communist Party. They worked as labor organizers; Buller was married to Harry Guralnik, an educator and activist in the Jewish left. The militant Jewish women lived their politics. The *Yidishe Arbayter Froyen Farayn* aimed to draw on Jewish working women, elevate them to a higher cultural level, and develop their class consciousness. They picketed in support of strikers, went to jail defiant and singing, were bailed out, and returned to the picket lines again and again.

Bessie Schacter, one of the leading members in the Montreal *Yidishe Arbayter Froyen Farayn*, emphasized the involvement of non-Jewish women in union struggles. She described the *Farayn*'s participation in a dressmakers' strike along with Italian and French-Canadian women. Lil Himmelfarb Ilomaki, a member of the Communist Party as well as the *Yidishe Arbayter Froyen Farayn,* was arrested no fewer than ten times from the time she was sixteen to twenty-six. She was also part of the Canadian Labour Defense League, the organization that acted to stop evictions by putting the furniture back in people's homes. Lil explained that she was known as "Red Lil," and because she could speak loudly, often became the spokesperson. She also loved to sing and write poetry.[15]

In 1925, the Toronto women had the idea of forming a camp and were soon followed by women in Montreal. These workers' children's camps were the projects of which the women were most proud. Becky Lapedes, one of the founders, credits the role of her friend, Rachel Watson. Becky Lapedes told her daughter, Sheyndl: "The people were so poor. They had to go to work and they didn't have where to leave their children . . . it was very idealistic but it certainly wasn't practical. We were only a group of over 30 women, married—with families to look after, it wasn't easy." They rented a furnished cottage from Sam Green, a member of the community and who donated supplies. "Each of us brought from our own homes pots, an ice box, silverware, and all the other things that were needed . . . The members of the *Farayn* volunteered for two week shifts of work in the camp. No one was paid for working; on the contrary we all paid for our own food. The parents paid from $3.50 to $4.00 according to the age of the child."[16]

The camp, called *Kindervelt* (kid's world), was started in 1925 in Long Branch, near Lake Ontario in Toronto. The following year *Kindervelt* moved to Rouge Hills where it remained for ten years. The Montrealers opened their children's camp in 1927 in the Laurentians across the road from the camp for adults called *Nitgedayget* (not to worry). In 1936, the Toronto camp moved to Eldorado Park in Brampton, purchased with the help of a Ukrainian comrade on land previously owned by the Canadian National Railways. There was a "gentiles only" sign posted at the entrance. In a period when Jews were restricted from visiting the Toronto Islands and were not welcome at the swimming pools, or many resorts, the camp, now called *Naivlelt* (new world), was visited by thousands each weekend. It was a lively place with concerts, plays, dances, reading circles, and, of course, romances. Children ingested the progressive politics through song.

Morris Biderman described in his memoirs how *Naivelt* was visited by thousands of people; both children and adults enjoying a chance to spend some time in the beautiful surroundings. "In the early years people would gather at 7 Brunswick Avenue on Sunday morning to take a truck ride to the camp for 35 cents. (There were not too many car owners among the members and friends in the Labour League in those years.)"[17] His son, Ron Biderman, who spent summers at the camp from the age of six until his teenage years, nurtured fond memories: "Younger people especially remember the summers they spent there. The intensity, which grew out of the concentration of so many young, dedicated, energetic and enthusiastic people in their teens, twenties and thirties was remarkable. The camp was a magnet drawing people into the ambit of the organization who would otherwise never have approached it."[18]

Rita Bergman recalled the beauty of the place from her first year in 1936; an opportunity to be in the country was a joyous privilege. "I loved the tent, especially when it rained. The nicest thing was to have your head hanging out of the tent watching the stars fall. Oh that was gorgeous."[19] Rachel Orlan, who met her husband while singing in the Choir, described the Friday night campfires, with readings and parodies in Yiddish, and the Saturday night dances and concerts. "We would gather under the 'Dach' sometimes with members of the Travellers and sing choir songs and songs of the day, and share stories till the wee small hours."[20] Jim Laxer recalled how he tried to explain to mystified friends that this camp with no horseback riding, no canoes, no lake, little hiking, and quite basic facilities, was the best camp ever.[21] Sherri Bergman, who spent almost every summer at *Naivelt* from 1948 to 1955, located the coming-of-age activities of her generation within the camp and its activities—one's first love, games, sports, campfires, and hikes. She also recalled learning through songs and how the activities at the camp developed an appreciation for socialist values and for Yiddish. Two of her three camp directors were Yiddish teachers in the winter.[22] The slogan describing the connection between the Yiddish-language school the children attended in the city in the winter, and their summers in *Naivelt*, was "*fun kemp tsu shul, fun shul tsu kemp*."[23]

Culture on the Left

For East European secular Jews on the left, culture was all-important. Reading, learning, and creating was as vital as breathing, and went hand-in-hand with the attempt to change the world through union activism. One way it was used was to emphasize traditional, or folk, culture. But culture also included the classics of European civilization and respect for the achievements of "high art"—music, literature, painting, sculpture, theatre, dance, and film—which these leftists viewed as transcending class. They rejected *shund* (trash), the cheap entertainments pandering to commercial interests.

In the 1920s, Alhambra Hall at 450 Spadina Avenue in Toronto became the gathering place for Jewish left-wingers. It was not much to look at. Philip Halperin, the first Toronto editor of *Der Kamf* described it as

> a large, stuffy hall without windows with dirty walls and doors and old decrepit floors. New people would turn up their noses. But, to the left, it was a special place. We loved every nook and cranny—every room and every corner was saturated with our struggle, with our hopes. How many dreams were dreamt within these walls. . . . It was here that the Kamf was born; the first dinners in honour of the Kamf were held. It was here that the Jewish workers' movement, the Labour League was founded; the athlete association forged, the cradle of the Frayhayt Gezangs Fareyn with the resounding sound of proletarian song.

Halperin recalled "the passionate discussions, the call to struggle for a new world in song, the proud steps of the worker sports groups, the fiery affirmations of the pioneers" that took place in Alhambra Hall. Singing was especially important, because it was in song that the distinction between "true" workers' culture and *shund* (trash) became clear.[24]

Alhambra Hall housed the newspaper, the Jewish Workers' Library, the *Yidishe Arbayter Froyen Farayn*, the Young Pioneers, the Mandolin Orchestra, the Jewish Drama League, the Progressive Arts Club, the *Frayhayt Gezangs Farayn* (the Freedom Singing Circle), and the Workers' Sport Association (Toronto Jewish Section Youth Division). Sam Kagan, the sculptor, recalled his education in the Jewish Workers' Library located in Alhambra Hall, where, after arriving in Canada from the Ukraine as a young man, he taught himself English:

> My learning was from Oliver Twist on one side, a dictionary on the other side, and each and every word had to be referred to the dictionary. . . . [W]e read political science books, philosophy, the reformers of the French Revolution, like Voltaire and Rousseau. We didn't go for the small stuff, or anything like that. Plus Yiddish literature and Mendele, that I had studied and read in the first government-sponsored Yiddish shules [in the USSR].[25]

Alhambra Hall Library holdings in Yiddish included not just the Yiddish poets and writers, and Marxist political economy, but translations of favorite classical works, including Tolstoy, Nietzsche, Zola, Dostoevsky, Rousseau, Shakespeare, Anatol France, Oscar Wilde, Goethe, and Victor Hugo. *Der Kamf* described the library's importance to the community:

> Here comes the Jewish worker to rest after a day of hard work, to read a newspaper, a journal or a book and through this enriching his intellectual store. . . . At present our libraries already have a tradition, a past. From saved pennies, they collected book by book, until the mighty libraries developed. In Alhambra Hall, which was until not long ago the centre of the leftist Jewish Workers, a large, comfortable room was set aside to the library, which also included a reading room. In the evenings the room used to be crowded with Jewish workers reading. Books were given out and borrowed. So was the library, the nicest, brightest corner in Alhambra Hall.[26]

Jewish leftists negotiated a terrain between self-identity—the preservation of language and culture that meant a great deal to them—and an equally profound internationalist revolutionary commitment. Particularly in the early 1930s, when Communist Party ideology criticized the attachment to ethnic loyalties as "nationalism," this was a difficult process. Yiddish leftists in the 1920s saw the Soviet Union leading the way in the development of a Yiddish proletarian culture in an egalitarian society. Yiddish was the vehicle through which revolutionary sensibilities were learned and reinforced. Whether it was Yiddish singing, drama, art, or sport, the idea was to impart revolutionary Bolshevik sentiments to participants. The creation of a Yiddish proletarian cultural movement also meant distinguishing it from other Jewish secular movements such as the Workmen's Circle or the left Zionist groups who they saw as lacking a militant activist approach to social change.

During the period in Toronto between 1929 and 1932, known by the left as "the terror," Toronto Police Chief Dennis Draper, convinced that foreigners' meetings were hotbeds of revolution, appointed a "Red Squad" and issued an edict forbidding all public meetings not held in English. He ordered jailed and/or deported as many troublemakers as he could.[27] Alhambra Hall, the meeting place of the Jewish left, was closed. The Frayhayt club had no place to meet and the choir literally sang on the street. The recently organized Labour League, the group that broke away from the Workmen's Circle in 1926, came to the rescue and provided a meeting place at their center.[28] The silencing of left voices became a Free Speech issue, supported by people such as sixty-eight professors from the University of Toronto, church officials from the United Church, and the Fellowship of Reconciliation, who maintained that the police commission did not have the right to interfere with civil liberties through licensing of public halls.[29] The Toronto Jewish Workers' Cultural Centre was officially founded on April 6, 1931, with 150 people attending their first meeting and 120 joining immediately. Despite the difficult living conditions, the anxiety, and the excessive police terrorization and persecution, an atmosphere of celebration and perseverance characterized the Centre in those early years.[30]

After Hitler came to power in Germany and the Communist Party initiated its new Popular Front policy to combat fascism in 1935, Jewish radicals had an easier time combining their Jewish identity with their revolutionary commitment. Yiddish and a Jewish identity were valued as a matter of survival and an important tool in the fight against fascism. The International Yiddish Culture Congress was a Popular Front effort, supported by a mix of socialists, communists, left Zionists and Yiddish secularists. Organized in Paris in 1937 by the writer, Khaim Sloves, it was a determined attempt to put aside the fierce internecine battles among the various ideological factions, which had dominated in the past, and come together to protect secular Jewish culture. Khaim Zhitlovsky, one of the organizers of the first Yiddish conference held in Czernowitz in 1908 and very prominent in the world of Yiddish culture, strongly supported the conference as necessary to transcend partisan and political differences in the face of the serious threats to Yiddish culture. The list of participants and supporters was a distinguished collection of writers and poets including Joseph Opatoshu, Peretz Hirshbein, H. Leyvik, and the communist writers Moyshe Olgin, Moyshe Katz, and Kalman Marmor. At the last minute the Soviet authorities did not allow the major Soviet Jewish writers Itzik Fefer, David Bergelson, and Izzy Kharik to attend.[31] The conference, attended by four thousand people with representatives from twenty-three countries, lasted four days. They formed commissions to promote the growth of Yiddish literature, theatre, schools, scholarship, and art, and created a new cultural organization called the YKUF. Nakhman Mayzel was named editor of YKUF's new monthly publication called *Yidishe Kultur* (*Jewish Culture*), offering non-partisan cultural contributions.

However, not all were ready to support this effort if communists were involved. The popular New York Yiddish paper, the *Forverts* (*Forward*) denounced the conference, as did the *Arbeter Ring*. Neither the Canadian Jewish Congress nor its counterpart, the American Jewish Congress, endorsed the event. Nevertheless, the conference, attended by many of the prominent Yiddishists of the time, sparked a renewed interest in Yiddish.[32] Under the aegis of the *Alveltlekher Yidisher Kultur Farband* (YKUF), reading circles formed throughout Canada. Many YKUF members were also strong supporters of the *shules* for the children.

Reading Circles

The secular community as a whole, and the left community in particular, valued learning. Gerry Kane, born in 1935, recalled that his mother, a member of Branch Six of the United Jewish People's Order, was part of such a YKUF reading circle most of her life:

> I used to sit at the top of the stairs, listening to my mother and a group of women read and discuss a book. What did they read? [Yiddish] novels—romance novels, lousy culture? No! . . . [Y]ears later, I was a director of the Committee for Yiddish at [the Canadian Jewish] Congress, and that was at a time when people like my mother were dying, and their kids would bring their mother's Yiddish books to the committee, and say that they didn't read or understand Yiddish, but could we take the books. And I remember getting a box of books from a prominent Toronto physician—they belonged to his mother, and he had no idea what they were. He had no idea who she was! Let me tell you what was in the box—Don Quixote in Yiddish, Lenin in Yiddish, poetry in Yiddish. Here was a woman working in shops all day long, putting money away for learning, and they learned together. They read so widely! It was amazing, to take a look at that box. I remember hearing my mother and the women discussing Sinclair Lewis in Yiddish. . . . Sometimes there was a leader; usually they each read. Sometimes someone prepared something. It depended. In my mother's *leyenkrayz* [reading circle], some were more argumentative, some were more

> passive—just ingesting what they heard. But these were women who never went to school.[33]

Cultural life was important for both adults and their children. In a Yiddish article in *Der Pen*, "A Shmues mit der Farangenhayt (a conversation with the past)," the author, Moishe Miller, who grew up in Winnipeg's North End, describes a visit with his mother in a Florida nursing home in the 1990s. She drifts in and out of knowing who he is and where she is, but her recollections of the Frayhayt Temple (Liberty Temple) in Winnipeg are very clear. Mrs. Miller had also been active in the *Muter Farayn*, the mother's group that supported the Sholem Aleichem *shule* in Winnipeg. Her son asks her in Yiddish, "I would like to know, why you sent us, all three children, to such a political left wing shule. You could have found a middle way—the Peretz school, or the religious Talmud Torah." She replies,

> "The simple answer is that we were free-thinkers and believed in a Yiddish education—with the language, history, culture and so forth. One can very well advance beyond the influence of Zionism or religion. Do you have complaints about this choice?"
>
> "No, but I believe that the school was extreme. At seven years of age, we knew about Lenin, Trotsky, Capitalism."
>
> "You don't have to be so dramatic . . . you also studied good literature, and there was gymnastics as well . . . not so terrible."

She remembered the large hall at the top of the stairs in Winnipeg's Liberty Temple. "I myself recited poetry many times for an audience." [In English] Your mother was a star. Do you know that your father was well known as a poet?[34]

Most of the people in this movement were workers, or perhaps small shopkeepers. It was not a good living. The hours of work were long, the living conditions of their homes cramped, but no matter—the focus of their lives were community halls of the left. Here was an opportunity to actively participate in cultural activities, and to be defined not as a "hand" or a disposable worker, but as an artist. For both children and parents, it meant a great deal. A disproportionate number of people from this community did indeed become prominent for their contribution to Canadian cultural life.[35]

The Choir was perhaps the most prominent of the cultural entities associated with the Labour League and the UJPO. It began as the Young

Socialist Choir, led by Hyman Riegelhaupt before World War I, but disbanded during the turbulent years of 1914–1918. When the progressive movement reorganized in 1925, the *Frayhayt Gezangs Farayn* (the Freedom Singing Circle) was born, with a group of twenty-five people. From 1925 to 1933, the choir, at first small in numbers, featured folksongs—songs that told of the lives of workers. The choir grew, both in numbers and popularity, and was renamed the Toronto Jewish Folk Choir in 1934.[36]

In the 1940s, under the leadership of Emil Gartner, a refugee from Austria, the Choir was performing in Massey Hall, with Metropolitan opera stars such as Jan Peerce, Regina Reznik, and Jenni Tourel. Paul Robeson was a frequent guest and a personal friend of the conductor. The eminent singer and actor from the United States was much beloved by the Choir, and he gave a number of concerts in Toronto and Montreal in the late 1940s, until his passport was revoked in 1950 and he was blacklisted. For choir members, singing when the guest was Paul Robeson was particularly memorable.

> The man was larger than life. He came in the early 1950s, just before they took his visa away at the height of the Cold War. He gave a concert, I think it was in the Queen Elizabeth Building of Exhibition Place and the entire place was surrounded by Royal Canadian Mounted Police, with their coats and hats, inside and out. Inside, the place was packed. He came out and walked onto the stage. There was a ten-minute ovation. It was unbelievable. He said hello, and the applause once again went and on. He had been told he couldn't speak, he could only sing. When Robeson did "Kol Nidre," that was the most moving thing.[37]

Merrily Weisbord described Robeson's prominence in the Jewish left of the 1940s and 1950s as follows: "Everyone knew the Spanish Civil War songs and everyone knew Paul Robeson. More than any other people's artist at that time, Robeson was spokesman, legend, bard."[38]

The Canadian State and the Canadian Jewish Congress

The Jewish left's struggles with the Canadian state and the Canadian Jewish Congress were a constant through most of the twentieth century, except for a brief reprieve during the World War II years, when the Western Allies and the Soviet Union were allies in opposing Hitler. The Labour Zionists came to dominate the Canadian Jewish Congress early on and they opposed the leftists for several reasons. The ideological differences were irreconcilable. Labour Zionists felt that the establishment of a Jewish homeland was the only solution to the problem of anti-Semitism. In their insecurity as new Canadians, they were anxious to prove that Jews were good Canadians. Militant activity challenging the government was therefore unacceptable. Thus, with Congress's desire to prove themselves loyal Canadians, any challenge to existing Canadian government policy was either silenced completely, or only taken with the utmost discretion through polite representation by the few elected Jewish politicians.

In both the United States and Canada, the organized Jewish community's fear of the association of Jews with communism led to supporting the state in the suppression of civil liberties in North America. The Canadian state's persecution of foreign radicals has a long history in Canada. Under the War Measures Act of 1914, many radicals were harassed and intimidated. In Winnipeg, "suspect" establishments such as the *Yidisher Vort* (*Israelite Press*) and the Frayhayt Temple were investigated, and books, newspaper and journals of a "dubious" nature confiscated from private homes in the Winnipeg's North End. The Russian, Ukrainian and Finnish radical organizations were outlawed altogether.[39] The Winnipeg General Strike of 1919, one of the most influential in Canadian history, was fought over the issue of union recognition and the right to bargain collectively. Shloime Almazov, a revolutionary Marxist and an active participant in the Winnipeg General Strike, argued that capitalism was the enemy of all workers; only socialism could secure cultural fulfillment and social equality for both Jews and non-Jews. A Jewish homeland was no assurance against capitalism and it was idealistic to assume that the creation of a Palestinian homeland automatically meant a socialist state. Furthermore, it would deflect from the class struggle.

Although few Jews were involved in the leadership, the Winnipeg *Free Press* ran cartoons depicting hooked-nosed Jewish radicals throwing bombs. When the strike leaders were arrested, those of British origin were allowed out on bail. The *Israelite Press* noted that the Jews and Ukrainians remained in prison without bail. In an effort "to arrest a movement, to deport a philosophy," three of the five "enemy aliens" arrested were Jews and charged under Section 41 of the immigration act, which gave the government broad powers to deport anyone they didn't like, activists who challenged government policy or big business interests.[40] Although they were radicals, they were not leaders in the strike and even under this restrictive legislation, there was not sufficient evidence to deport them in this case.

Section 41 however was effectively used to deport communists and trade unionist radicals by the thousands.

Section 98 of the Criminal Code was added following the Winnipeg General Strike and made Canada the world's only democracy banning the Communist Party. The legislation included the general provision that prohibited "unlawful association." Under [S]ection 98, this was applied to anyone who had attended meetings, spoken out in favour or distributed literature for a named organization. Property could be seized by police without a warrant and forfeited to the Crown, and any person claiming to be a representative of the unlawful association was guilty by association. Civil libertarians were alarmed at this provision and a coalition of communists, leftists and liberals from the League for Social Reconstruction opposed it.

Section 98 was repealed by the federal government in the thirties, and replaced with a broader sedition clause in the Criminal Code. In Quebec, Maurice Duplessis, the autocratic premier of Quebec, soon replaced Section 98 with a provincial law, called the Padlock law. Armed with this legislation he was able to wage a virtual war against unpopular minorities during his reign from the thirties, and again in the fifties, when he was reelected after losing power. The Padlock law, passed in 1937, has the dubious distinction of being considered by civil rights groups as the most offensive piece of legislation violating individual right in a generation. It gave the attorney general the right to literally close down a building by placing a padlock on the front door of any premises containing material deemed subversive by the authorities. There were no criteria, and no appeal. The law was finally struck down in the Supreme Court of Canada in 1957.

On January 27, 1950, twenty-one officers descended on the Morris Winchevsky Cultural Centre of the left Jewish Organization, the UJPO in Montreal, and padlocked it, carting away several truckloads of office machines, organizational records, files, correspondence, and library books. They also raided the home of the secretary of the order, Benny Silverberg, and the home of Bess Shockett, who described how the police confiscated "every book with a red cover."[41] No charges were laid against the organization, or allegations that any of the activities engaged in were not lawful. Under the terms of the Padlock law, contentions did not need to be proven in court, or the police actions justified. Following the Quebec raid, the Toronto Jewish Welfare Fund decided to halt support of the Toronto Winchevsky Shule. In Vancouver, too, funds for the left-wing Peretz Institute were terminated.[42]

Protest resolutions from across Canada indicated a strong reaction amongst the Canadian public. *Saturday Night* magazine was outraged at the use of a law that made Duplessis "policeman, prosecutor, judge, sheriff and hangman." In one of several editorials, *Saturday Night* pointed out that UJPO had not only not been not been proven guilty of any criminal offense but had not even been charged. "He is depriving them of their property by his own absolute power, conferred upon him by the Quebec Legislature. . . . They are of course a minority, but there was a time when Quebec was supposed to be solicitous about the rights of minorities."[43] Some of those who spoke up included the Civil Liberties Union in Montreal and Toronto, the Montreal Labour Council, the Ontario Federation of Labour, students at McGill University, the *Ottawa Citizen* and the Montreal Presbyterian Presbytery. Forty-three clergy and ministers published their petition to Duplessis in the *Montreal Daily Gazette*, calling the padlocking a flat contradiction of "our accepted democratic tradition."[44] UJPO quickly drafted a petition and mobilized its members to canvas for signatures. Thousands signed.

The leadership of the Canadian Jewish Congress decided that the closure of the Winchevsky Centre in Montreal was not a Jewish issue. Some organizations affiliated with the Canadian Jewish Congress had a different view. The Jewish Junior Welfare Committee, a member of the Women's Liaison Committee of the CJC, condemned the use of the law "under any circumstances whatsoever," and "heartily" endorsed any positive action the Canadian Jewish Congress might take in an effort to undo the wrongs.[45] Saul Hayes, the national Executive Director replied, asking them to "leave the matter in abeyance" until the Joint Public Relations Committee of Congress met.[46] The Youth Councils in Toronto and Montreal also passed protest resolutions as did he Winnipeg Jewish Youth Council, requesting the Eastern Division of the Joint Public Relations Committee to take up the matter.[47] However, the CJC felt the need to warn the community of the dangers of "Communism."[48] Pro-Soviet positions were being equated with Communist Party membership.

In 1943, when Canada had been fighting the Nazis, and Russia was an ally, the left had been invited to be part of Congress, and leftists became active participants in Congress. Not long after the war ended there was widespread concern in the Jewish community about the rearmament of Germany. The UJPO organized a campaign, initially supported by all branches of Congress, in opposition. When the Canadian Jewish Congress sent a delegation to meet with Lester Pearson, the Minister of External Affairs, Pearson informed the delegation that the Canadian government supported rearming Germany to contain the expansion of communism. Following this meeting, the CJC president, Saul Hayes, recommended that the campaign be abandoned.[49] However, the UJPO was convinced that German rearmament constituted a critical danger to world Jewry and continued their mobilization.[50]

Two other world issues at that time were the Korean War and the Stockholm Peace Petition. In opposition to Congress, UJPO wholeheartedly supported the petition while it vigorously opposed the Korean War. Congress, following Canada's position on both issues, supported the Korean War and opposed the Stockholm Peace Petition and urged people not to sign it. The peace petition called for an absolute ban on nuclear weapons. The drafters and signatories included Reverend James Endicott of Canada, Lionel Pauling, Marc Chagall, Pablo Neruda, Duke Ellington, and a long list of artists and poets. It was signed by millions of people throughout the world.

While antiwar sentiments had been popular in the pre-World War II period, the postwar climate had shifted. The foe however was no longer Hitler and fascism, but a return to the threat of communism.[51] The New York Anti-Defamation League office denounced the Stockholm Peace Appeal, characterizing it as a "despicable divide and conquer tactic" and a pro-communist tactic, provoking groups to violence. Still, in Canada, 300,000 signatures were collected at street demonstrations and street corner meetings.[52] Ben Shek, in high school at the time and in the youth group of the UJPO, recalls how peace supporters faced police harassment and physical threats as they circulated through the community for signatures.[53]

The leadership of the Canadian Jewish Congress was outraged at the left's refusal to abide by Congress's decision and expelled the UJPO, maintaining that the views and actions of the left-wing oriented group stemmed from an ideology rooted outside of Canadian Jewish life. In the Congress archives one can examine the flurry of memos, all marked "Personal and Confidential," which passed between Saul Hayes and the presidents of the regions, changing the rules of who can vote and how voting should take place to ensure that the proposal would pass. Jewish left-leaning organizations were no longer to be considered part of the Jewish community. Given UJPO's organizational strength at the time and active presence in the political and cultural life of Canadian Jewry, this was not easy to accomplish. However, with the resurgence of a Cold War climate and the fears that it engendered in all of Canada, expulsion was possible.

What was at stake in this decision was not necessarily defense or opposition to the UJPO's views, but rather the right to hold views with which

Congress leadership didn't agree, and some of the questionable methods Congress used to rid itself of quite a powerful group. The claim was that these left groups were not Jewish and not Canadian.[54] Within the context of Cold War Canada, the parallels to these events within the Jewish community and what was happening in other organizations is unmistakable. Similar processes of ousting pro-communist elements were found in the union movement (United Electrical Workers, Canadian Seaman's Union, Mine and Mill, and in the Needle Trades) as well as in other ethnic communities. Any position that challenged Canadian government policies was deemed to be disloyal and "un-Canadian."

Until the terrible revelations of the twentieth Party Congress in 1956 when people realized that their beloved Soviet Jewish artists and poets had been murdered, the left organizations were indeed pro-Soviet, with a leadership who were Communist Party members. Members of the Jewish left organizations understood the difference between being pro-Soviet and being a communist organization. Aside from attending fewer meetings, they supported the policies that made sense to them. A Winnipeg activist who was "never a party person" described her support for a worldview of "equality, justice, socialism and the new world order," rather than a directive from "some higher up." She described intense debates over policy, but a community united in support of candidates such as Joe Zuken, the Communist alderman from Winnipeg's North End. She felt there was "an integrity there, and an honesty that you didn't find with others."[55]

Until 1956, the Soviet Union was admired as the model for what these revolutionary idealists were trying to achieve in Canada. They learned that they were sadly mistaken. Virtually all Jewish Communists left the Communist Party, and much of the UJPO leadership who were Party members left both the Party and the Order. However, many rank-and-filers remained and a new leadership emerged. The UJPO itself continues. The Winnipeg UJPO has grown in the first decade of the twenty-first century, although the Montreal organization is no more. Vancouver is the home of the *Outlook,* a progressive Jewish magazine in English that began publication in 1960. UJPO members are often the only visible Jewish organizational presence at social justice rallies for human rights and labor rights. Their criticisms of Israeli government policies continue to be denounced as the traitorous sentiments of "self-hating Jews." The UJPO was invited to rejoin the Canadian Jewish Congress in 1995. However, in 2011, Congress itself was abolished, replaced by the Centre for Israel and Jewish Affairs. There is, however, growing concern in the Jewish community about this move as it leaves Canadian Jews without an organization to address national and local issues.

In 2008, a group of children and teenagers in Camp *Naivelt* learned about a commune run by youngsters in the Soviet Union in the 1920s, through the memoirs of Manya Lipshitz. As a teenager, she had been part of the twelfth children's work commune in Vitebsk. The journals produced by the children resurfaced some fifty years later. Inspired by how these children who had survived terrible losses were able, by working together, to make a difference in their collective lives, the *Naivelt* kids recreated the commune. Adopting the persona of the children from the journals published in the original commune, they approximated as closely as they could the life in the commune. This weeklong experience was followed by a play called *Oy di Velt*, named after the song by Morris Winchevsky. The play was a history of the left movement in Toronto and the camp, through dance, acting and singing, and excerpts of archival interviews.

Naivelt, where this reenactment took place, is part of the United Jewish People's Order. In Toronto, the Winchevsky Centre on Cranbrooke Avenue and Camp *Naivelt*, located in the back of El Dorado Park in Brampton, are very much alive. The community is no longer Yiddish speaking, and indeed not exclusively Jewish, but it has a "Yiddishn tam"—a Jewish taste—and a tradition of progressive radicalism that is nonsexist and welcoming to all variations of families. Is the legacy a vanished one? The young people from the summer of 2008 are a reminder that sometimes one can, if not learn from the past, be inspired by the idealism of earlier times.

Notes

1. Stephen A. Speisman, *The Jews of Toronto: A History to 1937* (Toronto: McClelland and. Stewart, 1979), 317.

2. *Canadian Jewry Today: Who's Who in Canadian Jewry*, ed. Edmond Y. Lipsitz (Downsview, ON: J.E.S.L. Educational Products, 1989).

3. Ian McKay, "Joe Salsberg, Depression-Era Communism, and the Limits of Moscow's Rule," paper presented to the seminar in honor of Gerry Tulchinsky, University of Toronto, 2013.

4. Gerald Tulchinsky, *Joe Salsberg: A Life of Commitment* (Toronto: University of Toronto Press, 2013).

5. Jim Mochoruk documents the fierce battles between officials on the Executive Committee of the CP and Ukrainian leaders, who did remain in the party,

but acted independently and in opposition to party's wishes. " 'Pop & Co' versus Buck and the 'Lenin school Boys': Ukrainian Canadians and the Communist Party of Canada," in *Re-imagining Ukrainian-Canadians: History, Politics and Identity*, eds. Rhonda L. Hinther and Jim Mochoruk (Toronto: University of Toronto Press, 2010), 331–75. Peter Campbell in "The Cult of Spontaneity: Finnish Bushworkers and the Industrial Workers of the World in Northern Ontario, 1919–34," *Labour/le Travail* No. 41 (1998): 117–46, documents the continued Wobbly influence in autonomous decision making, even after most of the former Wobblies had become Communist Party members.

6. Joan Sangster, *Dreams of Equality: Women in the Canadian Left, 1920–1950* (Toronto: McClelland and Stewart, 1989); Ruth Frager, *Sweatshop Strife: Class, Ethnicity and Gender in the Jewish Labour Movement of Toronto, 1900–1939* (Toronto: University of Toronto Press, 1992); and Mercedes Steedman, *Angels of the Workplace: Women and the Construction of Gender Relations in the Canadian Clothing Industry, 1890–1940* (Toronto: University of Toronto Press, 1997).

7. Antonio Gramsci, *Selections From the Prison Notebooks* (London: Lawrence and Wishart, 1971).

8. Paulo Freire, *The Politics of Education: Culture, Power and Liberation* (Westport, CT: Praeger, 1985), 67–120.

9. Stuart Hall, "Cultural Identity and Diaspora," in *Social Theory*, 2nd ed., ed. Roberta Garner (Toronto: University of Toronto Press, 2010), 563.

10. Richard Stites, *The Women's Liberation Movement in Russia: Feminism, Nihilism, and Bolshevism, 1860–1930* (Princeton, NJ: Princeton University Press, 1978).

11. Rachel Haltman, "Der Haym un Kooperativa Virtshaft," *Der Kamf*, March 12, 1926, 4.

12. F. Frumet "Vilde Shtik: unzer Sivilizatsye un di Froyen," *Der Kamf*, April 2, 1926, 4.

13. Rachel Watson, "Di Froy in di Kapitalistishe Lender un in Sovyetn Farband," *Der Kamf*, May 14, 1926, 4.

14. A saleslady, "Di shklaferishe Badingunden fun di Farkoyferin," *Der Kamf*, March 21, 1930, 3.

15. Lil was a neighbor of mine, and I have some of her poetry celebrating the history of the UJPO. Singing we did occasionally, although I don't know if she ever was part of the Choir. She married a Finnish Communist, Max Ilomaki.

16. Becky Lapedes, "A Camp is Born," *Souvenir Book for the 20th Jubilee of the Camps in Brampton*, 1956.

17. Morris Biderman, *A Life on the Jewish Left: An Immigrant's Experience* (Toronto: Onward, 2000), 70.

18. Ron Biderman, quoted in Morris Biderman, *A Life on the Jewish Left*, 71.

19. Rita Bergman, "The Most Beautiful Memorial," in *Unzer Zumer Haim* (Toronto: Camp Naivelt Souvenir Booklet, 2000), 11.

20. Rachel Orlan, "Naivelt Memories," in *Unzer Zumer Haim*, 12.

21. James Laxer, conversation with the author, April 2001.

22. Sherry Bergman, "My Home, My Heart," in *Unzer Zumer Haim*, 18–19.

23. Ben Shek, correspondence with the author, February 2001. The phrase can be rendered "from camp to school, from school to camp."

24. Phillip Halperin, "Alhambra Hall," *Der Kamf*, March 12, 1937, 6 (reprint from March 29, 1929).

25. Karen Levine interviews with Sam Kagan, deposited at the Multicultural History Society of Ontario, Toronto. In the 1970s, Karen Levine interviewed a number of Jewish radicals.

26. M. Mindes, "Di Arbeter Bibliotek: a Vikhtiger ring fun Proletarishe Kultur-front," *Der Kamf*, April 19, 1929, 4.

27. In August 1933 Police Chief Dennis Draper ignored Mayor William Stewart's instructions that there was going to be trouble between Nazi hooligans and a largely Jewish baseball team, called the Harbord Playground, at a ball park, and he did nothing. The result was the Christie Pits riot. See Cyril H. Levitt and William Shaffir, *The Riot at Christie Pits* (Toronto: Lester & Orpen Denys, 1987), for a fuller description of the incident.

28. M. Biderman, "Frayhayt *Gezangs Farayn* un der Labour League," in *10 Years Labor League* (Toronto: Supreme Printing, 1936).

29. "Police Board Usurp Power given Council," *Toronto Star*, Jan 16, 1931, 1–2.

30. Benjamin Katz, "On the First Anniversary," *Der Kamf*, May 13, 1932, 5.

31. Matthew Hoffman, "From Czernowitz to Paris: the International Yiddish Culture Congress of 1937," in *Czernowitz at 100: the First Yiddish Language Conference in Historical Perspective*, eds. Kalman Weiser and Joshua Fogel (New York, 2010), 160. All three authors were later victims of Stalin's purges in the 1930s and beyond.

32. Ibid., 151–64.

33. Interview with the author, May 2000.

34. Moishe Miller, "A Shmues mit der Fargangenhayt," *Di Pen*, May 1995, 18–22. Thanks to Roz Usiskin for bringing this article to my attention.

35. Phllip Halperin, "Alhambra Hall."

36. J. S. Chaikoff, "Past and Future of the Toronto Jewish Folk Choir," in *Twenty Fifth Anniversary Program of the Toronto Jewish Folk Choir*, Toronto, 1950, third page (unnumbered).

37. Author's interview with Mollie Klein, March 1996. The concerts were held on May 25,1946, March 25, 1947, November 19, 1947, December 4 and 6, 1948, and December 3 and 5, 1949.

38. Merrily Weisbord, *The Strangest Dream: Canadian Communists, The Spy Trials, and The Cold War* (Toronto: Lester & Orpen Dennys, 1983), 85.

39. Roz Usiskin, "The Winnipeg Jewish Community: Its Radical Elements, 1905–1918," *Manitoba Historical Society Transactions*, Series 3, No. 33, 1976–77.

40. Barbara Ann Roberts, *Whence They Came: Deportation from Canada, 1900–1935* (Ottawa: University of Ottawa Press, 1988), 95

41. Author's interview with Bess Schockett, April 2007.

42. Faith Jones, "Between Suspicion and Censure: Attitudes Towards the Jewish Left in Postwar Vancouver," *Canadian Jewish Studies* 6 (1998): 1–24, describes the expulsion of the Vancouver UJPO from the Vancouver Jewish Administrative Council, causing the Peretz Institute to lose its funding from the United Jewish Appeal. Although the school was independent, many members of UJPO participated in the school.

43. *Saturday Night* editorials of February 7, 1950, and February 21, 1950; Canadian Jewish Congress Archives, Montreal [hereafter CJC Archives], ZA 1950, Box 11, File 107.

44. *Civil Liberties Bulletin*, Nos. 3 and 4, February and March 1950; *Canadian Tribune*, Feb. 13, 1950; CJC Archives, ZA 1950, Box 11, File 107.

45. Letter from Mrs. Sahila M Bordo, President, Jewish Junior Welfare League to Saul Hayes, Executive Director, CJC, Feb 8, 1950; CJC Archives, ZA 1950, Box 11, File 107.

46. Letter from Saul Hayes, National Executive Director, CJC to Mrs. Saila M Bordo, President, Jewish Junior Welfare League, March 2, 1950; CJC Archives, ZA 1950, Box 11, File 107.

47. Letter from H. Frank, Executive Director, CJC Western Division to Saul Hayes, Feb 22, 1950; CJC Archives, ZA 1950, Box 11, File 107.

48. Gerald Tulchinsky, *Branching Out: The Transformation of the Jewish Community (*Toronto: Stoddart, 1998), 123.

49. Ibid.

50. "Statement of the National Executive Committee of the United Jewish Peoples Order to the Jewish People in Canada." Virtually all UJPO members understand this to be the reason for the later expulsion. Personal communication, David Abramowitz, National President, UJPO; Ben Shek, National Secretary, UJPO.

51. Victor Huard, "Armageddon Reconsidered: Shifting Attitudes Towards Peace in English Canada, 1936–1953," PhD thesis, Queen's University, Kingston, ON, 1995.

52. Stephen Endicott, *James G. Endicott: Rebel out of China* (Toronto: University of Toronto Press, 1980), 267.

53. Interview with Ben Shek, April 2004.

54. Memorandum B: "On the admissibility of Leftist groups within the Canadian Jewish Congress"; CJC Archives, ZA 1950, Box 11.

55. Author's interview with Roz Usiskin, May 2006.

7

Jews in the Communist Party of Great Britain

Perceptions of Ethnicity and Class

Stephen M. Cullen

Failing to Account for Jewish Support for the CPGB

Despite its small size and generally poor electoral performances the Communist Party of Great Britain (CPGB) always attracted a good deal of attention throughout its seventy-one years of existence. In 1995, just four years after the CPGB's dissolution, the well-known British journalist Francis Beckett published his sympathetic but critical general history of the Party, *The Enemy Within: the Rise and Fall of the British Communist Party.*[1] Beckett was able to take advantage of recently opened archives in Moscow, interviews with ageing but well-known communist activists, and the reflective, critical atmosphere that the failure of Soviet Communism had engendered, to produce a successful popular history. He rehearsed key themes in the CPGB's life, among which was the fact that "without Jews from London's East End and Scots from the Red Clyde, the CP would have been a very poor thing indeed."[2] Beckett also noted the impact of the decline then the collapse of Jewish support for the CPGB, as population movements, the *embourgeoisement* of the Jewish community, the foundation of the State of Israel, and, critically, revelations of Soviet anti-Semitism meant that, for example, in 1957 the general secretary of the party, John Gollan, had to ask Moscow for a reintroduction of direct financial support for the CPGB.[3] Yet, despite this awareness of the historic link between large sections of the

Jewish community and the CPGB, which coincided with the period of the Party's greatest success from the mid-1930s to the late 1940s, Beckett did not really attempt to engage with issues of Jewish ethnicity and membership and support for the CPGB.[4] However, Beckett was in no way exceptional in this regard, as the historiography of the CPGB has been characterized by only passing, or incidental recognition of the Jewish contribution to the CPGB, and almost no engagement with the interplay of class and ethnicity in relation to Jewish support for communism in the United Kingdom (UK).

Explaining the failure to engage with the issue may well have two, opposing, ideological sources. First, histories of the CPGB, like those of other communist parties, are frequently written by partisans of communism, and as such, are unsurprisingly focused on class. In this respect, what is most important about Jewish support for the CPGB is the working-class experience of Jews in the East End of London, Manchester, Leeds, and Glasgow. This approach puts the class struggle of Jewish workers and their families at the center of the picture, with, for example, the Stepney Tenants' Defence League (STDL), which was dominated by Jewish rent payers, being viewed almost entirely through an economic lens. For example, the famous account of the CPGB's campaigns in the 1930s and 1940s, *Our Flag Stays Red*, by one of the Party's most successful and well-known activists, Phil Piratin, provided an account of the CPGB's successes in mobilizing Stepney rent payers in the STDL, which is, in effect, an account of the mobilization of a significant section of the Jewish community in that borough, but that is implied rather than clearly stated.[5] More interestingly, a recent Stalinist biography of Piratin, while acknowledging Piratin's Jewishness and, moreover, the importance of ethnicity in the politics of the East End of London,[6] fails to come to grips with the complexity of Jewish support for communism. Piratin's own family trajectory, from his father's refugee origins in the Ukraine to his son's education at the Royal Grammar School, High Wycombe, and his legal career and, indeed, Phil Piratin's own later career as a successful businessman and director of a merchant bank,[7] was typical of many Jewish families who had immigrated as refugees into the UK in the late nineteenth and early twentieth century. What was unusual was Phil Piratin's lifelong adherence to communism, but what was more typical was his continued self-identification as a Jew as well as a communist:

> Piratin had renounced Judaism and embraced atheism. His view was unequivocal—he was a communist, even though this change of doctrine had caused schisms within his own family.

> Nonetheless, he still proclaimed his own identity as a "good son of the Jewish people" and addressed matters of particular concern to Jews.[8]

Despite this recognition, Marsh and Griffiths made little effort to unpack this complexity of motivations and self-identification, and provided only a sketchy view of, for example, the collapse of Jewish support for the CPGB. Indeed, the authors appear to believe that Soviet anti-Semitism amounted to little more than "allegations in the [Western] press."[9]

In addition to a class-focused historiography, it has been argued that the Jewish contribution to the Communist movement has been deliberately underplayed by Stalinist historiography. This view has been most forcefully put by Martin Sugarman in his introduction to his roll call of Jews who served in the International Brigades (IB) during the Spanish Civil War. Sugarman notes that around a quarter of all International Brigaders were Jewish, and that proportion was certainly much higher for Jews from Poland (45 percent of 5,000 volunteers) and the United States (38 percent of 1,250), while France (15 percent of 1043) and the UK (between 11 and 22 percent)[10] also saw disproportionately large numbers of Jews from those countries fighting with the IB. In the light of these figures, which are probably an underestimate, Sugarman argued,

> [T]he marginalization of the huge part played by the Jewish fighters in Spain is due to the tight grip held by old fashioned Stalinists who have been "Keepers of the Memory" of the IB in the post war period and right up to the 21st century—especially in the UK and the USA. To acknowledge the incredible role of the Jews is to have to admit that many went to Spain as proud Jews as much as proud Socialists, and that many were also Zionists, especially the large number [300–500 . . .] who came from Mandate Palestine/Israel.[11]

This might not be the whole story, however. It may very well be that contemporary anti-fascists and anti-Nazis were attempting to counter the perception that "bolshevism was Jewish," something that has had historiographical implications. It is also questionable whether many communist Jews in the IB were to any degree Zionist. But, nonetheless, it is the case that for many years the Jewish contribution to the defense of the Spanish Republic was overlooked, and the approach of Sugarman's "old fashioned Stalinists" might be at root as much of a reflection of the fundamental Marxist-Leninist approach to nationality and national questions as a simple extension of the recurrence of periodic Soviet anti-Semitism. Stephan Wendehorst, in his recent history *British Jewry, Zionism, and the Jewish State, 1936–1956*, has highlighted that the CPGB's much-vaunted claim that the Soviet system had "solved" the "Jewish question" was, the Jewish Autonomous Region of Birobidzhan notwithstanding, little more than an ultra-assimilationist "solution" that would mean, eventually, that any sense of a Jewish nation or people would dissolve as proletarian culture finally overcame all vestiges of bourgeois culture, of which national identity was one.[12]

If class-based or unreconstructed Stalinist historiography accounts for some of the failure to examine all aspects of Jewish support for the CPGB, then the shadow of fascist and Nazi anti-Semitism provides the second explanation. In 1913, Lenin wrote of Jews outside Russia that

> there the great and universally progressive features of Jewish culture have made themselves clearly felt; its internationalism, its responsiveness to the advanced movements of our times (the percentage of Jews in democratic and proletarian movements is everywhere higher than the percentage of Jews in the general population).[13]

Lenin's stress on the "universal" aspects of Jewish culture, and its "internationalism" represents, in all probability, an accurate insight into two underlying explanatory variables that help explain Jewish support for communism. Indeed, Wendehorst identifies the universalist appeal of communism to Jews, especially from the mid-1930s until the early 1950s, as a key to understanding that support.[14] However, by the mid-1930s, what had been a Tsarist tool of anti-Semitism had become, in the aftermath of the Russian Revolution a much more widespread and fatally potent Nazi propaganda slogan, that "Bolshevism was Jewish." The success of that slogan, its widespread acceptance, and not only by those on the ultra-right, and the implications for all Jews, whether communist or not, meant that a focus on the Jewish contribution to communism was avoided by many. For example, the British Communist Tom Wintringham, a founder of the CPGB's main propaganda vehicle, *The Daily Worker*, and, briefly, commander of the British Battalion of the International Brigades, deliberately underestimated the outstanding contribution of Jewish fighters to the International Brigades precisely because he did not wish to give credence to the slogan "Bolshevism is

Jewish." Far from acknowledging that British Jewish volunteers might have made up to 22 percent of the British International Brigaders (when Jews only made up 0.5 percent of the British population), Wintringham said in his post-Spanish Civil War memoir, *English Captain*, published in 1939, that Jews made up only 3 percent of British volunteers. Henry Srebrnik has argued that this was intentional as Wintringham sought to deny anti-Semites ammunition with which to attack the Jewish community and the international Communist movement.[15]

The Beginnings of a Reassessment of Jewish Support for the CPGB

The impact of this inheritance of underestimating, ignoring, or failing to fully engage with Jewish support for the CPGB has been long-lasting, and only now, nearly sixty years since "the end of the affair"[16] is the subject attracting the attention it deserves. Henry Pelling's early history of the CPGB, *The British Communist Party*, was atypical in that it devoted some space to specific discussion of the issue, noting that "the Jewish population of the East End rallied to the party in fair numbers."[17] Kenneth Newton's *The Sociology of British Communism* did address the issue of Jewish support, but Newton's work was a contemporary study, and by the early 1960s the heyday of Jewish membership of the party was long over. Nonetheless, Newton did make some interesting points about Jewish Communism in the 1930s, stressing the combination of factors that underpinned that support, as well as arguing that, "even without the pressures of Fascist anti-Semitism [in the 1930s], it is probable that a number of Jews in the East End [of London] would have joined the Party, for there are certain affinities between Communism and Judaism."[18] This is an area that needs a good deal more work, but at least Newton addressed some issues that had linked British Jews to the Party. By contrast, Noreen Branson in *History of the Communist Party of Great Britain, 1927–1941*,[19] and, later, Willie Thompson in *The Good Old Cause*,[20] paid scant attention to the question. Finally, two notable works by Jewish Communists were Joe Jacobs's *Out of the Ghetto*,[21] which presented an important contrast to Piratin's account of the CPGB and anti-fascism in East London, and Raphael Samuel's reflections on his upbringing in a communist family, which first appeared in the *New Left Review* in 1985–87. However, discussion of Jacobs's work has centered on the arguments surrounding approaches to anti-fascism, while Samuel's memoir-based piece has not perhaps received the recognition that it merits.

This lack of attention began to be addressed by two ground-breaking historians, Elaine Rosa Smith and Henry Felix Srebrnik, both of whom wrote doctoral theses on the subject and produced the first of a number of important articles during the 1980s.[22] Srebrnik, in particular, has continued to extend our knowledge of the relationship between Jews and British Communism in a series of articles, and his writing has acted as a focus of debate, with Jason Heppell challenging some key elements of Srebrnik's analysis.[23] James Hopkins's study of the British contribution to the defense of the Spanish Republic, *Into the Heart of the Fire*, recognized the contribution of British Jews, and noted the linkage between "militant anti-fascism," particularly Jewish anti-fascism, in Britain and volunteering for Spain.[24] This contribution also receives some recognition in Richard Baxell's *Unlikely Warriors: The British in the Spanish Civil War and the Struggle Against Fascism*, but it is largely in passing, and one gets no sense of the disproportionate numbers of British Jews who went to Spain with the International Brigades.[25] More generally, other historians have continued to add to our understanding of the communist experience in Britain, with, for example, Andrew Thorpe taking advantage of new archival sources to discuss CPGB membership, reinforcing our knowledge of the general pattern of membership, with areas where the Jewish community was relatively strong—particularly East London, Manchester, Leeds, and Glasgow—also being areas of Party strength in the 1930s.[26] But while Thorpe discussed the gender, class, and age profile of the Party, he failed to engage with the ethnic profile. Similarly, Thomas Linehan's richly textured account of communist lives in his *Communism in Britain, 1920–39* unfortunately provides no insight into the lives of Jewish Party members "from the cradle to the grave,"[27] while his account of communist activism, in which he conceptualizes communists as belonging to a "political religion," again makes no mention of Jewish influences and experience, despite Raphael Samuel's earlier exegesis of the linkage between religious faith and communism.[28] However, Linehan has briefly noted the importance of Jewish anti-fascism in his recent discussion of communist culture.[29] More usefully, Kevin Morgan, Gidon Cohen, and Andrew Flinn's landmark study of British Communists, *Communists and British Society 1920–1991*, devotes some space, and interesting reflections, on the relationship of Jews to the CPGB, and, in the process, suggested future research paths for the topic.[30] The most recent, and valuable, contribution, Wendehorst's *British Jewry, Zionism, and the Jewish State, 1936–*

1956, includes some important reflections on the shifting, and complex, nature of Jewish adherence to the CPGB, and tensions over the Zionist project, especially from the mid-1940s onwards.[31]

Developing the Debate

A key issue that has emerged with regard to the Jewish contribution to British Communism is the degree to which Jews in the Party separated themselves from their sense of ethnic identity. This is a central academic argument concerning the history of British Jewish involvement in the CPGB, and is an issue that has yet to be resolved. Jason Heppell has used the lack of interest in the work of the Jewish Bureau of the CPGB, which was established in 1936, to examine the question of what constitutes "Jewish politics," and to argue that the overwhelming majority of Jewish members of the Party "were Communist Jews not Jewish Communists," and that these members were "Jews separated from their ethnic community by their Communist beliefs." Heppell's use of the terms "Communist Jews" and "Jewish Communists" is, perhaps, confusing, but has been used here as Heppell's arguments concerning the supposed separation of Communist Jews from their ethnic background lie at the heart of the debate. This view received support in Morgan, Cohen, and Flinn's work, where they argued that the "non-Jewish Jew" was more typical of CPGB Jewish membership than that of the Jewish Communist "ethnic politician." Heppell supported his argument, in part, by arguing that in the 1930s and early 1940s, there was typically an intergenerational rift between the largely young Jews in the Party, usually second- or third-generation British Jews, and older members of their families and community, often immigrants into Britain. Heppell advanced this argument in opposition to that of Srebrnik, who presents Jewish involvement in the Communist movement in the 1930s and early 1940s as being a significant part of the working-class Jewish experience of the time, with Jewish members of the CPGB being "Jewish Communists," as opposed to Heppell's categorization of "Communist Jews." Although Heppell does not engage with the work of Smith, it is worth noting that her approach more closely mirrors that of Srebrnik, with Smith arguing that "the Communist Party provided East End Jews with a means of expressing their Jewish identity within the framework of a secular political culture. One contemporary witness has even suggested that East End Jewish Communists 'were Jews before they were Communists.' "[32]

Smith's use of an interview with Bessy Weinberg—the "contemporary witness"—points the way to the use of oral history work to add an additional dimension to research centered on the question of the nature of Jewish involvement with communism. Both Heppell and Srebrnik's work relied on Party literature and records, but not on self-reflective testimony from Jewish members of the Party. Marsh and Griffiths, in their biography of Piratin, also make the pertinent observation that "while Communist Party of Great Britain (CPGB) archives are substantial, they contain little to indicate the role of individuals in decision-making and specific activities."[33] They might have also added that such archives, or that other major source of archival material, the reports of the police and the security services, rarely provide the type of self-reflective personal testimony that would enable historians to begin to understand the impact and importance of personal perceptions of identity, ethnicity, class, and ideology—the motivating forces behind individual adherence to the CPGB. In a piece published in *Socialist History* in 2012,[34] I attempted to enhance understanding of the experience of Jewish support for the CPGB in the 1930s, and, in the process examine the "Jewish Communists" or "Communist Jews" argument. In order to approach this issue from the perceptions of Jews who were active members of the CPGB in the 1930s, a series of recorded interviews, held at the Imperial War Museum (IWM), London, were utilized. The aim was to provide a textured account of the nature of Jewish support for the CPGB at a time when it was most enthusiastic. The convergence of changes in communist strategy (particularly with the adoption of the Popular Front model), the threat of fascism at home and abroad, combined with, in the East End of London in particular, socioeconomic problems and a very strong sense of Jewish communal identity, created a "perfect storm" of factors leading to enhanced support for the CPGB. In that context, the oral history material held at the IWM enabled particularly Jewish experiences, histories, and understandings to be examined, for example, in relation to Jewish involvement in pre-Bolshevik radicalism and Jewish family, sports, and social life.

The material from the IWM sound archive was drawn from a valuable group of recordings relating to the Spanish Civil War of 1936–1939. The interviews form part of the IWM's Spanish Civil War oral history project, which began in 1976, stimulated by the 40th anniversary reunion of the International Brigade Association. The IWM described the purpose of the project as being "to create a significant body of information where there were few specific documentary or written sources."[35] The IWM's catalogue of this project indicates that there were at least 122 individuals who were interviewed who had served with a variety of Republican units.[36] Of the 122, 113 interviewees were British, including a small number who had dual nationalities. The interviews typically cover a good deal of the lives of the interviewees, both before and after the Spanish Civil War period. As a result, accounts usually provide details of the interviewees' childhood and family background, their working lives, political development, active service (if applicable) in the Spanish Civil War, experiences during the Second World War, and subsequent life. This includes material relating to fascism and anti-fascism in Britain and in Spain. In particular, there are thirty-four recordings of active British anti-fascists, including twenty-four men who fought for the Spanish Republic. Of these thirty-four anti-fascists, eighteen were Jewish anti-fascists, all of whom were members of the CPGB, the Young Communist League (YCL), or the communist-organized National Unemployed Workers' Movement (NUWM). The eighteen interviews provide important insights into Jewish membership and support for the CPGB, and represent a hitherto underutilised source that provides valuable primary data on the topic. The reminiscences provide a valuable insight into the interviewees' perceptions of their early lives, family backgrounds, political engagement, and the meaning of these experiences to each interviewee. As such, the interviews, like all historical data sources, are subjective interpretations of history—in this case of personal histories by the interviewees. What is of particular value is that this personal reflection, and the attributing of meaning to past experiences by the interviewees, enabled the question of whether they were "Jewish Communists" or "Communist Jews" to be addressed. Assessments of the impact of Jewish engagement with the CPGB on ties to family and community can be effectively explored using such personal history work. Adopting a micro-historical approach, I attempted to address the question of Jewish support for the Party by giving "a voice and the capacity to make meaning [. . .] to those who act[ed] out the practices of everyday life"[37] as communists.

Testing a Model of Jewish Support for the CPGB

The intention here is to review the findings and conclusions of my earlier piece based on the IWM sound recordings, and to develop those conclusions further by drawing on additional recorded interviews with two notable Jewish members of the CPGB, Sir Alfred Sherman (1919–2006) and Mick Mindel (1909–1994). These two were interviewed at length by the British journalist and researcher Andrew Whitehead in 1990 and 1988, respectively.[38] Analysis and comparison of the Sherman and Mindel interviews are of particular value as a heuristic device to test the model of Jewish support for the CPGB that I developed in my *Socialist History* article. The interviews come from a different source than the IWM interviews, and they are interviews with two lifelong, politically engaged Jews who are fascinating in their own right. Further, Mick Mindel and Sir Alfred Sherman were Jews whose trajectories converged in the 1930s to the CPGB, only to diverge later. Alfred Sherman moved from communism to Zionism and, later, was famous for his closeness to the British Prime Minister, Margaret Thatcher, while, by contrast, Mick Mindel maintained a lifetime's commitment to communism and trade unionism. The interviews with both men were conducted in the final stages of their lives, and the focus of much of their accounts was on their Jewishness, their communism, and their understanding of the relationship between the two. As such, these data provide a tool for further exploring the conclusions built on the reflections of the IWM interviewees, and, it is hoped, add further depth to our understanding of the perceptions, motivations and attitudes to questions of ethnicity and class on the part of British Jews in the Communist Party of Great Britain in the peak period of Jewish support for the Party.

The evidence from the IWM interviewees enabled a number of key themes to be identified that help explain Jewish adherence to the CPGB, particularly in the East End of London, and especially from the mid-1930s until the late-1940s. These themes are:

- The issue of Jewish national identity, anti-Semitism and the "Jewish question"
- Fascism and anti-fascism, both in the UK and abroad, particularly in Spain
- Socioeconomic deprivation
- Territorialism, particularly in the East End of London
- The history of radicalism among Jews who immigrated in the late nineteenth and early twentieth century
- Jewish life: family, leisure, and culture.

Each theme is dealt with in turn here, with the evidence and analysis of the IWM interviews being presented, then tested ("Testing it out") in the light of data drawn from the Mindel and Sherman interviews.

The CPGB and the Jewish Community

External Factors Underpinning the Appeal of the CPGB to British Jews

The 1930s saw the steady growth of the link between significant sectors of the Jewish working class and the CPGB. Although the Party had difficulties in defining its stance on Jewish ethnicity, its attitude to the Jewish community in Palestine (the *Yishuv*) and Zionism, difficulties that would eventually contribute to the weakening of links between British Jews and the CPGB,[39] the Party developed a strategy for building its base among working-class Jews. Srebrnik, Smith, and Heppell have argued that the CPGB had a policy of attempting to build a core of solid support for the Party in Jewish areas. The intention was to create "Little Moscows," areas where the Party would enjoy localized hegemony, and from which the CPGB could expand its influence. In the East End of London, the Party was able in the early 1930s to build upon the activism of the Stepney Communist Party (leading elements of which were Jewish) and Harry Pollitt's strong showing in the Whitechapel by-election of November 1930[40] (a month after the Labour government published its White Paper proposing restrictions on Jewish immigration into Palestine), to become a significant force within the Jewish community. The early work of the CPGB in the East End stood it in good stead once the main British fascist party, Sir Oswald Mosley's British Union of Fascists (BUF), began to expand into the area, particularly from 1934 onwards. The CPGB took maximum advantage of this threat. In his 1951 account of the CPGB, Douglas Hyde, former news editor of the *Daily Worker* wrote of the CPGB's focus on the Jewish community in the context of anti-fascism: "Quite deliberately we used the Jewish fear of fascism and anti-Semitism for our own political ends. It made the Stepney branch our strongest, with over 1,000 members. It was the Party's greatest asset in Jewish areas all over Britain."[41] The scope that the CPGB had to turn predominantly Jewish areas of the East End into "Little Moscows" (along with Jewish areas of Manchester,[42] Leeds, and to a lesser extent, Glasgow) increased as international events developed over the decade, especially following the Nazi victory in Germany and the consequent realigning of Comintern policy in 1935. That move to the Popular Front stance also greatly facilitated the CPGB's ability to deepen its appeal to British Jews:

> It was during those periods in which Communist parties adopted popular front tactics, from 1935 to 1939 and from 1941 to

> 1946, that the CPGB was most accommodating to specific Jewish concerns and most successful at tapping reservoirs of Jewish sympathy [. . .] It thus became possible for the CPGB to seek the support of Jews *qua* Jews, not only as members of the working class.[43]

The combined effect of the attempt to create "Little Moscows," the consequent focus on Jewish concerns, and the emergence of the Popular Front strategy, all contributed to a situation where "through sustained agitation based upon the set of issues informing Jewish concerns, Jewish Communism for a brief period gained political hegemony within the East London Jewish community."[44]

The evidence of the IWM interviewees provides a clear underpinning to the picture of the CPGB's policy of focusing on Jewish concerns, particularly in East London. In terms of the "Jewish question," the Party presented a class analysis of the problems faced by Jews throughout the world, and argued that a Zionist solution would simply strengthen British imperial interests in the Middle East, and that "separatism" was not a viable solution to anti-Semitism. At the same time, much emphasis was placed on the creation, in 1934, of the Jewish Autonomous Region of Birobidzhan in the Soviet Union, which, it was claimed, added a specifically Jewish dimension to the Soviet utopian project. The CPGB's view was summarized in a party pamphlet from 1934, specifically aimed at the Jewish community:

> The Soviet Union—with its full equality for the Jews in every direction, with its policy of training an enlightened industrial working class out of millions of former pedlars, hucksters and petty artisans, and with its building up of a self-governing Jewish territory of Birobidjan in co-operation with other peoples, and not at their expense—shows what the workers and peasants can do, even in a poor and undeveloped country, provided they follow the leadership of Lenin.[45]

This summary of the communist position exhibits the view that the development of a proletarian future would create a new "enlightened industrial working class" out of what is characterized as a culturally and economically decayed Russian Jewish community, while making a passing sideswipe at those who thought that the establishment of a Jewish state in Mandatory Palestine would offer a "solution" to the "Jewish question." The belief that anti-Semitism had been eradicated in the Soviet Union, and that it was a model for working-class Jews to aspire to, was part of the explanation for the failure of other potentially competing groups to extend their influence among East London Jews. Jack Louis Shaw, who joined the YCL at the age of seventeen in 1934 and worked as an office boy with the *Daily Worker*, recalled his perceptions of the Soviet Union as a young Jewish boy prior to joining the Party:

> For a lot of us, Russia was the utopia. It was the utopia for the working class. Although we belonged to no political party, we were always attending meetings. At the corner of Wallace Road and Whitechapel there were always speakers on platforms. There were the Zionists, which we didn't take notice of, there was the Communist Party, which we did take notice of, there was the Socialist Party of Great Britain, which we never took notice of, and there were the Trotskyists, who we thought were terrible people.[46]

This view was also stressed by Maurice Levitas, an Irish-Jewish anti-fascist who moved with his parents to East London in 1931, and at the age of twelve joined the YCL in 1936. He noted that Jews "knew that the Soviet Union had abolished anti-Semitism, and was against anti-Semitism. So there was a natural sympathy for the Soviet Union if you happened to be a Jewish worker."[47] Indeed, the postwar revelations that, in fact, the Soviet Union had not abolished anti-Semitism proved to be a key moment in the dissipation of the links between sections of the Jewish community and communism.[48]

The sense that the interviewees regarded the Soviet Union as a "utopia" is strong, but, interestingly, there are no mentions of Birobidzhan as a specific "solution" to the Jewish national question. It is probable that the Communist movement's propagandist stress on the Jewish Autonomous Region was simply absorbed into the general perception that the Soviet Union had abolished anti-Semitism and "solved" the Jewish question; nonetheless, it is worthy of note that Birobidzhan was absent from the testimony of this group of British Jews.

What is also interesting in Shaw's statement is that among the groups that he and his young friends "didn't take notice of" were the Zionists. Other interviewees also note the lack of purchase that Zionism had on young Jews drawn to the CPGB, with, for example, Louis Kenton,[49] a member of Stepney YCL, claiming that he knew nothing at all about the Zionist anti-fascist group the "Legion of Blue and White Shirts," founded in 1936.[50] Shaw commented that the group "was too Jewish," and that, therefore, he was not attracted to it. Historians, such as Paul Kelemen, have argued that the CPGB consistently over-estimated the attraction and influence of Zionism for British working-class Jews in the 1930s, and the interviews seem to bear this out.[51] However, the focus of the Party on Jewish concerns incorporated consistent attention to the Zionist project in Palestine, analyzing it in a framework of British imperialism, and the class interests of the Jewish bourgeoisie. There was no sense that the Party was able to see that Zionist sectarianism in Palestine incorporated the Jewish working class, via its trade unionism, into the Zionist national project. Yet, the strength of working-class Jewish support for the CPGB ensured that the Party continued, throughout the 1930s, to focus on issues of concern to the community.

TESTING IT OUT

Mick Mindel was a young boy when news of the Russian Revolution began to dominate the discussions in his home in the flats of the Rothschild Buildings in Spitalfields, East London. What he remembered was the excitement and expectation among his father's friends—mostly radical refugees from the old Tsarist Russia. Their central hope and belief was that the success of the Bolshevik Revolution had finally ended anti-Semitism:

> There was this *tremendous* hope that the Russian Revolution would solve the problems of the Jewish people—anti-Semitism would be eliminated, into the past, all the economic problems of the Jews would be resolved, and much more that could be associated with this tremendous expression and confidence that the Jewish intelligentsia in particular had towards the Russian Revolution.[52]

Nine decades later, Mick Mindel's nephew, the famous British journalist Jonathan Freedland, would give more detail of the discussions in the Mindel's flat in his history of the Freedland family and the meaning of Jewishness and belonging. Jewish neighbors of the Mindels were preparing to return to Russia:

> He [a neighbour] and the others tried to persuade the Mindels that the Russia they had all left behind—of pogroms and press-ganged service in the tsar's army—was now a thing of the

> past. Only a bright future awaited the Jews in the new Soviet Union. "Look who's in charge now," said the neighbour [. . .] "Trotsky, Zinoviev, Kamenev, Radek—most of the central committee are Jews!"[53]

Interestingly, given this list of ill-fated Bolsheviks, Mick Mindel noted that his father, who was a Bundist, never believed that the Bolshevik Revolution or the establishment of the Soviet state would solve either the problem of anti-Semitism or the economic problem. This led to "tremendous conflict [. . .] in later years with my father in discussions of the political scene," as the Communist Mindel followed the CPGB line on the Soviet utopia. Mindel admitted, years later, that his father's view was "on reflection, a very profound thing to say." But despite this and despite the shock of the Hitler-Stalin Pact in August 1939, which Mindel called "the tremendous policy problem of Russia and Germany," he remained in the CPGB and loyal to the Party line.

By way of contrast, Alfred Sherman's reflections in 1990 throw doubt on the idea that Jews in the CPGB were "really" Jews. In the terms of the current debate, Sherman argued that these members of the CPGB were "Communist Jews," rather than "Jewish Communists." Sherman held that it was a desire to escape from their Jewishness that led so may young Jews to join the CPGB in the 1930s, but, ironically, the geographic concentration of Jews in Britain meant that they then found that they had, in fact, "escaped" into another world that was still disproportionately Jewish:

> In a sense, the Jew contains two concepts—of being a Jew and of ceasing to be a Jew. Throughout history, a large number of Jews have ceased to be Jews, and the Jews who joined the Communist Party were, for the most part, people who did not feel anything positive, Jewishness meant foreignness, it meant speaking bad English, it meant being an alien. And therefore you tried to get away from that [. . .] and by joining the Communist Party you ceased to be a Jew, you were a member of a worldwide movement in which you were no longer a Jew, you were a person, a Communist. It was only later you realised that you had simply joined another Jewish faction.[54]

As in Mindel's account, there is a very clear sense of a generational shift from the older radicalism of Yiddish-speaking immigrants located within the mindset of the ghetto, to the newer Soviet-style radicalism of young

English-speaking Jews who wished to step outside the mindset of their parents and grandparents. Indeed, it was during this period that Yiddish began an intergenerational decline among radical British Jews, one that, perhaps, marked a difference between the British community and Jews in other countries. But there is less of a feeling of the abandonment of a sense of Jewishness in Mindel's account than in Sherman's version. It should be noted however, that Alfred Sherman had long abandoned his communism (he left the CPGB in 1948), replacing it both with Zionism and, in the British context, support for the free-market-based liberties of Thatcherism.

Fascism and Anti-Fascism

If there was one overriding issue of concern in the period, it was the struggle against fascism, both in Britain and abroad. As Louis Kenton, a member of the Stepney branch of the YCL said, "in the early 1930s, the movement against fascism became the main thing in the life of most political people in East London, certainly of my group."[55] The focus of the IWM interviews is the Spanish Civil War, but the eighteen interviewees all talk about the anti-fascist struggle in Britain, which they saw as being part of the wider struggle that took them to Spain. The accounts are dominated by a number of themes: the CPGB's role in challenging fascism in the form of the BUF; involvement in the Party's attempts to build its presence in Jewish areas, but also in other areas, like Bethnal Green, where the BUF was strong; the role of street meetings and demonstrations; physical clashes at BUF meetings; and casual street violence at other times that were seen as part of the fascist/anti-fascist struggle.

The CPGB led the struggle against the BUF, although other groups, like the Labour League of Youth (LLoY), and the Independent Labour Party (ILP) were also involved in active opposition to the BUF. In the East End of London, and, in particular, in Stepney, the anti-fascist field was left open to the CPGB partly because of the ambivalent attitude of the local Labour Party. A good deal has been written about the ethnic dimension of politics in East London and the difficulties created in relation to the fascist/anti-fascist struggle. The strength of the Labour Party in Stepney was built on the ethnic Irish vote, and Catholic issues loomed large. In consequence, the fear of communism, both at home and, from 1936 in Spain, meant that the Stepney Labour Party resisted being drawn into the anti-fascist struggle.[56] Indeed, one of the comments made by Jack Shaw was that in "the Labour movement in Stepney there was more anti-Semitism than anywhere else."[57]

The fascist/anti-fascist struggle in the East End was frequently punctuated by violent confrontation between the two elements. The CPGB did not have, in fact, a single view on the best way to combat the BUF, something that was highlighted in the contrasting accounts of Phil Piratin and Joe Jacobs. Piratin's recollections in *Our Flag Stays Red* stressed the importance of political action on a wide front, whereas Jacobs, in *Out of the Ghetto*, was an advocate of the physical force policy. It is clear that whatever the official CPGB line, violence was a key element in the Party's anti-fascism. An example was that given by Joe Garber in relation to the BUF rally at Olympia in 1934. As Garber explained, the violence was not limited to the meeting itself, or to Blackshirt stewards:

> Then someone said, "Look, there's a building site nearby." We [communists] broke it open, and there were all sorts of things in there, bricks, scaffold poles, and there was a lorry, a small lorry. And we waited, and a load of Blackshirts from the provinces, all the county, and the counties, all in their coaches [. . .] and, all of a sudden, one brick went, and a [scaffold] pole, right through the bleeding coach window, and there were screams [from inside].[58]

The use of bricks and scaffold poles is also a reminder that weapons were a far from unknown feature of anti-fascist violence, and appear to have been more frequently used by anti-fascists, compared to fascists.[59] Piratin's account of his struggles within the Stepney party focused on the need for a much broader approach to anti-fascism. In his account, after watching a large crowd of BUF supporters in Bethnal Green, some of whom "wore trade-union badges," he argued that fascist support in the area came from people who

> were living miserable, squalid lives. Their homes were slums, many were unemployed. Those at work were often in low-paid jobs. Therefore we urged that the Communist Party should help the people to improve their conditions of life, in the course of which we could show them who was really responsible for their conditions, and get them organised to fight against their real exploiters.[60]

Piratin claimed successes in this strategy, with BUF members switching their allegiance to the CPGB thanks to the rent strike movement organised by the communists. However, the evidence is that despite this, the majority of Stepney communists were drawn from the Jewish community, who suffered the same socioeconomic conditions.

TESTING IT OUT

Perhaps unsurprisingly, both Mindel and Sherman focused on the issue of fascism and Nazism abroad and in Britain as key factors in their political lives in the 1930s. Famously, Alfred Sherman fought with the International Brigades in Spain[61] prior to wartime service with the British Army, but although Mick Mindel did not go to Spain he did have the extraordinary experience, for a British Jew, of being in Berlin the day that Hitler came to power. Mindel explained how his family background, his studies of Marxism-Leninism, and the political views of his friends drew him closer to the CPGB. This move was confirmed by his experiences of Nazism in Germany and fascism in Britain:

> The question of Hitlerism [was increasingly important], and I had quite an experience of that because I was in Germany in 1932 and I went to Berlin on the day that Hitler came to power, so my need for political analysis turned more to the Communist Party because it was only through the Communist Party that I saw a struggle against fascism. But whether that was absolutely true or not is another political question. But if you ask me how I came to the Communist Party I think it was largely because [of] seeing [. . .] the Blackshirts on the streets of East London.

Alfred Sherman was a little more dismissive, in his old age, of his service in Spain with the International Brigades, saying that volunteering to fight was "the tradition of Byron, of the English part of my background, of Englishmen going to fight valiant causes." There was, in all probability, more to it than that, although, just as Mindel subsequently questioned the CPGB's claim to be the only movement fighting fascism in Britain, Sherman noted that

> [t]he fascist danger [in Britain] was very much deliberately overrated by the Communists, and wherever possible the Communist *provoked* the fascists in order that they should have something to defend against. It was grist to the mill. If it hadn't been for

> the Communists provoking for something to be against, one would have heard very much less of the fascists.

Interestingly, this reflects the view of the Jewish "establishment," in particular the Board of Deputies of British Jews, at the time in Britain, who called upon Jews to stay away from fascist events. Whatever the merits of Sherman's later view, it is certainly the case that the fear of fascism at home as well as abroad was certainly a key driver for Jewish membership of the CPGB in the 1930s.

Socioeconomic Conditions

Poor housing conditions, unemployment, underemployment, and sweatshops were all dominant features of life for many in the Jewish community in East London. As Max Colin explained about his parents' experiences, "they lived in Stepney, in very poor circumstances [. . .] and went through a pretty rough time."[62] The CPGB was to the forefront in opposing landlord abuses, and attempted to tackle the conditions of sweated labor that characterized the garment and cabinet-making industries in particular. Sweating also created hostility among Christian East Enders, as it was seen to be an endemic Jewish issue that was characterized by the BUF and others keen to make anti-Semitic capital, as an example of unfair competition. The Stepney YCL activist Louis Kenton noted that the CPGB ran "a continuing battle in the tailoring industry, which was very, very badly exploited."[63] All these conditions acted as yet another influence on Jews, and references to socioeconomic pressures feature throughout the IWM interviews. The effect was, in Louis Kenton's view, that "[i]n East London it [the CPGB] was a very widespread movement and conditions in East London were such that most people gravitated to the Labour Party and the Left, it was a natural result of the conditions of the period."[64] However, the Labour Party was, as we have seen, dominated by other ethnic interests in Stepney, and, in consequence, the main political choice on offer for Jews was, in the 1930s, the CPGB,[65] both in terms of anti-fascism, and in relation to pressing socioeconomic issues.

TESTING IT OUT

Looking back on a life of political activism, Mick Mindel placed his communism in both an international and a local context. If "socialism was the answer [with] Russia as the first socialist country, the example of Russia was the example that we used," then the questions that needed answering were "anti-Semitism [. . .] unemployment, hunger marches [. . .] the means test" and, where Mindel lived in the East End, "housing conditions, evictions." For Mindel, the CPGB members in Stepney were "part of the people of Stepney," experiencing the same socioeconomic conditions as their neighbors. In his account, Sherman identified areas of Britain that continued to suffer extremes of socioeconomic conditions throughout the inter-war period. Further, he linked the socioeconomic appeal to the ability of the CPGB to make successful ethnic appeals—"it [the CPGB] was, as it were, the party of the 'outs,'" appealing to workers on Clydeside, Merseyside, South Wales, and in Irish and Jewish areas. However, what is interesting here is that the CPGB was far less successful in appealing to the Irish in Britain than it was in appealing the Jewish community, especially following the outbreak of the Spanish Civil War.

Territorialism

The Jewish community in the East End of London was a product of the emigration of refugees from Russia and Romania following a series of pogroms from 1871 to the aftermath of the 1905 Revolution in Russia, which latter exodus saw the largest number of Jewish refugees enter Britain.[66] The nature of the emigration, the background of violent anti-Semitism, and the poverty of the refugees combined to create a Jewish presence in Britain that was quite different from the existing Anglo-Jewish population, characterized by dispersal, and relative socioeconomic prosperity and status. Instead, the Jewish community that emerged in the East End (and, to a lesser extent, in Manchester, Leeds, Glasgow, and Dublin) effectively re-created the ghetto environments of Russia and Romania. As Srebrnik has argued, "by almost any criterion developed by scholars of ethnicity, the Jews of East London in the first half of the twentieth century were a distinct, highly visible, homogenous ethnic group [. . .] They were a community with social solidarity and subjective self-awareness, and they were perceived as such by outsiders."[67] This strong sense of community and the associated sense of neighborhood and territorialism was replicated among Christian East Enders, and in the distinct, pre-Blitz, pre-regeneration geography of the area, that universal sense of community and territory fed into ethnic tensions. Benjamin Lammers has argued that the 1930s saw a slow erosion of this sense of competing ethnic communities thanks to generational changes among Jews, the impact of the cinema (which appealed across cultures), and anti-fascism, in particular the experience of the "Battle of Cable Street."[68] However, the picture presented by the IWM interviewees is of a strong sense of territory, something that was mirrored in accounts by their fascist opponents.[69] Louis Kenton, who was born in Mile End, explained in his interview that people had a clear sense of which streets they could, and could not, safely walk down, noting that "there were always a few streets that were totally non-Jewish, and one or two Blackshirts who lived there would attack us. But it wasn't a thing that happened very often."[70] This territorialism based upon ethnic concentrations was intensified by ethno-political loyalty. Jack Shaw remembered an occasion when he and others attacked unsuspecting fascists who were unfamiliar with the ethno-political geography of the area:

> One lot [of fascists] had a meeting in the Mile End Arena, in Mile End, Blackshirt meeting. And when they came out, they got on the tram, and they didn't realise they were going right into enemy territory, and we got on the tram as well [. . .] quite a few of us. And we beat them up. This was in 1935.[71]

It was this combination of urban territorialism, concentrations of differing ethnic populations in particular streets, associated political loyalties, and youth that helped create a situation where casual violence was far from infrequent.

TESTING IT OUT

There is little doubt that Mick Mindel's experience of day-to-day life and politics in Stepney in the 1930s was highly localized. He was deeply embedded in the life of the community and the workplace in "his" part of the East End. For Mindel his "main love [was] the workers' Jewish unions," and those unions were largely located in the Jewish areas of the East End of London. For all his understanding of Marxism and belief in a materialist concept of history and progress that gave him the "confidence that Marxism was right, that we [communists] knew all the answers to *all* the problems," Mindel's activism was overwhelmingly focused on local people and his understanding of their problems. This appears to have been less the case for Alfred Sherman, according to his testimony. Nonetheless, his pre-Spanish Civil War activism was focused on his home locality of Hackney, where the local CPGB "was mainly Jewish. Jews formed a disproportionately large number in relation to the population [of Hackney]. In a sense, we lived in a semi-ghetto, and the Communist Party was an intellectual and emotional ghetto of its own." So, even for Sherman, who later argued that Jews in the CPGB were in some way no longer Jews, his early experience of communist activism was within the context of a heavily Jewish local communism.

Being Jewish and Choosing the CPGB

In addition to those factors, which can be seen to have drawn Jews to support the CPGB—the "Jewish question," fascism and anti-fascism, socio-economic deprivation, and territorialism and community—there were still other factors that helped propel many Jews toward the Party. These latter factors can be seen to be internal to Jewish life in the period. The evidence provided by the IWM interviewees indicates that family and community histories of radicalism were strong influences that effectively prepared the ground for the appeal of the CPGB. In addition, the IWM data suggest that Heppell's argument that young Jews who supported the CPGB did so at the price of distancing themselves from family and community life was, at the least, a far from universal experience. Instead, the interviewees' evidence indicates that Jewish communal and family life was often integral to their communism; even though there were increasing differences between the generations, marked most clearly by the decline in the use of Yiddish as a daily language, with younger British-born Jews being English speakers with an uncertain fluency in Yiddish. It was also the case that being part of the Communist movement enabled many Jews to look outside of their semi-ghettoized existence, but not at the expense of their Jewish identity or life. Instead, key Jewish organizations, such as Jewish sports clubs and the Jewish Lads' Brigade were essential institutions in the building of Jewish support for the CPGB. David Dee has argued that, for some young Jews at least, sport was an avenue away from their self-identification as Jews toward a more Anglicized identity.[72] However, the evidence of the IWM interviewees does not support this in general, although the difference here may well be as simple a matter of the individual interests of young Jews—sport and politics not necessarily, even in the 1930s, attracting the same enthusiasm. However, the evidence presented here supports the contention of Srebrnik and Smith, that these communists were "Jewish Communists," as opposed to "Communist Jews."

A History of Radicalism

A constant in the majority of interviewees' accounts of their backgrounds is the radicalism of their parents' generation. Fifteen of the interviewees were the children of immigrant Jewish parents, most of whom had come from Russia. They had brought with them histories of involvement with radical politics—anarchism, revolutionary socialism, and Bundism. The majority of the interviewees' parents were no longer active in politics, but family life was marked by political awareness. The interviewees gave very similar accounts of their parents' backgrounds and political beliefs, but with some interesting family history "twists" to their stories. For example, Max Colin's father had been in the Russian army, but his experience of Tsarist anti-Semitism had led him to immigrate to London to avoid service in the Russo-Japanese War of 1905; his wife joined him from Russia the following year and family tensions colored family politics:

> My father professed to being a communist. Actually, he was an anarchist, but, there you are, he got the *Daily Worker* [. . .]. We didn't like our father very much, so we took our mother's side, and we used to say, "Well, if you are a communist, to hell with communism!"[73]

Nonetheless, Max Colin joined the YCL after experiencing police anti-Semitism at the time of the BUF's 1934 Olympia meeting, and went on to serve as a mechanic and ambulance driver in Spain.

Maurice Levitas's father had a radical political background that was a little closer to London. Originating in Lithuania, he had immigrated to Dublin at the end of the nineteenth century along with Levitas's Jewish Latvian mother. In Dublin, Levitas senior was involved with the socialist wing of the Irish Republican movement, and was an acquaintance of James Connolly. The family then moved to the East End of London, via Glasgow, and his father suffered from under-employment, with Maurice Levitas noting that the family was "poverty stricken." Maurice Levitas went on to be the secretary of the Bethnal Green branch of the YCL, and served as a rifleman in the British Battalion of the International Brigades. He remained a communist, and worked as a schoolteacher in the German Democratic Republic from 1985–1991.[74] A further example of this early exposure to radical politics via family life is provided by the parents of Louis Kenton, who said of his parents, "they were both, of course, Jewish, but they were also involved in the Social Democratic movement at that period [prior to the 1905 pogroms] in Kiev."[75] Kenton noted that, once in London, his parents "didn't take a very active part" in politics, but that he, like others, was affected by the general family and community background of radicalism:

> Living in the East End there was a natural radical element throughout my whole youth, so, without being aware of it, I found myself sympathising with the Labour section of the movement, and later the Communist movement [. . .] When I was about 19, 20 [1927 or 1928] I seemed to gravitate naturally towards the [Communist] movement, and I joined the Young Communist League.[76]

The radicalism of the older, first-generation Jewish immigrants was a product of the Jewish experience of life in the Russian Empire, characterized for most of them by a powerful mix of ghettoization, anti-Semitism, poverty, and consequent involvement with radical politics focused on social and economic emancipation and a solution to the "Jewish question" of ending anti-Semitism. It was this background, and the knowledge of it that was transmitted to a new generation of British-born Jews, that made the working-class Jewish community in the East End such an obvious focus for the CPGB. The inheritance of radicalism had, however, undergone a transformation from that which characterized radical, refugee immigrant Jews in the nineteenth and early twentieth century. The children and grandchildren of those Jewish immigrants were British citizens, and no longer legally confined, as had been the case in Tsarist Russia, to the ghetto. Most tellingly, the use of Yiddish went into decline among British-born Jews. By the inter-war period, younger Jews might use Yiddish to talk to their grandparents, but among themselves English was their language. The political importance of this was that the older Jewish radicalism had found expression in Yiddish-speaking organizations and Yiddish-language newspapers and propaganda, and that radicalism was in decline in terms of its generational appeal. Instead, the success of the Russian Revolution and the prestige which that endowed the new Bolshevik parties of the world with, opened up a more modern, more successful revolutionary radicalism that, furthermore, was not confined to Yiddish-speaking refugees.

TESTING IT OUT

There is a very close match between the arguments of men like Max Colin, Maurice Levitas, and Louis Kenton regarding the influence of the older, immigrant refugee radicalism and the views of both Mindel and Sherman. Being a decade older than Sherman, Mick Mindel had a clearer personal picture of the lively, active continuation of Jewish radicalism that, in Mindel's case, his parents had brought with them from Vilna. His father, Morris, was a very active Bundist and librarian of the Workers' Circle, heavily committed to Jewish working-class education, often in Yiddish. As a child, Mick Mindel was also familiar with Jewish anarchists who made their mark in the East End, particularly before the First World War. Even though these currents had, like the Yiddish that sustained them, begun to wane in the aftermath of the Russian Revolution, they had created a fertile seedbed among working-class Jews in Britain, one that the CPGB was able to take advantage of. Alfred Sherman, who was born in 1919, appears to have been less personally aware of the impact of the radical tradition, but he was aware that the older, pre-CPGB, tradition was dying in the East End of London, just as the Yiddish that sustained it was: "In the '30s and '40s, you wouldn't have got very far with Yiddish [. . .] in the heart of the East End [. . .] by and large Yiddish would have been used by the Bund more, who were trying to revive in this country the large Jewish organisation they had in the Russian Empire." This decline in the significance of Yiddish for radical Jewish politics in Britain is of interest in that it seems to be at odds with the continuing importance of Yiddish in the worldwide Jewish Communist movement. Why this was the case is unclear, but, speculating, one might connect the fact that Britain in the 1930s was not only still a premier global power, but was also the mandatory power in Palestine. As such, developments in terms of Jewish migration to Palestine, or support for Jewish settlement there, depended to a large degree on Britain. The language of the key power, therefore, was English, and, for many, it seemed that English would be of significance for Jews with an interest, whether Zionist or not, in the future status of Palestine. Indeed, it was that connection, between the British Empire, Palestine, and Zionism that underpinned official communist hostility to Zionism as a force allied to imperialism. Given this background, it may have been these influences that helped accelerate a drift away from Yiddish among young, English-speaking Jewish Communists in Britain, particularly in London, the imperial capital.

Jewish Life: Family, Leisure, and Culture

Raphael Samuel gave a rich account of his communist childhood and youth, which revealed a family life that combined elements of communist and Jewish culture, and one that was not characterized by a generational rift resulting from the younger family members' allegiance to communism. For example, Samuel remembered "my grandmother, a religious woman, was tolerant of this family Communism, and the Passovers which we held out of respect for her would begin with Hebrew prayers and end with Soviet songs."[77] Younger Jews might have newer political loyalties and speak English, but there were still very strong family and community ties. Among the IWM interviewees there is no sense either of generational divisions as a result of younger family members' communism. In part, this may be a result of the bias of the interview sample, with interviewees coming from families that already had a history of radicalism; however, there is no sense that the interviewees did not regard themselves as Jewish. Only one interviewee, the Slough-born Frank Frankford, who was a member of the Hackney branch of the CPGB and the NUWM, said that, "unfortunately, I can't claim to be Jewish because my mother was a Gentile. My father was a Jew, he was on the Manchester Jewish Board of Guardians."[78] Interestingly, Frankford left the CPGB because "I got fed up with the Communist Party, because they didn't seem to have any opinion until they'd read the next day's *Daily Worker*."[79] He went on to fight for the Spanish Republic as part of the ILP contingent with the POUM, and had a somewhat controversial history there, becoming embroiled in dangerous intra-left rivalry.[80] By way of contrast, another interviewee, Julius "Jud" Colman, came from an Orthodox Jewish background, his parents being émigrés from Lithuania and Latvia. Colman made no mention of intergenerational tensions in his account of communism in Cheetham, Manchester, where he joined the YCL as a 15-year-old in 1932.[81]

Although there is no evidence in the interviewees' accounts of intergenerational division caused by allegiances to communism, there is a sense that, for some of the interviewees at least, communism was welcomed, in part, because it was a way of making contacts outside the Jewish community. For example, Jack Shaw made a strong point about his preference for a broad alliance, based on class and anti-fascism, rather than on Jewish interests alone:

> I joined the YCL because that was the only organisation that was fighting fascism, and we got an education [in that] we learned how to mix with Christian people, not to be suspicious of them.

> [. . .] There was a Jewish organisation called the Blue and White Shirts, but, to me, it was nothing. To me it was too Jewish. And I didn't believe in it. We should be, not just Anglicized, but the Christian people are with us, not just one Jewish section.[82]

A very similar point was made by interviewees in relation to anti-fascists involved in the Cable Street demonstration, and, more generally, in terms of the CPGB, with, for example, Maurice Levitas noting that although a lot of the CPGB and YCL members in Bethnal Green were Jews, "some of them were not, these were non-Jews who understood what fascism meant."[83]

The other common experience of the interviewees was their involvement in youth clubs, which were centers of Jewish community life, sport and culture, and politics. Foremost among these clubs were those formed by the YCL, but also by groups like the Jewish Lads' Brigade (JLB). The clubs provided places to enjoy boxing, athletics, cycling, and the interviewees also describe how they were, in effect, foci for young Jewish social and political life. Charlie Goodman remembered, "at that time [mid-1930s] there were 18 Jewish youth clubs in [. . .] Stepney, Poplar and Bethnal Green [. . .] and we were all into boxing and football."[84] The same applied in Cheetham, Manchester, according to Julius Colman, who was in the local Jewish Lads' Brigade. Colman explained that almost all of the members of his local brigade joined the YCL club too.[85] The CPGB appears to have taken advantage of the potential for comparatively large-scale recruiting among Jewish youth clubs. Colman explained that in Cheetham, most of the Jewish Lads' Brigade were also members of the local branch of the YCL, and, together, they formed the core of a wider anti-fascist group that was active not only in anti-fascist politics, but also in other campaigns:

> We used to sell *Challenge*, the [YCL's] newspaper, we used to have meetings a lot, we used to chalk, political campaigns [. . .] When the fascists got stronger, we formed what was called the "Youth Front," a group, all anti-fascist, communist controlled, naturally [. . .] it was a Jewish area, [and] a mixed area, a lot of politics [. . .] there were non-Jews in it, but mostly Jews.[86]

Maurice Levitas also gave an account of how important the Jewish Lads' Brigade was to the YCL in Bethnal Green, with the membership of the JLB forming a leading element in the CPGB's attempts to challenge the BUF in its East London heartland. Levitas noted that winning over the JLB was

> one of the big beginnings of the YCL [in Bethnal Green]. In fact, we had the whole of the Jewish Lads' Brigade bugle band [. . .] who came over to the YCL. And that bugle band headed our marches down from the Salmon and Ball [public house] down to BUF headquarters in Roman Road.[87]

These Jewish youth groups proved important for the CPGB, not only as recruiting centers, but also for the potential they represented for quickly mobilising young anti-fascist activists. Max Colin remembered how he and other members of his largely Jewish YCL club were mobilized for the BUF Olympia meeting in June 1934. Colin was in the YCL club (although not at that time a member of the YCL) for social and sporting reasons, and, in fact, met Blackshirts in his job as a mechanic as he was responsible for servicing the BUF vans:

> I was very non-political. But, a particular night in the club one of the other chaps said, "Don't forget boys, all out at Olympia! Against Mosley! All out at Olympia against Mosley!" So, [me and] my mate, who also wasn't very political [went].[88]

For Colin, the Olympia meeting was "an eye-opener," not because of the BUF as he did not see any of the violence, but because of anti-Jewish remarks made to him and his friend by two policemen who told them to "get back to the fucking East End, you Jew bastards."[89] That incident, in addition to seeing police horses being ridden at anti-fascists near Olympia, pushed him into the YCL.

The picture created by the IWM interviewees is one where there was a close intermingling of Jewish youth clubs and organizations and the Young Communist League. There is no sense that being a member of the YCL, or the CPGB, had any negative impact on membership of Jewish youth organizations. The young Jewish members of the JLB, or a Jewish sports club did not sacrifice their standing among their Jewish peers by joining the YCL, or the CPGB, rather they appear to have enhanced it.

TESTING IT OUT

Both Mindel and Sherman gave a clearer sense of intergenerational tensions surrounding the role of the CPGB than did the IWM interviewees. The foci of those tensions was, in Mindel's case, his father's Bundism and his father's more accurate assessment of the veracity of the boast that the Soviet Union had "solved" the "Jewish question." In Sherman's assessment, the tensions grew out of younger, English-speaking Jews finding their Jewishness problematic and wishing to find "a new religion, a new identity—so you became a communist." But if Sherman was, in effect, arguing that Jews in the CPGB were "Communist Jews" rather than "Jewish Communists," he was also aware that because so many younger British Jews joined or followed the CPGB they ended up "mixing up with [even more] other Jews in the search for this [new] identity." Sherman's much later view of this, as a Zionist, was that he and his fellow "Communist Jews" had merely been "whoring after strange gods." Nonetheless, Sherman's argument, as he was aware, still meant that Jews who joined the CPGB had not strayed that far from their Jewishness, precisely because so many other Jews had done the same thing. Just as, later, so many more Jews, including former members and supporters of the CPGB, would shift their allegiance to Zionism.

Conclusions: Jews, Jewishness, and the CPGB

I have attempted here to review the slow recognition of the importance to the CPGB of support from the Jewish community in Britain, particularly from the mid-1930s until the early 1950s. The linkage between significant parts of the working-class Jewish population, particularly in the East End of London, but also in other areas such as Manchester, Leeds, and Glasgow, has only recently begun to gain the historical attention that it deserves. However, only a small number of writers have attempted to understand the meaning of that adherence to Jews who joined or followed the CPGB. A key issue in interpretations of Jewish support for the CPGB revolves around the degree to which such supporters were "Jewish Communists" as opposed to "Communist Jews." In this chapter, I have attempted to examine a six-part model of Jewish support for the CPGB in the 1930s that I developed in an earlier article in the journal *Socialist History*. In that piece I drew upon oral history holdings at the IWM, and while it is the case that "no single source or combination of them can ever give a picture of the total complexity of reality,"[90] this source allowed a textured and detailed picture of this group of activists' accounts of their lives, their communism, their anti-fascism, and their sense of their Jewishness to be created. I have further attempted here to test that model by using two detailed and lengthy interviews carried out by Andrew Whitehead with two significant figures—the lifelong Jewish trade unionist and communist, Mick Mindel, and the communist Spanish Civil War veteran, but later Zionist and British Conservative, Sir Alfred Sherman. The perspectives of these two Jewish activists, whose paths converged for a time in the 1930s and 1940s, while different in detail, particularly given Sherman's Zionism, still enables a conclusion that although "the ethnic identity of Jews [is] fluid, formed in interaction with other forms of identity and in a process determined by specific social and historical conditions,"[91] for very many working-class Jews, particularly in the East End of London (but also in Manchester, Leeds, and Glasgow), their contribution to the CPGB was as "Jewish Communists." For the majority of these communists their ideological commitment to Marxism-Leninism did not mean that they had abandoned a sense of their Jewishness.

Notes

1. Francis Beckett, *The Enemy Within: The Rise and Fall of the British Communist Party* (London: John Murray, 1995).

2. Beckett, *Enemy Within*, 129.

3. Beckett, *Enemy Within*, 147.

4. Interestingly, Beckett might have been regarded as well placed to discuss the questions of Jewishness, identity, and ideology. He subsequently wrote a poignant life of his father, John Beckett, whose own mother came from an Orthodox Jewish family which disowned her when she married "out." John Beckett's own political trajectory followed the not uncommon interwar path from ardent socialist to fascist, but, despite his maternal inheritance, he went on to become one of Britain's most infamous Nazis, and a close friend of William Joyce. Francis Beckett, whose partner, and the mother of his children, was Rosa Cohen, dealt with the difficult subject of his father's life in *The Rebel Who Lost His Cause: The Tragedy of John Beckett MP* (London: Allison and Busby, 1999).

5. Phil Piratin, *Our Flag Stays Red* (London: Thames, 1948; Lawrence and Wishart edition, 1978), 33–49.

6. Kevin Marsh and Robert Griffiths, *Granite and Honey: The Story of Phil Piratin, Communist MP* (London: Manifesto Press, 2012), 35.

7. Marsh and Griffiths, *Granite and Honey*, 192–93.

8. Marsh and Griffiths, *Granite and Honey*, 59.

9. Marsh and Griffiths, *Granite and Honey*, 161.

10. Martin Sugarman, "Against Fascism—Jews who served in The International Brigade in the Spanish Civil War": http://www.jewishvirtuallibrary.org/jsource/History/spanjews.pdf. Accessed, June 25, 2013.

11. Sugarman, "Against Fascism," 1.

12. Stephan E. C. Wendehorst, *British Jewry, Zionism, and the Jewish State* (Oxford: Oxford University Press, 2012), 89–90, 238, 245.

13. Quoted in R. F. Andrews, *What Lenin Said About the Jews; Extracts from His Writings* (London: Utopia Press, 1934), 9.

14. Wendehorst, *British Jewry, Zionism, and the Jewish State*, 106.

15. Henry Felix Srebrnik, *London Jews and British Communism, 1935–1945* (London: Frank Cass/Vallentine Mitchell, 1995), note 5, 202.

16. The term (borrowed from the title of Graham Greene's 1951 novel) is Stephan Wendehorst's description of the estrangement of many Jews from communism from 1956 onwards. Wendehorst, *British Jewry, Zionism, and the Jewish State*, 104–07.

17. Henry Pelling, *The British Communist Party: A Historical Profile* (London: Adam and Charles Black, 1958), 83 (1975 paperback edition).

18. Kenneth Newton, *The Sociology of British Communism* (London: Allan Lane, 1969), 80.

19. Noreen Branson, *History of the Communist Party of Great Britain, 1927–1941* (London: Lawrence and Wishart, 1985).

20. Willie Thompson, *The Good Old Cause* (London: Pluto Press, 1992).

21. Joe Jacobs, *Out of the Ghetto: My Youth in the East End: Communism and Fascism, 1913–1939* (London: Simon, 1978).

22. See in particular, Henry F. Srebrnik, "The Jewish Communist Movement in Stepney: Ideological Mobilization and Political Victories in an East London Borough, 1935–1945" (PhD thesis, University of Birmingham, 1984); H. F. Srebrnik, "The British Communist Party's National Jewish Committee and the fight against Anti-Semitism during the Second World War," in *The Politics of Marginality: Race, the Radical Right and Minorities in Twentieth Century Britain*, eds. Tony Kushner and Kenneth Lunn (London: Frank Cass, 1990): 82–96; and H. F. Srebrnik, "Communism and Pro-Soviet feeling among the Jews of East London, 1935–45," *Immigrants and Minorities* 5, No. 3 (1986): 285–304; Elaine Rosa Smith, "Jewish Responses to Political anti-Semitism and Fascism in the East End of London, 1920–1939," in *Traditions of Intolerance: Historical Perspectives on Fascism and Race Discourse in Britain*, eds. Tony Kushner and Kenneth Lunn (Manchester: Manchester University Press, 1989): 53–71; and Elaine Rosa Smith, "East End Jews in Politics, 1918–1939: A Study in Class and Ethnicity" (PhD thesis, University of Leicester, 1990).

23. See, in particular, Jason L. Heppell, "A Question of 'Jewish Politics'? The Jewish Section of the Communist Party of Great Britain, 1936–45," in *Jews, Labour and the Left, 1918–1948*, eds. Christine Collette and Stephen Bird (Aldershot: Ashgate, 2000): 93–121; and Jason L. Heppell, "A Rebel not a Rabbi: Jewish Membership of the Communist Party of Great Britain," *Twentieth Century British History* 15, No. 1 (2004): 28–50.

24. James K. Hopkins, *Into the Heart of the Fire: the British in the Spanish Civil War* (Stanford, CA: Stanford University Press, 1998), 143–44.

25. Richard Baxell, *Unlikely Warriors: The British in the Spanish Civil War and the Struggle Against Fascism* (London: Aurum Press, 2012). Apart from acknowledging the impact of fascism in Britain and abroad as a motive for Jewish volunteers for Spain, Baxell says little more; his most pertinent comments can be found on pages 41, 56, and 71.

26. Andrew Thorpe, "The Membership of the Communist Party of Great Britain, 1920–1945," *The Historical Journal* 43, No. 3 (2000): 777–800.

27. Thomas Linehan, *Communism in Britain, 1920–39: From the Cradle to the Grave* (Manchester: Manchester University Press, 2007).

28. Thomas Linehan, "Communist Activism in Interwar Britain: Motivation, Belonging and Political Religion," *Socialist History* No. 32 (2008): 1–17; Raphael Samuel, "The Lost World of British Communism," *New Left Review* No. 154 (1985): 3–54.

29. Thomas Linehan, "Communist Culture and Anti-fascism in Inter-war Britain," in *Varieties of Anti-Fascism: Britain in the Inter-War Period*, eds. Nigel Copsey and Andrzej Olechnowicz (London: Palgrave Macmillan, 2010), 49.

30. Kevin Morgan, Gidon Cohen, and Andrew Flinn, *Communists and British Society 1920–1991* (London: Rivers Oram Press, 2007), particularly 184–96.

31. Wendehorst, *British Jewry, Zionism, and the Jewish State*, especially 92–104.

32. Heppell, "A Question of 'Jewish Politics?,'" 108.

33. Marsh and Griffiths, *Granite and Honey*, viii.

34. Stephen M. Cullen, "'Jewish Communists' or 'Communist Jews'? The Communist Party of Great Britain and British Jews in the 1930s," *Socialist History* No. 40 (2012): 22–42

35. Imperial War Museum, *The Spanish Civil War Collection: Sound Archive, Oral History Recordings* (London: IWM, 1996), ii.

36. Also included in the archive are civilian reminiscences of the war, women involved in Spain or in the Aid Spain movement, journalists and a small number of volunteers with the Nationalists. The catalogue is a little unclear in some ways, with double counting, for example, of men who fell under more than one category of interview. Further, a few additional interviews have been added to the sound archive since the publication of the catalogue.

37. John Brewer, "Microhistory and the Histories of Everyday Life," *Cultural and Social History* 7, No. 1 (2010): 99.

38. I am extremely grateful for Andrew Whitehead's permission to use his valuable recordings of Alfred Sherman and Mick Mindel. Andrew Whitehead had the great foresight to interview a range of Jewish political activists from the early and mid-twentieth century, and this oral history, informed by his historical fascination with London life and politics, has made a real contribution to our understanding of the topic under discussion here. See, http://www.andrewwhitehead.net/. Accessed June 26, 2013.

39. See Paul Kelemen, "British Communists and the Palestine Conflict, 1929–1948," *Holy Land Studies* 5, No. 2 (2006): 131–53; and Henry Felix Srebrnik, "Sidestepping the Contradictions: the Communist Party, Jewish Communists and Zionism, 1935–1948," in *Opening the Books; Essays on the Social and Cultural History of the British Communist Party*, eds. Geoff Andrews, Nina Fishman, Kevin Morgan (London: Pluto Press, 1995): 124–41.

40. Smith's comment on the by-election was that "Pollitt aimed his campaign almost exclusively at Jewish voters." Smith, "East End Jews in Politics," 194.

41. Douglas Hyde, *I Believed* (Kingswood: William Heinemann, 1951), 187–88.

42. Manchester had been a key area for Jewish involvement with the CPGB even in the 1920s; see, Morgan, Cohen, Flinn, *Communists and British Society 1920–1991*, 190–91.

43. Wendehorst, *British Jewry, Zionism, and the Jewish State*, 93–94.

44. Srebrnik, *London Jews and British Communism, 1935–1945*, 19.

45. R.F. Andrews, *What Lenin Said About the Jews*, 2–3.

46. Jack Louis Shaw, IWM sound archive, 13547.

47. Maurice Levitas, IWM sound archive, 16358.

48. Thompson, *The Good Old Cause*, 93–94; Tony Kushner, "Jewish Communists in Twentieth-Century Britain: The Zaidman Collection," *Labour History Review*, 55 (1990): 71; Pelling, *The British Communist Party*, 167–69; Wendehorst, *British Jewry, Zionism, and the Jewish State*, 104–07.

49. Louis Kenton, IWM sound archive, 9374.

50. Smith, "East End Jews in Politics," 271. The Legion had its headquarters in Whitehorse Lane, Mile End.

51. Kelemen, "British Communists and the Palestine Conflict," 143–44.

52. Mick Mindel, recorded interview with Andrew Whitehead, March 13, 1988. Unless otherwise stated all subsequent quotations from Mick Mindel are from this source.

53. Jonathan Freedland, *Jacob's Gift: A Journey into the Heart of Belonging* (London: Hamish Hamilton, 2005): 96.

54. Sir Alfred Sherman, recorded interview with Andrew Whitehead, Feb. 29, 1990. Unless otherwise stated all subsequent quotations from Alfred Sherman are from this source.

55. Louis Kenton, IWM sound archive, 9374.

56. See, for example, Srebrnik, *London Jews and British Communism*, 4–11; Henry Felix Srebrnik, "Class, Ethnicity and Gender Intertwined: Jewish Women and the East End London Rent Strikes, 1935–1940," *Women's History Review* 4, No. 3 (1995): 283–99; and Thomas P. Linehan, *East London for Mosley: The British Union of Fascists in East London and South-West Essex, 1933–40* (London: Taylor an Francis, 1996), 80–84. For a more positive, and nuanced view of inter-ethnic relations and the fascist/anti-fascist struggle, see Benjamin J. Lammers, "The Birth of the East Ender: Neighborhood and Local Identity in Interwar East London," *Journal of Social History* 39, No. 2 (2005): 331–44.

57. Jack Louis Shaw, IWM sound archive, 13547.

58. Joe Garber, IWM sound archive, 12291. Garber served for a while as a machine gunner in the 15th International Brigade, then spent nearly two years as a secret policeman with the Servicio de Investigación Militar (SIM).

59. Stephen M. Cullen, "Political Violence: the Case of the British Union of Fascists," *Journal of Contemporary History* 28, No. 3 (1993): 245–67.

60. Piratin, *Our Flag Stays Red*, 18.

61. The most recent history of British volunteers in the Spanish Civil War contains a photograph of a fine sketch portrait of Sherman by Clive Branson,

drawn at San Pedro de Cardeña. Baxell, *Unlikely Warriors*, illustration between pages 244 and 245.

62. Max Colin, IWM sound archive, 8639.

63. Louis Kenton, IWM sound archive, 9374.

64. Louis Kenton, IWM sound archive, 9374.

65. The Jewish community had a previous strong link to the Liberal Party, which dated back to formative experiences for east London Jews, particularly anti-alien agitation, and the 1904 Conservative government Aliens Bill, but during the 1920s, the Liberal Party was a declining force.

66. Catherine Jones, *Immigration and Social Policy in Britain* (London: Tavistock Publications, 1977), 66–117.

67. Srebrnik, *London Jews and British Communism*, 4.

68. Benjamin Lammers, "The Birth of the East Ender: Neighborhood and Local Identity in Interwar East London." For an introduction to debates surrounding Cable Street, see the essays in Tony Kushner and Nadia Valman, *Remembering Cable Street: Fascism and Anti-fascism in British Society* (London: Vallentine Mitchell, 2000).

69. Interviews with former East End members of the BUF, undertaken in the mid-1980s by the present author, also present the East End as an area characterized by community, neighborhood, street, family, and, hence, a strong sense of territory. See Stephen M. Cullen, "The British Union of Fascists, 1932–1940: Ideology, Membership and Meetings" (MLitt thesis, University of Oxford, 1987), 108–47.

70. Louis Kenton, IWM sound archive, 9374.

71. Jack Shaw, IWM sound archive, 13547.

72. David Dee, " 'Too Semitic' or 'Thoroughly Anglicised'? The Life and Career of Harold Abrahams," *The International Journal of the History of Sport* 29, No. 6 (2012): 868–86; " 'The Hefty Hebrew': Boxing and British Jewish Identity, 1890–1960," *Sport in History* 32, No. 3 (2012): 361–81. See also Dee's unpublished paper, "A Means of 'Escape'? British Jewry, Communism and Sport, 1920–1950" (paper presented at the Social History Society Annual Conference, March 25, 2013).

73. Max Colin, IWM sound archive, 8639.

74. Maurice Levitas, IWM sound archive, 16358.

75. Louis Kenton, IWM sound archive, 9374.

76. Louis Kenton, IWM sound archive, 9374.

77. Raphael Samuel, "The Lost World of British Communism," 50.

78. Frank Frankford, IWM sound archive, 9308.

79. Frank Frankford, IWM sound archive, 9308.

80. Frankford was well known for his dislike of George Orwell, whom he met in Spain, and, more controversially, for his accusations (made under duress) that the POUM militia were a fascist "Fifth Column"; on this see, for example, Gordon Bowker, *George Orwell* (London: Little, Brown and Company, 2003), 218 and 234; and Bernard Crick, *George Orwell: A Life* (Harmondsworth: Penguin, 1992 edition), 346–48. This account also provides Frankford's version of events and the *Daily Worker*'s subsequent interpretation of his statement.

81. Julius "Jud" Colman, IWM sound archive, 14575.
82. Jack Louis Shaw, IWM sound archive, 13547.
83. Maurice Levitas, IWM sound archive 16358.
84. Charlie Goodman, IWM sound archive, 16612.
85. Julius "Jud" Colman, IWM sound archive, 14575.
86. Julius "Jud" Colman, IWM sound archive, 14575.
87. Maurice Levitas, IWM sound archive, 16358.
88. Max Colin, IWM sound archive, 8639.
89. Max Colin, IWM sound archive, 8639.
90. Valerie Yow, *Recording Oral History: A Guide for the Humanities and Social Sciences* (Walnut Creek, CA: Altamira Press, 2005), 21, quoted by R. Kenneth Kirby, "Phenomenology and the Problems of Oral History," *The Oral History Review* 35 (2008), 29.
91. Kelemen, "British Communists and the Palestine Conflict," 133.

8

Jewish Communism in Australia

PHILIP MENDES

Jewish Communism in Australia was a relatively minor affair. There was only a small group of working-class Jews in Australia, and the Communist Party displayed minimal interest in the Jewish community as a potential constituency. Consequently, the Jewish presence in the Communist Party and its associated trade unions and front groups was relatively small compared to most other English-speaking countries. Nevertheless, for a short period of time from approximately 1942–1950, Jewish Communists and their allies—primarily the nominally non-Communist Melbourne Jewish Council to Combat Fascism and Anti-Semitism and associated groups in the other major Jewish population center of Sydney[1]—attained a significant presence in the Jewish community.

This influence reflected a number of factors including the wartime alliance between the Western Allies and the Soviet Union from 1941 through 1945, the consistent stand of Australian Communists against anti-Semitism, and the strong support from the Soviet Union and local Communists for the creation of the State of Israel. Conversely, the onset of the Cold War and associated McCarthyism quickly narrowed the parameters of acceptable Jewish political behavior. Groups such as the Jewish Council and the associated Jewish Progressive Centre were quickly excluded from the mainstream Jewish community. The Jewish Communists' apologia for Soviet Anti-Semitism via their defense of the Slansky Trial in Czechoslovakia in late 1952 and the Doctors' Plot in the Soviet Union in early 1953 led to their permanent marginalization.

In part one, we examine the early manifestations of Australian Jewish Communism as a mostly Eastern European immigrant phenomenon. In part two, we examine the Jewish role in the Communist Party including associated Jewish Communist groups such as the Jewish Progressive Centre and the Kadimah Youth Organisation. In part three, we consider the rise and fall of the Jewish Council. In the conclusion, part four, we discuss why Jewish Communism in Australia was so short-lived and relatively insignificant.

Part One: Beginnings

Prior to the 1920s, Australian Jewry was small in number, comprising a relatively assimilated community of approximately 22,000 persons, mostly of British or German origin. A few individual Jews joined left-wing groups including the Communist Party,[2] but there was no organized Jewish-left subculture. This situation changed with the migration of 2,000 European Jews from Eastern Europe to Australia between 1921 and 1930, of whom about 1,400 settled in Melbourne. Further substantial pre-war and post-war immigration lifted Jewish numbers to approximately 35,000 by 1947. Many of these immigrants struggled to make a living at the lower end of the socioeconomic spectrum.[3]

Stan Robe, a Polish-born Jew who arrived in Melbourne in 1926 at the age of seventeen recalls the impact of this Eastern European immigration:

> They were poor Jews in the main. They came from little townships, from factories and workshops in the bigger cities, occasionally from the professional and entrepreneurial class. Their politics in the land of their birth had been, for the most part, tending towards the Left. Bundist, Labour or extreme Left were the spheres in which they lived and on arrival here they tried to reproduce the atmosphere of home including their political outlook.[4]

The new immigrants congregated in the Melbourne suburbs of Carlton and Brunswick, and promptly developed their own religious and cultural life, social groups, welfare services, and political organizations. The first political institution founded by the newcomers in 1928 was called the Jewish Polish Cultural Society. Formed by a group of mostly small businessmen, the Society attempted to provide a forum for political discussion amongst radically inclined Polish-speaking Jews. In 1929, the name of the Society was changed to the Jewish Socialist Group in an attempt to create a more specifically political organization open to Jews from all backgrounds.[5]

The first major Jewish-left group, the Gezerd, named after a Soviet organization settling Jews on agricultural farms, was formed by leaders of the Jewish Socialist Group and other immigrants active in the Friends of Yiddish Schools in Poland group in 1930. It was followed shortly after by a smaller Sydney Gezerd. The aim of the Gezerd, meaning "back to earth," was to support the settlement of Jews in the Soviet region of Birobidzhan, a faraway Asiatic province of the USSR where the Bolsheviks hoped to establish a Jewish homeland. A pamphlet published by the Sydney Gezerd praised the assistance given by the Soviet Union to the persecuted Jews of the world: "Here is the one corner in the world where the Jew is given security in the present and hope for the future . . . Russia has given the Jew the opportunity of remaking himself into a self-respecting, self-supporting member of a Socialist society."[6]

The Gezerd described itself as a Socialist organization committed to Jewish national culture. Anti-communists in the Jewish community quickly and aggressively contested its claim to represent a legitimate Jewish viewpoint, yet by 1933 the Gezerd had several hundred members and supporters and had become the most vocal and active anti-fascist organization in Jewish circles. Initially, the Gezerd included a range of left-wing perspectives including Bundists, Poale Zion supporters, some Communists, and other non-aligned leftists. There were friendly but informal links with the Communist Party, which at times exerted a dominant and doctrinaire influence on the organization. For example, a leading Bundist (and member of the founding Gezerd Committee), Sender Burstin, was publicly expelled in 1932 as an alleged "social fascist" for opposing imposition of a narrow pro-Soviet agenda. About thirty other Bundists resigned in sympathy.[7]

In addition to raising significant funds for Birobidzhan, the Gezerd participated in various left-wing campaigns to combat war, oppose unemployment and associated housing evictions during the Depression, support the Spanish Republic, and defend free speech. It also formed a joint committee in 1935 with the anti-communist Jewish Labour Bund to boycott German goods and campaign against Nazi Germany, but this alliance was short-lived due to a political disagreement. The Gezerd established its own headquarters titled "Cultural House" in Rathdowne Street, Carlton; created a functioning Youth Section; organized a library; and offered English classes and lectures on Australian history to new immigrants. However, the organization declined during the war due to its narrow immigrant base and its sectarian support of the Soviet Union, particularly at the time of the unpopular Nazi-Soviet pact. It was dissolved in 1944.[8]

Part Two: The Rise and Fall of Jewish Communism

It has been estimated that only a few hundred Australian Jews were active members or supporters of communist groups at any one time, and they never comprised a numerically significant grouping within Australian Communism.[9] This remains the case even when taking into account both the relatively small membership of the Communist Party of Australia (which peaked at 23,000 in 1945 and quickly declined to 12,000 in 1947 and about 6,000 by 1952),[10] and the relatively small Jewish population discussed above.

Nevertheless, for a short period of time from approximately 1942 to 1950, communists were visible within the Jewish community, not only within marginal left-wing groups such as the Gezerd and later the Jewish Progressive Centre, but also within more mainstream organizations ranging from the pro-Soviet but nominally non-communist Melbourne Jewish Council to Combat Fascism and Anti-Semitism to the Melbourne Jewish Youth Council. Memoirs from the period suggest that communists were viewed as a legitimate component of Jewish life seriously competing with Zionists and Bundists for ideological dominance.[11]

Jews were drawn to the Communist movement by a number of factors. Foremost was the strong opposition of the Communist Party of Australia (CPA) to anti-Semitism, and its stated commitment to equality for Jews. As early as 1939, for example, the Communist Party's chief political spokesman, Lance Sharkey, condemned anti-Semitism "as a menace to the Labor movement." Sharkey pointed out that anti-Semitism—despite the exploitative practices of some Jewish employers—served the purposes of political reaction by diverting the workers from the class struggle against the real capitalist enemy. Sharkey refuted Nazi allegations of Jewish control of international capitalism and finance, noting that none of the big capitalists in Germany, the United States, Great Britain, or Australia were Jewish.[12] Similarly, the Party's youth organization, the Eureka Youth League (EYL), issued a pamphlet condemning anti-Semitism, which it associated with machinations by big employers to suppress workers' rights.[13]

The EYL provided a warm welcome to Jews participating in its activities. One member of the Kadimah Youth Organization who attended its summer holiday camp commented:

> That Jews, especially Jewish youth, should feel at home in such an environment is easily understood . . . Nowhere else in this country have I yet witnessed such a feeling of equality between gentiles of different creeds and Jews . . . We sang some Yiddish folk songs, which were heartily appreciated. In sports activities, we had an all-Jewish volleyball team. We called ourselves "Judeans." For the duration of the camp we were a group of young Jews, who made no attempt to hide their identity, simply because to have done so would have been a thing unheard of in EYL activities. We felt equal—we were equal—not just merely being tolerated.[14]

Another important factor was the Party's strong support for Israel during the 1947–1948 conflict. Despite its historical anti-Zionism, the CPA welcomed the United Nations' decision to partition Palestine into Jewish and Arab states in 1947, stating that they "rejoice with the Jewish people in the decision of the United Nations, which opens up the possibility of a new future for the Jews in Palestine."[15] The CPA consistently supported Israel during the war. A pamphlet written by Ralph Gibson equated the Jewish struggle in Palestine with similar anti-imperialist struggles in China, Vietnam, and Greece. He denied that there was any explicit conflict between Jews and Arabs in Palestine, and claimed that the Palestinian Arabs who "outnumber the Jews by two to one could not be incited to violence against them on any large scale. The present war on the Jews is being waged by kings from outside the country." He attacked the British imperialists and the Arab reactionaries for their "barbarous attacks" on the new state of Israel, and demanded that the Australian Government immediately recognize Israel.[16]

Jewish support for the CPA took three principal forms. First, there were three identifiable organized Jewish blocs within the Party. The earliest Victorian Jewish CPA faction existed in the 1930s and consisted of approximately a dozen persons. This faction was led by Nat Seeligson, the secretary of the Victorian Branch of the Movement against War and Fascism, and included both Jews actively involved in the Gezerd and those whose links with the Jewish community were more tenuous. A similar small Jewish faction was formed in Sydney under the leadership of Polish-born Bella Weiner, which was instrumental in establishing a Jewish Youth Theatre. However, both fractions were dissolved by the Party in 1943 under the pretext that the Party could not tolerate ethnic separatism.[17]

Far more important was the revitalized Jewish fraction of the late 1940s and early 1950s, which included some forty to forty-five mainly youthful and mostly immigrant activists from the Melbourne suburb of Carlton. These were Jewish-identifying Communists who were actively engaged with Jewish life and culture. Many of these young people were politicized during the war by participation in informal discussion groups conducted by students at local high schools. Some joined the Carlton Branch of the Eureka Youth League, and in later years both the Melbourne University Labour Club and the University Communist Party branch.[18]

A number became active in specifically Jewish youth groups such as the Melbourne Jewish Youth Council, the Jewish Students Study Group, and the Kadimah Younger Set (KYS), which was based at the large Yiddish-speaking Kadimah Cultural Centre in Carlton. In 1946, a small group of communist and pro-communist activists took control of the KYS, and renamed it the Kadimah Youth Organization (KYO). The KYO, which consisted of about 250 young people aged ten to thirty years, published a journal called *Jewish Youth*, which addressed a range of topics in English, Hebrew, and Yiddish, and held numerous public forums on specifically Jewish and broader political and cultural issues. The KYO formed close links with the Jewish Council, and its older members became active in the Council's Youth Section. It was influential within the Melbourne Jewish Youth Council, which incorporated thirteen youth groups representing Zionist, student, cultural, and social perspectives. The KYO was later expelled from the now Bundist-dominated Kadimah Centre in 1951 after voting to send a delegate to the Soviet-controlled Berlin Youth Festival. [19]

A third Jewish grouping consisted of the older Yiddish-speaking Polish Jews involved in the Jewish Progressive Centre, which we discuss below.

In addition, a number of Jews played prominent roles in the CPA leadership. They included leading figures such as the Aarons brothers, Laurie, Eric, and Sam; Bernie Taft and his son Mark Taft; Harry Stein; the writer Judah Waten; and Teachers Federation leader, Sam Lewis. But only Bernie Taft, who spoke both Hebrew and Yiddish, seriously identified with Jewish life. He stated:

> I never felt my Jewishness to be in contradiction to my Communist views. I was somewhat proud to be a Socialist and a Jew, particularly looking at the Jewish contribution to history and to culture. I always regarded my Jewishness as an extra gift and bonus.[20]

In contrast, most of the other leaders of Jewish background were arguably non-Jewish Jews[21] as reflected in their biographies, which suggest little or no engagement with Jewish culture.[22] And whilst Judah Waten included a number of Jewish themes in his novels, he mainly exploited his Jewish background to defend the Soviet Union's anti-Jewish policies.[23]

Nevertheless, the Aarons brothers and other leading CPA Jews were still regarded by some observers as representative of a specifically Jewish politics. Right-wing anti-communists and even internal Party critics used their prominence as an excuse to openly display their anti-Semitic prejudices. And even the local Soviet Embassy representative, concerned about the CPA's "liberalist" political deviations in the late 1960s, complained that there were too many Jews in the Party leadership.[24]

Many other Jews—often migrants of longer standing who were well integrated into Australian society—were also active in Party life, but retained (with some notable exceptions) only minimal links with organized Jewish activities.[25] There is also some evidence of significant Jewish financial support for the CPA during the immediate postwar years.[26] The daughter of one major Jewish Party donor recalls rather cynically:

> It was not surprising that many of the younger generation became ardent Socialists and Communists, because they had grown up in an atmosphere of political idealism combined with material success, and so theorising was quite a comfortable non-risk activity. Many of the Carlton businessmen, brought up to regard themselves as social underdogs, were bound by conscience and a history of personal persecution to revolutionary movements as a matter of course. They supported the Communist Party both morally and financially on emotional as well as rational grounds . . . It was ironic that many of the North Carlton capitalists voted Labor whilst giving considerable sums to the Communist Party and paying their workers not a penny more than was necessary.[27]

However, once it became clear that the Soviet Union was actually persecuting rather than defending Jews, these donations quickly declined. The Communist Party's unqualified defense of the Slansky Trial (November 1952) and the Doctors' Plot (January 1953) eroded remaining Jewish support for Communism. The weekly Communist paper, *Tribune*, denied that these events were influenced by anti-Semitism which was declared to be illegal and nonexistent in the Communist countries due to the defeat of capitalism. The paper provided a critique of Zionists and Jewish capitalists, and alleged that critics of the trials were trying to drag the world into war.[28]

Many Australian Jewish Communists seem to have been unconvinced by the official explanations. A report by Communist Party of Australia (CPA) Central Committee official, Eddie Maher, of a meeting of Jewish members held in Sydney on February 2, 1953, suggested that the majority were "uneasy" about recent developments in the Soviet Union, and were not convinced that there was no anti-Semitism involved in the Doctors' Plot.[29] Maher's report appears to have concerned the Party leadership. A subsequent report by CPA leader Jack Blake noted that some Jewish Party members were unable to properly distinguish between Zionist and Communist beliefs, and consequently had been influenced by the allegations of anti-Semitism in the Communist countries. Blake argued that Zionism was incompatible with Communist Party membership, and demanded that Jewish members attack Jewish capitalists no less than other capitalists. He added that anti-Semitism was also incompatible with membership in the Party.[30]

As a result of Blake's report, a public meeting was held by the Communist Party in Sydney to "explain the reasons for the just trials by the USSR of the murderous Doctors." The Party asked Jewish members to distribute pamphlets and write letters to all Yiddish newspapers exposing the class nature of the Zionist movement, and "attacking Zionists for their capitalist pressure on workers." The Party also called for the destruction of disloyal traitors and enemies within the Party membership.[31] It would appear that some Jewish members were shocked by Blake's rhetoric, and chose as a result to either resign from Party membership or cease active involvement.[32] Three years later, Jack Blake publicly apologized to Jewish Communists for his defense of the Doctors' Plot, and his associated attacks on alleged Zionists within the Party.[33] But his apology did little to restore Jewish support for the Party, which continued to deny the existence of anti-Semitism in the Soviet Union.

It was to take almost another decade before the Party, influenced by a concern emanating from Italian Communists for greater openness and democratic discussion within the international Communist movement, issued a number of official admissions of the existence of anti-Semitism in the Soviet Union. In general, these official CPA statements were cautious and ambivalent. They acknowledged that there were anti-Semitic feelings and tendencies in the Soviet Union, but denied that there was any evidence of systematic anti-Jewish persecution or discrimination. Nevertheless, the official public criticisms that CPA leaders made regarding Soviet anti-Semitism were unprecedented for a Communist Party, and had a significant impact in encouraging other Communist Parties to address the Soviet Jewry issue.[34]

In a not unrelated development, the Vietnam War era produced a minor revival of Jewish support for the CPA as a number of younger Jews, mostly the children of older leftists, joined the Party. However, in contrast to the older generation, their association with the CPA principally reflected broader universalistic, rather than specifically Jewish concerns.[35]

The Jewish Progressive Centre

The Jewish Progressive Centre (JPC), a small pro-Soviet, Yiddish-speaking organization, was established in 1946 by former leaders of the Gezerd, augmented by newly arrived postwar Polish Jewish refugees. The JPC members maintained a Jewish Communist subculture, but few actually joined the Communist Party due to concerns about their alien status and the threat of potential persecution or deportation.[36]

The JPC aimed to develop a specifically Jewish progressive culture, to fight anti-Semitism and other forms of racism, and to promote democratic rights and world peace. It advanced this agenda by holding public forums on issues such as anti-Semitism in Australia, the war in Palestine, the anniversary of the Bolshevik revolution, and the commemoration of the Warsaw Ghetto uprising, and by forming links with similar-minded overseas groups in Poland, Canada, and elsewhere. The JPC also raised funds for Communist-linked health and education organizations in Israel.[37]

A particular concern was to refute charges of Soviet anti-Semitism. The JPC provided evidence of alleged Jewish progress and achievements under Communism, and denied that there was any official campaign to suppress Yiddish culture in the Soviet Union.[38] In response to the Slansky trial, the JPC issued a leaflet stating:

> The sentencing of 14 persons in Prague is being interpreted in both the Jewish and non-Jewish press as an anti-Semitic verdict. For many years now, there has been an intensive propaganda drive to the effect that the USSR and the Peoples' Democracies have embarked on a policy of anti-Semitism. This is a malicious lie. This is a deliberate attempt to incite the Jewish population against the Peoples' Democracies and to enlist the Jewish masses in the widespread warmongering hysteria . . . Neither the Jews nor Israel

> were on trial in Prague, but the Embassy of Israel. They supported the anti-Socialist forces in Czechoslovakia, and carried out spying activities. Should we protect them?[39]

However, following Nikita Khrushchev's 1956 revelations of Stalinist anti-Semitism, the JPC held a number of large general meetings at which many rank-and-file members expressed their "horror and disappointment" at the events that had taken place in the USSR.[40] As a result, the JPC wrote a number of letters to the Soviet Society for Cultural Relations with Foreign Countries condemning Stalin's treatment of the Jews and urging the reconstruction of Jewish culture.[41] These letters were published by Communist Party newspapers in Poland, Israel, Canada, Argentina, and other countries. However, the JPC later returned to an unequivocal defense of the Soviet Union, including a denial of ongoing discrimination against Soviet Jewry.[42]

The membership of the Centre at its height was approximately 150, predominantly of the older generation, and only a small group among them was active. The 1967 Six-Day War and the formation of the pro-Soviet Socialist Party as a breakaway group from the CPA caused a split within the Centre, which terminated in 1969.[43]

The JPC was succeeded by two groups. One was a small group called the Jewish Progressive Group for Peace in the Middle East, which publicly criticized anti-Semitism in the Soviet Bloc with particular attention to the 1968 anti-Jewish campaign in Poland, and the use of anti-Zionism as a cover for anti-Semitism. The group dissolved in 1971.[44]

The second was a larger pro-Soviet group of about seventy to eighty people, the Itzhak Wittenberg Group, named after the Communist leader of the Jewish resistance in the Vilna Ghetto. Headed by long-time CPA activists Saul Factor, Micha Frydman, and Manny Biederberg, the group consisted mainly of elderly, Yiddish speaking, Polish-born Communists. A number had been jailed in pre-war Poland, and many had their lives saved during World War Two by the Soviet Union. The group held annual commemorations of the Warsaw Ghetto uprising and the Russian revolution, and attained some notoriety in 1982 for its vigorous criticism of Israel's Lebanon War. Most of its members have now passed away, and the group has ceased to exist.[45]

Jewish Trotskyists

The Australian Trotskyist movement was relatively tiny until at least the 1960s, totaling fewer than fifty people nationally.[46] However, some Jews were prominent in the small Sydney Labour Socialist Group, including Issy Wyner, Anatol Kagan, and Ben Palley. Kagan and Wyner were both long-time collaborators of the famous activist, Nick Origlass.[47] Much later in the 1970s and '80s a number of Jews were active in newer Trotskyist groups such as the Democratic Socialist Party, and the International Socialist Organisation. Some of these Jews were prominent in the formation of the Jews against Zionism and Anti-Semitism group, which campaigned for the elimination of the State of Israel.[48]

Judeo-Communism in Australia

In contrast to the popular constructions of Judeo-Communism in Europe,[49] there seems to have been little public identification in Australia of any connection between Jews and communism. The only open allegations of Jewish Communism emanated from small far-right groups such as the League of Rights, which published the *Protocols of the Elders of Zion*, and in one case from a maverick Carmelite priest, Father Patrick Gearon, who alleged Jewish control of the Bolsheviks.[50] To be sure, the Australian Security Intelligence Organisation (ASIO) obsessively investigated alleged links between Jews and Communism from the early 1930s until at least the late 1960s, targeting not only left-wing groups such as the Jewish section of the Communist Party and the Jewish Council, but even the mainstream Jewish peak bodies.[51]

To at least some extent, this investigation of Jews reflected a belief in an intrinsic connection between Jews and Communism. For example, as early as October 1943, a Security Service document on the Jewish Council drew attention to "the numbers of Jewish persons who have been attracted to communism. Reference has been made frequently to the circulation of Russian newspapers through little cliques of Jewish people, principally in racial or national groups."[52] Later ASIO reports made similar reference to the numbers of Jews holding communist or pro-communist sympathies, and to the potential security risk posed by the Jewish Council.[53] Nevertheless, there is little evidence to suggest that ASIO acted on these prejudices in any politically significant way.[54]

Not unrelated were the May 1950 police interrogations of twenty young people belonging to the left-wing Kadimah Youth Organisation and the Zionist youth group Hatikvah in the Melbourne suburbs of Carlton, North Carlton, St. Kilda, and Elwood, concerning their alleged involvement in anti-British and Communist activities. Some of their parents were also approached and intimidated, and a number of overseas-born activists were threatened with deportation. The interrogations, which seem to have been inspired by the introduction of the Communist Party Dissolution Bill into the federal Parliament, caused great consternation within the Jewish community. But Prime Minister Robert Menzies specifically denied in Parliament that any Commonwealth officer or minister had authorized or organized the police actions. And similarly the Victorian Premier, J. G. B. McDonald, provided assurances that the Jewish community had not been singled out, and that no such actions would reoccur in the future. From there the matter fizzled out.[55]

In addition, Jewish CPA member and businessman Isaac Gust was publicly named as a prominent donor to the Party (and labelled a "Russian Jew") during the Victorian Royal Commission into Communism. The Commission alleged that a Jewish meeting organized by Gust had raised the large sum of 1,500 pounds for the Party. The report also named left-wing Jews, Zelman Markov and Sam Brilliant, as Party donors, and referred in passing to about ten other Jewish supporters of the CPA including Jewish Council Secretary Judah Waten.[56] But none of these investigations or allegations produced any significant anti-Jewish manifestations. Nor did the fact that some members of the Soviet spy ring in Australia known as the Klod Group appear to have had a number of Jewish friends and possible collaborators.[57] None of these associations were made public at the time, and there was certainly no Australian version of the Rosenberg spy scandal, or even the jailing of Fred Rose and Sam Carr in Canada.

Part Three: The Melbourne Jewish Council to Combat Fascism and Anti-Semitism

The most significant Australian Jewish Left group was the Melbourne Jewish Council to Combat Fascism and Anti-Semitism, formed in 1942 to counter the growth in anti-Semitism associated with pre- and postwar Jewish immigration, and the impact of Nazism. Leaders of the Council advocated an activist and high-profile approach to fighting anti-Semitism, rather than the traditional low-key, inconspicuous strategy favored by the established Anglo-Australian Jewish leadership. The Council was always influenced by the Communist Party and its sympathizers, but in its early years enjoyed broad communal support. Its emergence reflected the wartime popularity of the Soviet Union, and the united front of all Jews—social democrats, communists, conservatives, Zionists, and leading rabbis—against Nazism and its local apologists. The Council included both established Eastern European immigrants, and a group of Anglo-Australian Jews who had not previously been involved in Jewish politics.[58]

In spite of its overt left-wing sympathies, the Council was a highly influential, if not dominant, organization in the Melbourne Jewish community of the immediate postwar years, acting as the official public relations representative of the Victorian Jewish Board of Deputies (VJBD). This meant that the Council took control of all action pertaining to anti-Semitism, communal relations, and political activity undertaken by the Board. The Council was also responsible for the public relations activities of the Executive Council of Australian Jewry whenever that body was based in Victoria.

The Council's emphasis on the joint struggle against the evils of fascism and anti-Semitism reflected the experiences of many Jewish refugees who had experienced persecution under anti-Communist regimes in Central and Eastern Europe. This emphasis suggested that potential dangers to Jews came principally from conservatives and the political right, and implied that anti-Semitism could not emanate from left-wing sources. The Council believed that left-wing groups and organizations were particularly sympathetic to Jews, and worked closely with the Australian Labor Party, trade unions, and the Australian Council for Civil Liberties.[59]

The Council's name and founding statement was almost certainly influenced by two overseas groups.[60] The first was the British Jewish People's Council against Fascism and Anti-Semitism (JPC), which was formed in 1936 by a broad alliance of Communists, Bundists, trade unions, ex-servicemen, Zionists, and synagogues. The JPC aimed to defend the Jewish people against attacks from Sir Oswald Mosley's British Union of Fascists, and to cooperate with other anti-fascist organizations including the Communist Party. As with the Council, the JPC argued that Jews should combat the broad political ideology and movement of fascism, rather than limiting their agenda to fighting specific manifestations of anti-Semitism. And similarly, commentators disagree on whether the JPC was merely influenced by, or instead controlled by, its Communist members.[61]

Another likely influence was the Soviet Jewish Anti-Fascist Committee (JAFC) formed in Moscow in 1942 to promote international Jewish support for the Soviet Union.[62] The JAFC inspired the establishment of Jewish friends of the Soviet Union groups throughout the world, including Australia. However, the local application of this strategy of combating fascism as well as anti-Semitism was always likely to prove problematic given that the

Left-Right split in Australian politics did not neatly fit this European model. There was little tradition of conservative anti-Semitism in Australia, and it was actually a conservative government, which first admitted a significant (if still inadequate) number of Jewish refugees in the late 1930s. There was also a significant history of Australian philo-Semitism emanating from non-Left sources including particularly the churches.[63] Conversely the Australian Left had only a limited tradition of defending Jews. This meant that the Council had adopted a model that unnecessarily narrowed its options toward securing support from only one side of the spectrum, and implicitly excluded the possibility of finding allies on the political Right.[64]

The Council's political perspective quickly came under attack with the beginnings of the Cold War in 1948. The Jewish political unity of the wartime period began to erode. Jewish support for the Soviet Union collapsed as increasing evidence of Stalinist anti-Semitism began to emerge. In addition, Jews locally and internationally were influenced by the growth of anti-Communism and the pressure to endorse new political alignments against the USSR. For example, in July 1949, a VJBD delegate, Trevor Rapke, proposed a motion calling for the expulsion of "any present or past Communist or Communist sympathiser or supporter" from the Jewish Council. Although the motion was rejected, a number of VJBD deputies aggressively questioned Council representative, Norman Rothfield concerning the involvement of known Communists such as Judah Waten in the Council. Concern was expressed that the employment of Waten as Secretary of the Council (and the rumour—later proven correct—that he would be named at the forthcoming Victorian Royal Commission into Communism) was feeding public perceptions of an association of the whole Jewish community with Communism.[65]

In late 1950, prominent lawyer and right-wing Labor Party activist, Maurie Ashkanasy, launched his campaign to eliminate the Council from the Victorian and national Jewish "roof" bodies. According to Ashkanasy:

> The community and the Victorian Jewish Board of Deputies are not led by President Ben Green and his Executive—nor is the Jewish Council guided by its President Joseph Redapple. The whole community is lead [sic] by a Mr. Judah Waten, paid Secretary of the Council whose left-wing tendencies have prejudiced the efforts of the community in the Anti-Migration campaign in Government circles. Our youth have become mixed up with Communists since Mr. Waten that cunning and brilliant diplomat took control.[66]

As a result of these attacks and the Council's refusal to condemn Soviet anti-Semitism, most of the liberals, conservatives, and Zionists who had been active in earlier years such as the leading Reform Rabbi, Herman Sanger, left the Council.[67] The Council gradually became a united front of the Jewish Left, rather than a united front of all Jews.

Since the Council rejected the Cold War consensus, and attempted to maintain its existing political links and strategies, it became involved in a series of public disputes and controversies, which progressively weakened its previously strong support within the Jewish community. These included the Council's participation in a deputation pressing for anti-fascist and group libel legislation; opposition to a proposed Police Offences Bill; public denunciations of the police interrogations of Jewish youth (discussed earlier); invitation to the prominent British pro-Soviet peace activist, Dr. Hewlett Johnson, to address a Human Rights Rally; and opposition to the government proposal to outlaw the Communist Party. What was common in all these controversies was the allegation that the Council's left-wing alliances were associating the Jewish community per se with Communist activities, and therefore creating, rather than combating, anti-Semitism.[68]

The allegation that the Council was a "front" group controlled by Communist or pro-Soviet factions to manipulate naïve non-Communists into supporting pro-Soviet policies has some merit,[69] but is also strongly linked to the Cold War politics of the period. On the one hand, there is little evidence of direct Communist Party control of the Council akin to that of the Australian Peace Council or the Union of Australian Women.[70] According to Rechter's study of Jewish Communism in Melbourne, the CPA regarded the Jewish community as peripheral. CPA official Ralph Gibson acted as a liaison with the Jewish fraction, but contact with sympathetic Jewish groups remained unofficial, and was regarded by the Party as relatively unimportant. The Party's main emphasis was on promoting the class struggle in Australia, not debating international events. No central direction was given to Jewish groups regarding either political views or activities.[71]

It is also arguably significant that the Council's pro-Zionist and pro-Israel viewpoint contrasted sharply with the pro-Arab policies pursued by the Soviet Union from about 1955 onwards. It is hardly surprising that the Council acted as a strong advocate for the State of Israel during the 1947–1948 war when the Soviet Union was aligned with Israel. But other than a brief flirtation with Stalinist anti-Zionism during the anti-Jewish show trials of 1952–1953, the Council remained broadly pro-Israel even whilst the Soviet Union forged a strong alliance with radical Arab enemies of Israel. This seems to confirm that little pressure was placed on the Council by outside actors to conform to Soviet positions, although it is important to remember that the State of Israel remained a very minor issue on the Australian Left until the Six-Day War.[72]

However, the lack of direct organizational links between the Council and the CPA does not necessarily preclude the Party from exerting indirect influence on the Council. It would appear, for example, that the Council was significantly influenced by a number of prominent Communist Party members and active sympathizers. CPA members such as Judah Waten, Saul Factor, Lawrence Collinson, Lou Jedwab, Salomea Genin, Ken Marks, Todd Trevaks, and Isaac Gust all held significant roles in the Council at various times. They were supported by prominent Labor Party personalities such as Norman Rothfield and Sam Goldbloom who shared their hardline support for the Soviet Union, and appear to have participated in a broader Jewish Communist or pro-Soviet faction.[73] In addition, the Council's Youth Section functioned informally as a Jewish Communist youth group, and many of its members joined the CPA.[74]

The Council also worked closely with the Communist Jewish Progressive Centre (JPC), and co-sponsored the JPC Journal, *The Clarion*, which promoted hardline support for the Soviet Union.[75] Further links were maintained with broader leftist groups sympathetic to the Soviet Union including the Australian Peace Council, the Democratic Rights Council, various left-wing unions, and the Australian Council of Civil Liberties. Many leading Council personnel were also active in these bodies and related groups.[76]

On the other hand, Australian Labor Party activists such as Sam Cohen and Walter Lippman (until the latter resigned from the Council in mid-1953) were influential both within the Council and within the broader Jewish peak ruling bodies. Other prominent social democrats within the Council included Aaron Mushin, a former president of the Jewish Kadimah Cultural Centre, Martin Ravech, Nubert Stabey, and Isaac Sher.[77] None of these figures held dogmatic pro-Soviet views. However, they still shared the reluctance of the Communist and pro-Communist activists to openly criticize the Soviet Union during the Cold War. When it came to the crunch, the pro-Soviet or Communist faction was generally able to impose its agenda upon the Council.[78]

The McCarthyism of the period tended to accentuate the significance of these associations, both in terms of exaggerating the extent of Communist involvement, and equally in reinforcing the reluctance of leftist non-Communists to openly join anti-Communists in voicing criticisms of the Soviet Union. These complex internal maneuverings within the Council led to repeated conjecture as to whether the Council was sincerely leading campaigns against anti-Semitism, or alternatively and insidiously pursuing veiled political agendas.[79] For example, one particular conflict occurred around the controversial Jewish campaign against the government plan to introduce 100,000 German (particularly Volksdeutsche, ethnic German refugees from Eastern Europe) migrants to Australia over a four-year period. The Jewish community feared that the immigrants would include many ex-Nazis who would introduce significant anti-Semitism into Australia. The campaign, which had been directed by the Jewish Council, was suspended by the Executive Council of Australian Jewry in April 1951 due to a belief that it had achieved its key objectives. However, the Council resolved not only to continue the campaign against German immigrants, but also to foster a broader campaign against West German rearmament. In contrast, the Jewish "roof" bodies were increasingly influenced by the State of Israel's reconciliation with West Germany, and the general Cold War concern to include the Germans in the Western alliance. Eventually, the Council was expelled from the Victorian Jewish Board of Deputies in July 1952 for refusing to cancel a protest demonstration against the new West German Ambassador.[80]

Nevertheless, the Council remained an influential body. It had a numerically significant membership including a number of active subcommittees, a vocal Youth Section, and interstate affiliates in New South Wales and Western Australia.[81] In addition, key Council personalities such as Norman Rothfield, Sam Goldbloom, Sam Cohen (later an Australian Labor Party Senator), and Walter Lippmann remained prominent in both the Jewish and broader Australian communities. The Council's robust approach to fighting anti-Semitism from traditional conservative sources continued to attract support from a cross section of the Jewish community.

However, the Council's inadequate response to Stalinist anti-Semitism destroyed its political credibility. In particular, the Council responded to the anti-Semitic Slansky show trial of November 1952 and the associated USSR Doctors' Plot of January 1953 by claiming that anti-Semitism and Communism were a contradiction in terms. According to the Council, any suggestions to the contrary reflected either temporary aberrations arising from the continued existence in Eastern Europe of popular pre-Communist prejudices, or alternatively, manifestations of Cold War propaganda. When pressed, the Council emphasized the alleged subtle difference in Communist rhetoric between anti-Zionism and anti-Semitism. The Council acknowledged that the Soviet Bloc was hostile to Zionism and the State of Israel, and argued that this hostility could be attributed to the Zionist movement's alignment with the West in the Cold War. However, the

Council consistently denied that any anti-Jewish manifestations per se were involved. According to the Council,

> [a]n Executive sub-committee was set up to consider all the available evidence, including reports of the Czechoslovakian trial. This committee, consisting of lawyers as well as laymen, came back with the conclusion that there was no evidence of Government-inspired anti-Semitism in the Eastern European countries, although it was evident that Zionism was in disfavour there. Of course it is true that Zionism is regarded as an ideology hostile to those States, but that does not amount to anti-Semitism any more than hostility to Slovakian nationalism can be regarded as evidence of a bias against the Slovak people. Nor is it denied that there are still relics of anti-Semitic tendencies amongst certain anti-Semitic forces in the East.

The Council went on to say that

> [a] study of statements by leaders of various Communist states and of the legislation making anti-Semitism illegal, which these countries have adopted and which is unique in world history, must lead to the inescapable conclusion that there is no foundation for the charges that in these countries there is a campaign aimed at the Jewish people . . . If the Jewish communities of the western world join in the hymns of hatred which are being sung in ever increasing volume without trying to appreciate the true facts of the situation, or if we fail to distinguish the happenings in Eastern Europe from the Nazi attempt to annihilate the Jewish people, then we only join in what is a deliberate attempt to aggravate a situation which is the basis of the fears leading to actions from which flow the injustices and the hardships of which we complain.[82]

Further pro-Soviet views were expressed by the leading Council activist, Norman Rothfield, who was visiting Moscow in early 1953 when the Doctors' Plot was announced. Rothfield praised the treatment of Jews in Poland, Czechoslovakia, and the Soviet Union, arguing that anti-Semitism was nonexistent. He even offered qualified support for the accusations against the Jewish Doctors, suggesting that they were not as absurd as might be thought.[83]

The Council did not join the Communist Party of Australia in formally endorsing the show trials, but the refusal (despite some internal dissent) to even seek a public clarification of the blatant presence of anti-Semitism in the Soviet Bloc trials does suggest the growing organizational influence, and probable dominance, of the Communists and their allies. In relation to these events, former Council leader Norman Rothfield retrospectively acknowledges how "ideological loyalty" led many supporters of the Soviet Union "to confuse truth with propaganda."[84]

The Council's apologia for Stalinist anti-Semitism destroyed its remaining influence in the Jewish community. The anti-Communist purge that followed had two distinct manifestations. The first was the widespread banning of the Council from access to Jewish halls. In addition, attempts were made to disaffiliate the Council's Youth Section from the Melbourne Jewish Youth Council. An associated development was the large number of resignations from Council membership. Despite concerted efforts, the Council leadership was unable to stem the loss of communal support. [85]

Then came the official purge. In March 1953, the Executive Council of Australian Jewry passed the following motion:

> The ECAJ unequivocally states that it is the personal duty of every Jew and Jewess in Australia . . . to withdraw from any organization and group which seeks to aid, defend or in any way justify any past or future actions of the Governments of the USSR and of her satellites against Jews, against Jewish institutions, or against the State of Israel.

A further motion called on State Boards of Deputies to

> terminate the affiliation of any group or organization deemed to be pursuing a policy to the interests of the Jewish people . . . It further authorizes constituent bodies to make known that any similar but unaffiliated group or organization within the States concerned is not recognized by the Jewish community as a bona-fide Jewish organization.[86]

Thus the Council, which had arguably been the most influential Australian Jewish organization only three years earlier, now found itself formally excommunicated by the community's national umbrella body. The grounds for this excommunication were that the Council's stated views on Stalinist anti-Semitism had demonstrated that it was controlled by a Communist or pro-Soviet, rather than Jewish agenda.[87]

The Council remained an active organization until its eventual demise in 1970. It had regained some prominence in the late 1950s due to the association of some of its key members with the dominant Left faction of the Victorian Branch of the Australian Labor Party.[88] However, the unfortunate Senator Sam Cohen Affair in 1962 left the Council once again stereotyped as "soft" on Soviet anti-Semitism. Cohen, a former Council president and Labor Party senator, opposed a parliamentary motion condemning Soviet anti-Semitism, and appeared to defend the Soviet Union's record on this issue. Cohen argued that Jews as individuals enjoyed civil equality in the Soviet Union, and that public protests against alleged anti-Jewish discrimination would only exacerbate the Cold War, and ultimately worsen rather than improve the situation of Soviet Jewry. He argued that the interests of Soviet Jews would be best served by international dialogue and peace.[89]

In its later years, the Council continued to be plagued by divisions over the Soviet Union, an ageing leadership, and a failure to attract new supporters despite the emergence of significant Jewish participation in the new radical student and anti-war movements.[90] The Council was not able to revise its ideology to adapt to the new world whereby the key threat to Jews came not from West Germany or a revival of Nazism, but rather from the Soviet Union both in terms of its internal persecution of Jews and its external support of Arab hostility to Israel. Nor did the Council engage with the newer passionate Jewish activism revolving around the issues of Israel and Soviet Jewry.[91] The Council was later succeeded by groups such as the Jewish Radical Association, Paths to Peace, and the still-existing Australian Jewish Democratic Society. These groups had different political agendas than the Council, and were left-wing pluralist rather than pro-Communist or pro-Soviet in their philosophy.[92]

Part Four: Conclusion

Compared to the significant Jewish Communist movements in most other English-speaking countries, Jewish Communism in Australia was relatively minor. There were no large Yiddish-speaking immigrant working class, no specific Jewish trade unions, and no numerically significant Jewish faction or grouping within the Communist Party. Jewish Communism attracted almost no public attention, and indeed little political recognition or hostility other than from a relatively harmless Intelligence Service and marginal far Right groups.

Nevertheless, Communism attained a brief prominence within the mainstream of Australian Jewry from approximately 1942 through 1950. This rise reflected the temporary international convergence of Jewish and Communist concerns. Jews and the Soviet Union were allied in the fight against Nazism, and later in supporting the creation of Israel. Equally, many Jewish immigrants in Australia and elsewhere struggled economically and sympathized with the communist notion of class struggle. And some Jewish Communists and pro-Communists were skilled in integrating mainstream Jewish and Communist agendas.

Conversely, the decline of Jewish Communism in Australia also mirrored events elsewhere. The Cold War and the influence of McCarthyism, increasing Jewish identification with Zionist rather than Socialist solutions to anti-Semitism, the upward social mobility of many Jews, the decimation of secular Yiddish culture, declining manifestations of anti-Semitism from mainstream conservatives, and finally the complete loss of faith in the Soviet Union engendered by Stalinist anti-Semitism all combined to render Jewish Communism marginal by about 1953. It was no longer possible to align a self-respecting Jewish identity and Communist politics.

Many of the younger Jewish Communists ceased active political involvement, and concentrated on building families and careers. Others switched their political endeavors from the Jewish community to broader work in Communist Party branches. A few became active in the Jewish Council.[93] A specifically Jewish Communism ceased to exist other than in isolated enclaves such as the Jewish Progressive Centre.

Notes

1. The Sydney group was originally founded as the Jewish Unity Committee in 1945, and then changed its name to the Sydney Jewish Council to Combat Fascism and Anti-Semitism in 1948. See Suzanne Rutland, *Edge of the Diaspora: Two Centuries of Jewish Settlement in Australia* (Rose Bay: Brandl & Schlesinger, 2001), 327–28.

2. At least two Jews seem to have been among the founding members of the Communist Party. They were Bob Brodney and Sam Wyner. See Hall Greenland, *Red Hot: The Life and Times of Nick Origlass 1908–1996* (Sydney: Wellington Lane Press, 1998), 62; Stuart Macintyre, "Foundation: The Communist Party of Australia," *Overland*, No. 132 (1993): 6–12.

3. David Rechter, "Beyond the Pale: Jewish Communism in Melbourne," MA diss., University of Melbourne, 1986, 9, 19–21, 63; W. D. Rubinstein, *The Jews in Australia* (Melbourne: William Heinemann Australia, 1991), 137.

4. Stan Robe, *From Shtetl to Melbourne: A Century of Jewish Life in Melbourne,* unpublished manuscript, 1989, 6.

5. David Rechter, "The Gezerd: The Jewish Left in Melbourne in the 1930s," Honors diss., University of Melbourne, 1984, 15; Rechter, "Beyond the Pale," 9–10; Robe, *From Shtetl to Melbourne*, 90.

6. Suzane Abramovich, "Introduction" to *The New Jew*, by Anna Louise Strong, (Sydney: Gezerd, 1935), 1.

7. Sender Burstin, "The Australian Gezert," *Melbourne Chronicle,* July 1976; Rechter, "The Gezerd," 18–26; Rechter, "Beyond the Pale," 39–65; Robe, *From Shtetl to Melbourne*, 92–97.

8. Lou Jedwab, "The Kadimah Youth Organisation in Melbourne: Reminiscences, 1942–53," *Journal of the Australian Jewish Historical Society* 12, No. 1 (1993):179–81; Rechter, "The Gezerd," 27–29; Rechter, "Beyond the Pale," 65–73; Robe, *From Shtetl to Melbourne*, 95–97.

9. Rechter, "Beyond the Pale," 29.

10. Alistair Davidson, *The Communist Party of Australia* (Stanford, CA: Hoover Institution Press, 1969), 93, 120.

11. See numerous accounts of the active participation of Communists in Jewish life in the Melbourne suburb of Carlton in *A Shtetl in Ek Velt: 54 Stories of Growing up in Jewish Carlton 1925–1945*, ed. Julie Meadows (Melbourne: Australian Centre for Jewish Civilisation, 2011), 21, 34, 79, 166, 185, 198, 205, 230.

12. Lance Sharkey, "Labor Movement Must Fight against anti-Semitism," *Tribune,* February 24, 1939; Lance Sharkey, "The Jews and International Capitalism," *Tribune*, March 14, 1939.

13. Eureka Youth League, *What's Going on in Palestine?* (Melbourne: EYL, 1948).

14. R. Ginter, "Kadimah Youth Organization and Eureka Youth League Camp," *Jewish Youth*, January–February 1947: 5. See also the report by Joe Kiers, "Together for Peace," *The Clarion* 2 (1952): 5–6, on the extensive Jewish involvement in the Communist Youth Carnival for Peace and Friendship; and Philip Mendes, "Jewish Involvement in the Communist Party of Australia," *Journal of the Australian Jewish Historical Society* 12, No. 3 (1994): 597.

15. See message from Ralph Gibson of the Victorian State Committee of the CPA to the Jewish people, *Tribune*, November 19, 1947.

16. Ralph Gibson, *War in Palestine* (Melbourne: Communist Party of Australia, 1948), 5.

17. John Docker, *1492: The Poetics of Diaspora* (London: Continuum, 2001), 158–67; Stuart Macintyre, *The Reds: The Communist Party of Australia from Origins to Illegality* (St. Leonards, NSW: Allen & Unwin, 1998), 310–11; Mendes, "Jewish Involvement in the Communist Party of Australia," 593; Rechter, "Beyond the Pale," 52–53, 59–60; Robe, *From Shtetl to Melbourne*, 103–04.

18. Rechter, "Beyond the Pale," 87–88, 106–09.

19. Moshe Ajzenbud, *60 Years of "Bund" in Melbourne 1928–1988* (Melbourne: Jewish Labour Bund, 1996), 43–45; Barrie Blears, *Together with Us: A Personal Glimpse of the Eureka Youth League and its Origins: 1920 to 1970* (Melbourne: self-published, 2002), 111–12; Jedwab, "The Kadimah Youth Organisation in Melbourne,"181–84; Rechter, "Beyond the Pale," 67, 88–99, 103–04, 132; Robe, *From Shtetl to Melbourne*, 64–65.

20. Cited in Mendes, "Jewish Involvement in the Communist Party of Australia," 600.

21. A term coined by the Marxist scholar Isaac Deutscher, in *The Non-Jewish Jew and Other Essays* (London: Merlin Press, 1968) to characterize those Jews who moved beyond the boundaries of Judaism to develop universal ideals and values.

22. For example, Eric Aarons, in *What's Left?* (Melbourne: Penguin, 1993) includes only a few minor vignettes referring to Jewish influences in his childhood; see pp. 2, 17, 24. Similarly, Harry Stein, in *A Glance Over an Old Left Shoulder* (Sydney: Hale & Iremonger, 1994) makes few references to his Jewish upbringing; see pp. 11–15, 56. Laurie Aarons describes himself as "a person of some Jewish genetic inheritance," as cited in Mendes, "Jewish Involvement in the Communist Party of Australia," 584. See also Mark Aarons, *The Family File* (Melbourne: Black Inc., 2010), 22–25, and John Sendy, *Comrades Come Rally: Recollections of an Australian Communist* (Melbourne: Nelson, 1978), 210–13 regarding the detail of the family background in the East End of London.

23. Rubinstein, *The Jews in Australia*, 528–29.

24. Eric Aarons, *What's Left?*, 158; Mark Aarons, *The Family File*, 182–83, 229, 233–34.

25. Robe, *From Shtetl to Melbourne*, 104. A summary of the many prominent Jewish writers, artists, lawyers, and intellectuals active at one time or another in the Party can be found in Philip Mendes, "From the Shtetl to the Monash Soviet: An Overview of the Historiography of Jewish Radicalism in Australia," *Australian Journal of Jewish Studies* 14 (2000): 70–71. See also Mendes, "Jewish Involvement in the Communist Party of Australia," 584–85, 587, 595; David Carter, "Judah Waten (1911–1985) Writer, Communist, Jew," *Australian Jewish Democrat* 1 (1995): 34; Bernard Smith, *Noel Counihan Artist and Revolutionary* (Melbourne: Oxford University Press, 1993), 68–81, 223–25, 290.

26. Pauline Armstrong, *Frank Hardy and the Making of Power Without Glory* (Melbourne: Melbourne University Press, 2000), 97–98; Charles Lowe, *Report of Royal Commission Inquiring into the origins, aims, objects and funds of the Communist Party in Victoria and other related matters* (Melbourne: Victorian Parliament, 1950), 41–42; Mendes, "Jewish Involvement in the Communist Party of Australia," 587, 600.

27. Miriam Kuna, "North Carlton: My Nation State," *Journal of the Australian Jewish Historical Society* 12, No. 1 (1993):141.

28. *Tribune*, December 3, 1952, 3; December 10, 1952, 3; December 17, 1952, 4; January 7, 1953, 12; January 21, 1953, 1, 4; January 28, 1953, 10; and February 18, 1953, 4. For further discussion, see Philip Mendes, "American, Australian, and other Western Jewish Communists and Soviet Anti-Semitism: Responses

to the Slansky Trial and the Doctors' Plot 1952–53," *American Communist History* 10, No. 2 (2011): 151–68.

29. Australian Security Intelligence Organization File, *Communist Party of Australia—Interest and Activities in Jewish Community, 1943–1954*, Report No. 3657: February 5, 1953.

30. Jack Blake, "Zionism and Anti-Semitism," *Communist Review* No. 136 (1953): 119–22.

31. Australian Security Intelligence Organization File, *Communist Party of Australia—Interest and Activities in Jewish Community, 1943–1954*, Report No. 3680: February 9, 1953.

32. Bernie Taft, *Crossing the Party Line* (Newham, VIC: Scribe Publications, 1994), 76.

33. "Meeting hears Blake on Soviet Doctors" Case," *Tribune*, August 23, 1956.

34. Philip Mendes, "A Convergence of Political Interests: Isi Leibler, the Communist Party of Australia and Soviet Anti-Semitism, 1964–66," *Australian Journal of Politics and History* 55, No. 2 (2009): 157–69.

35. Philip Mendes, *The New Left, the Jews and the Vietnam War 1965–1972* (Melbourne: Lazare Press, 1993), 36.

36. Rechter, "Beyond the Pale," 116–17; Robe, *From Shtetl to Melbourne*, 141–42.

37. Rechter, "Beyond the Pale,"119–25; Lou Jedwab, "Jewish Progressive Centre," unpublished manuscript, 1992.

38. *Jewish Clarion*, No. 2 (May 1952): 9. This magazine was published by CPA activist Manny Biederberg for the Jewish Progressive Centre. See also Jedwab, "Jewish Progressive Centre," 3.

39. JPC leaflet (December 1952) cited in Ajzenbud, *60 Years of "Bund" in Melbourne 1928–1988*, 37.

40. Jedwab, "Jewish Progressive Centre," 5.

41. Jedwab, "Jewish Progressive Centre," 5–11.

42. Jedwab, "Jewish Progressive Centre," 13; Isi Leibler, *Soviet Jewry and Human Rights* (Melbourne: Human Rights Publications, 1965), 62–63.

43. Rechter, "Beyond the Pale,"125–26.

44. Philip Mendes, "The Melbourne Jewish Left 1967–1986," *Journal of the Australian Jewish Historical Society* 11, No. 3 (1991): 506, 521.

45. Susan Faine, "Interview with Heniek Kalmusz," *Itzak Wittenberg Study Group Oral History Project* (Canberra: National Library of Australia, 2003); Robe, *From Shtetl to Melbourne*, 160.

46. Davidson, *The Communist Party of Australia*, 188.

47. Greenland, *Red Hot*, 61–63, 73, 109–13.

48. Philip Mendes, "Denying the Jewish Experience of Oppression: Australian Jews against Zionism and Anti-Semitism and the 3CR Controversy," in *Rebels Against Zion: Studies on the Jewish Left Anti-Zionism*, ed. August Grabski (Warsaw:

Institute of Jewish History, 2011), 178; John Percy, *A History of the Democratic Socialist Party and Resistance* (Sydney: Resistance Books, 2005), 128, 168, 182–83, 208.

49. André Gerrits, *The Myth of Jewish Communism* (Brussels: Peter Lang, 2009).

50. Rodney Gouttman, "The Protocols and the Printer," *Journal of the Australian Jewish Historical Society* 11, No. 1 (1990): 155–59; Colin Thornton-Smith, "Echoes and Resonances of Action Française: Anti-Semitism in Early Issues of the Australian Catholic Worker," *Journal of the Australian Jewish Historical Society* 11, No. 3 (1991): 473. Gearon's book was called *Communism—Why Not?* (Melbourne: no publisher, 1943).

51. Vic Alhadeff, "When ASIO Monitored the Jews," *Australian Jewish News*, December 13, 1991; "ASIO"s Secret Files on Jews," *Australian Jewish News*, April 24, 1992; Glenn Gordon, *Guardians of Zion: The Shomrim in Australia 1939–1944* (Sydney: Mandelbaum Trust, 1995),125–29; David McKnight, *Australia's Spies and Their Secrets* (St. Leonards, NSW: Allen & Unwin, 1994),103, 148–51; Rechter, "Beyond the Pale," 51–52.

52. "Communist Party Interests in Jewish Council to Combat Fascism and Anti-Semitism," Security Service file dated October 21, 1943.

53. Ibid., January 26, 1945 and October 15, 1946. See also Fiona Capp, *Writers Defiled* (Melbourne: McPhee Gribble, 1993), 30–31, 166–67.

54. W. D. Rubinstein, "The Cold War, the Australian Jewish Community, and the Marginalisation of the Jewish Left, 1942–1960," *Australian Journal of Politics and History* 41, No. 3 (1995): 385.

55. Philip Mendes, "Rogue Police Action: The Melbourne Jewish-Communist Controversy of May 1950," *Recorder: Australian Society for the Study of Labour History Newsletter* No. 266 (2010): 2.

56. Lowe, *Report of Royal Commission*, 41–42. See also Isaac Gust, *Such Was Life: A Jumping Narrative from Radom to Melbourne* (Melbourne: Makor Jewish Community Library, 2004), 199–200; Amirah Inglis, *The Hammer & Sickle and the Washing Up* (Melbourne: Hyland House, 1995), 75, 82.

57. McKnight, *Australia's Spies and Their Secrets*, 4, 51, 97, 99.

58. Rechter, "Beyond the Pale," 82, 85, 110–12; Norman Rothfield, *Many Paths to Peace* (Melbourne: Yarraford Publications, 1997), 15–17.

59. Robe, *From Shtetl to Melbourne*, 131.

60. Rechter, "Beyond the Pale," 82–83.

61. Jason Heppell, "A Question of Jewish Politics? The Jewish Section of the Communist Party of Great Britain, 1936–45," in *Jews, Labour and the Left, 1918–48*, eds. Christine Collette and Stephen Bird (Aldershot, UK: Ashgate, 2000), 100; Gisela Lebzelter, *Political Anti-Semitism in England 1918–1939* (London: Macmillan, 1978), 140–42, 152–53; Elaine Smith, "But What Did They Do? Contemporary Jewish Responses to Cable Street," in *Remembering Cable Street: Fascism and Anti-Fascism in British Society*, eds. Tony Kushner and Nadia Valman (London: Vallentine Mitchell, 2000), 51–53.

62. Heppell, "A Question of Jewish Politics?," 100–02.

63. Michael Blakeney, *Australia and the Jewish Refugees 1933–1948* (Sydney: Croom Helm, 1985), 198–212.

64. Philip Mendes, "The Enemy is on the Right: Re-evaluating the Formative Ideology and Political Strategy of the Melbourne Jewish Council to Combat Fascism and Anti-Semitism, 1942–47," *Australian Jewish Historical Society Journal*, 24, No. 2 (2008): 285–92.

65. Victorian Jewish Board of Deputies question time, July 4, 1949, cited in Philip Mendes, "Constructions of Judeo-Communism: The Unravelling of the Melbourne Jewish Council to Combat Fascism and Antisemitism, 1949–50," *Australian Jewish Historical Society Journal* 20, No. 1 (2010): 114.

66. Cited in Sarah McNaughton, "Liberalism and Anti-Communism," MA diss., University of Sydney, 1984, 78.

67. Mendes, "Constructions of Judeo-Communism," 117.

68. Philip Mendes, "Jews, Nazis and Communists Down Under: The Jewish Council's Controversial Campaign Against German Immigration," *Australian Historical Studies* 33, No. 119 (2002): 76–77; Mendes, "Constructions of Judeo-Communism."

69. See Rubinstein, "The Cold War, the Australian Jewish Community, and the Marginalisation of the Jewish Left, 1942–1960," 379–80, for a serious argument in favor of the "Communist front" allegation.

70. Davidson, *The Communist Party of Australia*, 104–06; McNaughton, "Liberalism and Anti-Communism," 54.

71. Rechter, "Beyond the Pale," 99–102.

72. Philip Mendes, "The Jewish Council, Communism and the State of Israel," *Australian Jewish Historical Society Journal* 14, No. 1 (1998): 459–67; Philip Mendes, "The Australian Left's Support for the Creation of the State of Israel, 1947–48," *Labour History* No. 97 (2009): 143–44.

73. Rechter, "Beyond the Pale," 100, 113. See also the comments regarding Communist influence within the Jewish Council by former CPA members Bernard Rechter, Bernie Taft, and Henry Zimmerman in Mendes, "Jewish Involvement in the Communist Party of Australia."

74. Rechter, "Beyond the Pale," 96–97.

75. Rechter, "Beyond the Pale," 116–17.

76. For the details of some of these links, see *Jewish Council Executive Committee Minutes*, January 22, May 13, July 8, August 12, October 7, 1952, and March 3, 1953. See also Allan Leibler, "The Jewish Council to Combat Fascism and Anti-Semitism: A Study in the Structure and Function of a Communist Front Organisation," BA Honors diss., University of Melbourne, 1967, 57–58.

77. Rubinstein, *The Jews in Australia*, 409.

78. Rechter, "Beyond the Pale," 113.

79. Philip Mendes, "The Cold War, McCarthyism, the Melbourne Jewish Council to Combat Fascism and Anti-Semitism, and Australian Jewry, 1948–1953," *Journal of Australian Studies* 64 (2000): 196–206.

80. Mendes, "Jews, Nazis and Communists Down Under: The Jewish Council's Controversial Campaign Against German Immigration," 88–91.

81. Rutland, *Edge of the Diaspora*, 327–28, 336.

82. Jewish Council Annual Report (1952/53), 3. See also *Australian Jewish News*, February 6, 1953, 4.

83. Norman Rothfield, "Address to Australian Jewish Peace Movement Conference," Melbourne, February 15, 1953. See also "Red Accusations not Absurd, Argues Rothfield," *Australian Jewish News*, February 27, 1953; "Soviet Trials," *Farrago*, April 29, 1953.

84. Rothfield, *Many Paths to Peace*, 43.

85. JCCFAS *Annual Report* (1952/53), 4; JCCFAS *Executive Committee Minutes*, July 8, 1952; February 18, February 24, March 3, March 24, April 21, May 5, and May 25, 1953.

86. "ECAJ directs Boards of Deputies to Disaffiliate all Organizations Opposed to Interests of Jewish people," *Australian Jewish News*, March 6, 1953.

87. Rechter, "Beyond the Pale," 143–44.

88. Philip Mendes, "The 'Declining' Years of the Melbourne Jewish Council to Combat Fascism and Anti-Semitism, 1954–70," *Australian Jewish Historical Society Journal* 17, No. 3 (2004): 375–88.

89. Philip Mendes, "The Senator Sam Cohen Affair: Soviet Anti-Semitism, the ALP and the 1961 Federal Election," *Labour History* No. 78 (2000): 179–97.

90. Philip Mendes, *The New Left, the Jews and the Vietnam War 1965–1972.*

91. Mendes, "The 'Declining' Years of the Melbourne Jewish Council to Combat Fascism and Anti-Semitism, 1954–70," 387–88.

92. Philip Mendes, "Jews and the Left," in *Jews and Australian Politics*, eds. Geoffrey Brahm Levey and Philip Mendes (Brighton: Sussex Academic Press, 2004), 77–81.

93. Jedwab, "The Kadimah Youth Organisation in Melbourne," 187; Rechter, "Beyond the Pale," 6, 136–38, 149–50.

9

Jews and Communism in South Africa

David Yoram Saks

The triumph of Bolshevism in post-revolutionary Russia was a catalyst for Communist sympathizers throughout the world to begin organizing themselves on a more ambitious scale. In the Union of South Africa, at the time a largely self-governing Dominion of the British Empire, the key date in this regard was July 30, 1921, when the inaugural conference of the Communist Party of South Africa (CPSA) took place in Cape Town. In the Party's Manifesto, the Jewish Socialist Society of Cape Town and Jewish Socialist Society (*Poalei Zion*) of Johannesburg are listed as being amongst its founding bodies.[1] None of the Party's other founder organizations were established at the behest of any specific ethnic or religious grouping.

Thus, from the outset there was a pronounced Jewish presence within the nascent Communist movement in South Africa. In this respect, South African Jewry was not unique. The world over, one finds the same disproportionate involvement of Jews in left-wing social and political movements. The record of Jewish involvement in the history of Communism takes on a special resonance in the case of South Africa, however. Whereas in Western democratic societies, Communism has been largely a fringe phenomenon, in the South African case, Communists actually succeeded in achieving political power with the overthrow of the white minority-rule apartheid system and the ushering in of multiracial democracy in April 1994. Elsewhere, it has generally been the fate of Jewish left-wing activists to end up on the sidelines, never having attained the political power necessary to put theory into practice. In the South African case, by contrast, significant numbers of

Jewish "Struggle"[2] veterans ended their careers as senior office-bearers within the ruling party, right up to Cabinet level.

This does not mean that post-apartheid South Africa itself adopted the Communist system, but certainly the ruling regime since the transition to democracy has been significantly influenced by the Communist legacy, both at the ideological level and in terms of the number of its members who come from that background. To this day, the CPSA forms part of the ruling Tripartite Alliance. Moreover, many members of the other two components of that alliance, the African National Congress (ANC) and Congress of South African Trade Unions (COSATU), have their ideological roots firmly in the Communist camp. The irony is that by the time these activists finally achieved power, the Communist moment on the global stage had passed. Twenty years later, the political right to participate in government had yet to translate into bringing about the social transformation envisaged by those Communist Party ideologues who had fought against the apartheid system.[3]

Here, a brief overview of the struggle against white minority rule and the latter's eventual replacement by multiracial democracy in South Africa is necessary. Thereafter, it will be shown how this process impacted on, and was itself significantly influenced by, those Jewish political activists firmly rooted in the Communist camp.

The nation state of South Africa today has its origins in the unification of the British colonies of the Cape, Orange Free State, Natal, and Transvaal on May 31, 1910. Until May 31, 1961, it was known as the Union of South Africa, and thereafter as the Republic of South Africa. In terms of the unification agreement, non-whites outside of the Cape Province would remain without voting rights; within the Cape, the existing qualified common roll franchise was retained. Instead of the principle of a qualified franchise, which had allowed at least some black and mixed race males in the Cape to vote, being gradually extended to the rest of the country, the opposite occurred. By the mid-1950s, all those classified as "non-white" had lost their right to vote on the common roll in the Cape Province. It was not long before even the right to elect, on a separate roll, a limited number of whites to represent them in the country's parliament was taken away.

Without political representation, non-whites were helpless to prevent the passage of ever-more discriminatory legislation. Whatever rights and liberties they did have were progressively eroded through laws that greatly limiting their freedom of movement and access to land, resources, employment, education, and public amenities. This system of race-based control came to be called apartheid (separateness) by the ruling Afrikaner-dominated

National Party after 1948. Later, such euphemisms as "Separate Development" were employed. The ultimate aim of the policy was to establish independent black homelands, within which the various black ethnic groups would have full citizenship rights and outside of which their status would be that of temporary, migrant workers. The area set aside for these homelands, nine of which were ultimately established, amounted to some 13 percent of the country's total land mass. For "Colored" (mixed race) and Asian (mainly Indian) South Africans, a system of parallel representative institutions subservient to the authority of the white political establishment was devised.

In response, the various non-white groupings established their own extra-parliamentary political organizations to lobby on their behalf. Blacks, at the time comprising around two-thirds of the population, in 1912 established the South African National Native Congress—later shortened to African National Congress (ANC). Indians and Coloreds likewise set up representative organizations, and separate black trade unions gradually emerged. Up until World War II, these organizations were generally weak and ineffectual. Lacking in resources and membership, they pursued a course of quiet diplomacy rather than of confrontation. By 1945, however, this approach had been discredited, leading to a more forthright, proactive leadership coming to the fore. During the 1950s, the ANC took the lead in mounting a sustained challenge to the apartheid system and the barrage of new racial legislation that followed the National Party's 1948 electoral victory. While unable to prevent the passage and implementation of those laws, it dramatically raised its own profile, increased its support, and brought numerous other organizations under its banner. White activists within the CPSA, and following the latter's banning in 1950 within the clandestine South African Communist Party (SACP), exercised a significant influence on the course of events. This continued even after the banning of the ANC, the imprisonment of many of its leaders, and the flight into exile of hundreds of others during the 1960s.

In exile, the ANC and SACP survived and worked symbiotically in organizing external resistance, including the so-called "Armed Struggle," against the apartheid regime. They received extensive financial and logistical support in this regard from the Soviet Union and other Communist nations, including China, Cuba, and East Germany. At the same time, they were increasingly assisted by the growing anti-apartheid movement within the Western democratic nations. Ultimately, the much talked about Armed Struggle never really got out of the starting blocks, but both within and outside South Africa mounting pressure was placed on the white minority regime. Externally, an international boycott gathered momentum, culminating in economic sanctions. Within the country, popular resistance reemerged more strongly than ever in the mid-1970s and continued apace throughout the following decade. By the end, the apartheid policy was recognized even by its architects as having failed hopelessly, while it was by then impossible to counter the growing tide of popular unrest. The turning point came in February 1990, with the lifting of the ban of the ANC, SACP, and other resistance organizations and the release of political prisoners, including Nelson Mandela. Negotiations commenced between the white government and resistance movements, headed by the ANC, and these culminated in the country's first democratic, non-racial elections on April 27, 1994.

What was crucial to the willingness of whites to relinquish power was the fact that the threat of a Communist takeover had by then receded. The Soviet Union was no more, having finally been consigned to history three years previously, and the hopelessly discredited ideology of communism as a whole was everywhere being abandoned. Thus, the specter of a post-apartheid South Africa following the disastrous trajectory of other post-independence African states that adopted some form of socialism was removed. Additionally, the National Party hence could no longer defend its policies on the grounds that South Africa was a bulwark against the "total onslaught" of international Communism.[4] Within the new ruling party, sentimental attachment to the Communist dream remained, but there has never been any question of actually implementing the program so optimistically envisioned by its proponents in the heyday of The Struggle.

Throughout this long, violent, and often tragic process, Jewish individuals featured prominently in the ranks of whites who took part in the defeat of the apartheid regime. A high proportion of these identified as Communists, convinced that the Soviet Union—the "emblem of liberation"—was "the singular hope of mankind for a socialist future."[5] Hence, much as they were motivated by their abhorrence for the apartheid system, a strong strain of secular messianism infused them with an added determination to resist the ruling white minority regime.

That Jewish organizations formed a constituent part of the CPSA at its founding has already been noted. Thereafter, Jewish individuals remained disproportionately involved in its activities, a fact that did not go unnoticed by the government of the day. Jewish Bolshevists, for example, were accused of being behind the country's worst bout of industrial unrest, the 1922 Rand Rebellion. The Immigration Quota Act of 1930, which greatly limited subsequent Jewish immigration from Eastern European countries, was to a significant extent motivated by this mistrust.[6]

It will never be possible to arrive at an exact figure for the proportion of white left-wing activists in South Africa who were Jewish. This might be feasible if there had existed a comprehensive, broadly agreed-upon listing of such activists from the early twentieth century onwards, but there is none and never will be. Much information is lacking, the areas of involvement (such as trade unions, journalism, law, academia, politics, armed resistance, etc.) too wide-ranging, and in any case, on what basis does one determine who qualifies as being an activist and who not? Was merely being a member of a left-wing organization enough to have earned for that person the "activist" tag, or was something rather more proactive required? The whole question starts to take on a McCarthyist flavor, albeit that in this case, for many, being labeled as a Communist was a badge of honor.

Obtaining a sense of the extent to which South African Jews were involved in the Communist movement must therefore necessarily be limited to specific historical case studies. One that is frequently cited is that of the Treason Trial, which commenced at the end of 1956 with the arrest of 156 anti-apartheid activists countrywide. Of those, twenty-one were white and at least thirteen were Jewish. The latter ranged from such leading figures in the anti-apartheid struggle as Joe Slovo, his wife Ruth First,[7] Ben Turok, and Lionel "Rusty" Bernstein[8] to those whose involvement was at a relatively low level. What all had in common, however, was that they were committed Communists, something not true in the case of several of the other whites arrested.

Jewish involvement was even more disproportionate in the case of the so-called "Rivonia Trial" (1963–64). All of the white activists that were amongst those arrested in the decisive police raid on the ANC armed wing's underground headquarters and shortly thereafter were Jews with Communist affiliations. They included the aforementioned Bernstein, Denis Goldberg, Harold Wolpe, Arthur Goldreich, Bob Hepple, and Hilliard Festenstein.[9]

During the mid-1960s, some thirty white anti-apartheid activists served prison sentences ranging from three years to life on account of their underground political activities. Twelve of these were Jews and again, all were communists of some stamp or other.[10] Of the non-Jewish prisoners, a number can be classified as radical liberals whose abhorrence of the apartheid system from a human rights and pro-democracy perspective had motivated them to carry out sabotage operations against the apartheid state; one such liberal campaigner, John Harris, was the only white activist to be executed for his actions.[11] However, being a liberal was not in itself sufficient cause for imprisonment; merely being an identified communist was, even if this entailed no more than possessing banned literature.

Further examples of disproportionate Jewish involvement in the Communist movement can be cited. In the period 1949–1953, as will be discussed later, three white Communist candidates were returned to Parliament on a separate roll to represent black Africans; all three were Jewish. Jewish Communists predominated in the ranks of whites involved in the establishment of the ANC's armed wing, *Umkhonto we Sizwe* ("Spear of the Nation"). The Transvaal membership list for the Congress of Democrats, formed after the banning of the CPSA in 1950, is more than 50 percent Jewish. Likewise, Jews were a powerful presence within the nascent non-white trade union movement, including such legendary figures as Solly Sachs, Ray Alexander, and Leon Levy.

Whatever the exact proportions were, therefore, the extent to which Jews were part of the Communist movement in South Africa was clearly very considerable, many times greater than one would expect for a community that never formed much more than 3 percent of the white population and over time shrank to much less than that. Other white ethnic minorities of similar size, such as the Greek, Italian, and Portuguese communities, did not produce anything like so high a number of left-wing activists; indeed, the complete opposite was true. It might be true that most Jewish-born Communists did not wish to define themselves, or be defined by others, as Jews, preferring instead to assume the identity of "citizens of the world" unbound by the strictures of ethnic, national, or religious particularism. That being said, the extraordinarily high proportion of white Communists in South Africa who were of Jewish origin shows conclusively that their Jewishness, however that is defined, must have been a significant factor in the course they chose to adopt. The question that various historians and writers on the subject have sought to answer is exactly why this was the case.[12]

An immediate problem one is confronted with is that while very many left-wing anti-apartheid activists were of Jewish origin, their actual identification with that fact tended to be tenuous at best. By virtue of their political beliefs, which went well beyond mere theorizing on systems of government and economic management to be the basis of their very identity, they were, as a matter of course, non-religious, non-Zionist, and internationalist. Ethnic, religious, racial, cultural, or linguistic differences were regarded as irrelevant in this worldview, if not as positively harmful retarding factors in the quest to establish a workers' utopia.

Over the past two decades or so, numerous Jewish former activists have published their memoirs, amongst them Ben Turok, Joe Slovo, Lionel Bernstein, Norman Levy, Lorna Levy, Baruch Hirson, Norma Kitson, Rika Hodgson, Pauline Podbrey, Albie Sachs, and Ronnie Kasrils. Bernstein's book, extraordinarily enough, makes no mention anywhere in its 300-plus pages of his Jewish origins.[13] In most of the other cases, the subject's Jewish background merits no more than a few lines. The Hirson and Slovo autobiographies are an exception. Hirson's early involvement in Zionist activities, particularly within the most left-leaning of the local Zionist youth movements, *Hashomer Hatza'ir*, clearly had a significant impact on his subsequent life and career and is dealt with accordingly. It is not insignificant that in later life he chose to use his Hebrew name, Baruch, rather than his "English" name, Bertram. From an ethnic-cultural point of view, Slovo's memoir is the most "Jewish" of all, being flavored throughout with characteristic Jewish irony and humor. Against this, however, is a marked antipathy toward the mainstream Jewish community while his anti-Zionism goes so far as to lay the sins of "genocide" and "ethnic cleansing" against the Jewish state.[14]

The majority of the South African Jewish population today trace their origins back to Lithuanian, Latvian, and Polish immigrants who arrived in the main between 1880 and 1914. One fairly straightforward reason for the preponderance of its members involved in left-wing politics was that at least some had been exposed to Marxist and related ideologies such as Bundism in their native Eastern Europe prior to immigrating. Others were born to parents of whom one or both had been so influenced, and hence grew up in a home environment that was at least knowledgeable of and sympathetic toward socialist ways of thinking. Seen in these terms, the Jewish role in South African Communism can to some extent be seen as a product of the revolutionary upheavals that took place in Eastern Europe in the early decades of the twentieth century.

The renowned trade unionist Ray Alexander was one of those already thoroughly immersed in left-wing activism at the time of her leaving for South Africa. Born Rachel Alexandrowich in Latvia in 1913, she became active in the underground Latvian Communist Party while still a teenager, and joined the CPSA just five days after her arrival in the country in 1929. Another was Jack Flior, also Latvian-born, who regarded himself as a "child of the [Russian] Revolution"[15] and was eventually compelled to flee his native land because of his communist activities. At an early age, he forsook the Jewish religion for Marxism, which he also regarded as a form of religious faith. Shortly after World War II, he rejected the Marxist god as well and withdrew completely from politics.[16]

Prior exposure to left-wing ideologies in Eastern Europe thus helps explain why some Jews (or at least their children) became similarly engaged on coming to South Africa. However, these in fact constituted a small minority of South African Jewish Communists, most of whom were born in South Africa and in general do not seem to have been unduly influenced by their parental upbringing. To determine why these embraced the Marxist cause, one needs to explore other possible avenues.

One reason commonly cited for Jewish involvement in liberal-left causes in general is that Jews are more sensitive to the oppression of others because of their own long history of persecution. Nelson Mandela has been amongst those who have suggested this, in his 1994 autobiography writing that in his experience, he had "found Jews to be more broad-minded than most whites on issues of race and politics, perhaps because they themselves have historically been victims of prejudice."[17] Undoubtedly, this was a motivating factor for a great number of Jewish anti-apartheid activists, whether in the left-wing or liberal camp. It is a theme that comes through consistently in recorded interviews with and the memoirs of such individuals.

That being said, it does not automatically follow that being a member of a traditionally oppressed group will exercise an added compulsion on members of that group to come to the assistance of others who are being persecuted. In fact, coming from such a background might just as easily push people in the opposite direction, since they will naturally feel more vulnerable and hence less inclined to put themselves and their community at risk by involving themselves on behalf of others. Indeed, some might even go so far as to support the oppressing party outright in order to demonstrate their trustworthiness and thereby ensure that they, too, are not targeted. Alongside the record of Jews who confronted the apartheid system, one finds that there were in fact such individuals, although their numbers were a great deal smaller. Percy Yutar, the State Prosecutor in the above-noted Rivonia Trial, was at least in part motivated by a desire to boost the standing of the Jewish community by demonstrating to the apartheid government that not all Jews were communists and subversives. Ironically, Yutar's religio-ethnic origins are today regularly invoked in contexts that can only reflect negatively on the Jewish community, whereas those of the many lawyers who served on the other side are forgotten.[18]

A noteworthy distinction to make between foreign-born Jewish leftists and first-generation South African-born ones is that the former were much more at ease in identifying as Jews, to the extent of sometimes organizing themselves along ethnic-cultural lines. Thus, there was a Yiddish-speaking branch of the International Socialist League, the forerunner of the CPSA, and Jewish Socialist societies in both Cape Town and Johannesburg, all established around the time of the Bolshevik Revolution. These are in addition to the Jewish Socialist Society of Cape Town and Jewish Socialist Society (*Poalei Zion*) of Johannesburg, two of the CPSA's constituent bodies.

More socially and culturally focused was the Jewish Workers' Club, established in Johannesburg in 1929. In its heyday, it provided a vibrant community forum for working-class Yiddish-speaking immigrants, organizing dances, concerts, lectures, and theatrical performances while also maintaining links with such left-wing groupings as the Left Book Club and the South African Friends of the Soviet Union. Unusually for its time, its activities were run along racially integrated lines. It was stridently anti-Zionist, and anti-religious to the point that Yom Kippur was regularly chosen as a day on which to hold picnics. Paradoxically, this very act of pointedly dissociating from traditional Jewish norms was itself an expression of Jewish identity. It survives to an extent to this day in the prominence otherwise completely unaffiliated Jewish-born leftists play in South Africa's growing culture of hostility toward the State of Israel.

Another noteworthy instance of collective Jewish activism being combined with left-wing ideology was the case of the Zionist youth movement *Hashomer Hatza'ir*. It was still possible in the early decades of the century to be both a Zionist and a Communist, and in fact a fair number of Jews who went on to become prominent anti-apartheid activists received much of their early political education within that framework.[19] This changed irrevocably once the Soviet Union denounced the new-born State of Israel as a colonial outpost of Western capitalism. However, for a time *Hashomer Hatza'ir* provided, in the words of activist Baruch Hirson, "a crucible of political development" for many young Jews who went on to join the political left.[20]

Interestingly, even whilst becoming increasingly aware of the greater injustices being perpetrated in their society, Jewish leftists were at the forefront of those Jews prepared to physically confront pro-Nazi right-wingers when the latter attempted to hold rallies in the main Jewish population centers. In part, this was certainly because of a general opposition to fascist ideologies, but certainly the rabidly anti-Semitic nature of the radical right was a significant factor in the high number of Jews involved in the many violent clashes that occurred in Johannesburg, Cape Town, and elsewhere during the 1930s. This did not mean that when South Africa entered the war against Germany, Jewish Communists joined their fellow Jews in enlisting in the Union's armed forces. The CPSA's position at the time was that the war was an imperialist struggle between Britain and Germany for "the re-division of the world's markets, colonies, raw materials and fields of investment" and hence Party members should stay out of it. What transformed the "imperialist war" to a "war of freedom" was the Nazi invasion of the Soviet Union commencing June 22, 1941. Doing an about face, the Party now committed itself to supporting the Allied war effort, and many of its future stalwarts went on to serve in North Africa and Italy. Norman Levy, who was too young to enlist, was amongst those tasked with explaining the Party's new position to its members and the public in general: "I repeated their explanations time and again, sometimes getting the logic confused and the sequences muddled, like the hapless sheep in Orwell's *Animal Farm*."[21] Joe Slovo remembered the most difficult thing as trying to convince the CPSA's black members as to why they should fight for the existing South African government, given its record of anti-black repression.[22]

Unlike their immigrant forebears, South African-born Jewish radicals who spoke English as a first language "did not need or desire the fellowship of a specifically Jewish milieu."[23] As a result, organizations like the Jewish Workers' Club and *Hashomer Hatza'ir* failed to attract a younger membership and inevitably faded from the scene.

A final likely reason for the attraction left-wing ideologies exercised for at least some East European Jewish immigrants was that the latter were in the main from working class or at best lower-middle class backgrounds. It was a struggle for these impecunious, Yiddish-speaking new arrivals to establish themselves in an unfamiliar, largely hostile environment. With little immediate prospect of transcending their circumstances, some immigrants naturally gravitated toward communist/socialist modes of identity. Even here, there were exceptions. Julius and Tilly First, parents of the renowned Ruth, were always well-to-do, to the extent of being able to render considerable financial support to fellow activists.

From the above, we can at least tentatively identify some of the factors that resulted in a disproportionate number of Jews joining the Communist movement in South Africa. Some had already been exposed to a variety of leftist ideologies in their native Eastern Europe.

The legacy of anti-Semitism provided a strong motivation for opposing injustice for many others. Within the Zionist movement, there was a strong left-wing strain, most notably within *Hashomer Hatza'ir*, where a number of future activists received their early political education. What can be said without equivocation is that traditional "Judaic values," particularly with regard to the Jewish religious heritage, played little or no part in fashioning the way Jewish leftists saw the world and their role in it. On the contrary, one gets the distinct impression that whole-heartedly embracing the Communist vision was a way of escaping their Jewish identity altogether. As Shimoni aptly expresses it, many of the Jews who took part in the South African freedom struggle "espoused a dogmatic communism and slavish obedience to the Soviet line, which commanded the disavowal of any Jewish identity and engendered a self-blinding indifference to the crushing of liberty for Jews in the Soviet Union."[24]

Hirson recognized that the preponderance of Jews in radical politics begged an explanation. Once, whilst serving his prison sentence, one of the guards posed the question to him, and he was unable to provide a satisfactory answer. Grappling with the question many years later, his conclusion was: "The ethnic origin and classlessness, the studentship and professionalism, the political awareness and the presence in prison were not entirely disconnected, at least in my case, from being born a Jew. It was a Jewishness that denied many of its attributes, but there was a residue, harking back to some past that helped mark out the trajectory along which I journeyed."[25]

Several anti-apartheid veterans have recognized a linkage between their communist affiliations and their Jewish heritage. Ronnie Kasrils, who joined the SACP in 1961 and sat on its Central Committee for twenty years from December 1986 on, commented that Jewish activists like himself were not aberrations of the Jewish community but on the contrary were products of the Jewish humanistic tradition. Pauline Podbrey likewise said that she had always felt that her Communist sympathies had their roots in Jewish ethics and morality.[26]

Other former activists, however, downplayed the role their Jewish origins played in the course they decided to take. Immanuel Suttner, in his penetrating afterword to his book *Cutting Through the Mountain: Interviews With South African Jewish Activists*, has this to say on the question:

> The network of family and friends they moved amongst while growing up were largely Ashkenazi Jewish, and so imbibed the fears, aspirations, strengths and interpersonal modalities of that community and culture. That all this was internalised was arguably reflected later in both their questioning and in their analytical

> ability, in their drivenness, in their desire to programmatically implement basic intuitions about justice, in their food, music and humour they liked, in their professional aspirations and family dynamics.[27]

If any single individual can be said to epitomize the phenomenon of South African Jewish Communism, it must be Joe Slovo. Born Yossel Maishel Slovo in Obeliai, Lithuania, he immigrated to South Africa in 1926 and joined the Young Communist League as a teenager. Thereafter, he rose to occupy key positions within both the Communist Party, before and after its banning, and within the ANC's armed wing *Umkhonto we Sizwe.* He was the latter's chief of staff in exile, was the first white to be elected to the national executive of the ANC and in 1986 was elected secretary general of the SA Communist Party in exile. After the transition to democracy in April 1994, he served as Minister of Housing under President Nelson Mandela until his death from cancer in January the following year.

As seen and depicted by the apartheid regime, Slovo was the personification of the Communist menace. By contrast, within South Africa's black population, he was accorded the status of a heroic fighter for their freedom, with a stature equivalent to that enjoyed by such iconic black resistance leaders as Oliver Tambo and Walter Sisulu, if not quite on the level of Nelson Mandela. In this regard James Campbell writes, "To the architects of apartheid, he was the arch-villain, a sinister 'KGB colonel' (always a colonel: for fifteen years, National Party demonologists denied him a promotion) who exemplified Communist domination of the African National Congress. To the young 'comrades' of the 1980s, he was a founding member and chief strategist of *Umkhonto we Sizwe*, a freedom fighter whose exploits were celebrated in story and song."[28] Slovo was instrumental in all the key policy decisions made by the SACP, both within South Africa and in exile. He was also a relentless, dogmatic enforcer of doctrinal orthodoxy within the movement, as many a "deviationist" sidelined for questioning the Party line discovered at first hand.

It would have been surprising had the preponderance of Jews in radical leftist politics gone unnoticed by the ruling regime and its supporters. Indeed, the question put by the unnamed prison guard to Hirson was repeated in various guises, sometimes directed at the activists themselves and sometimes, more menacingly, at the mainstream Jewish leadership. In mid-1963, following the capture of some two dozen members of *Umkhonto we Sizwe* in a police raid on its Rivonia headquarters and the subsequent dramatic escape from custody of two of them, Arthur Goldreich and Harold Wolpe, anti-Jewish suspicions within the shaken white establishment were particularly strong. According to a *Time* magazine report, the Rivonia raid and escape of Goldreich and Wolpe "touched off ominous rumblings" against South African Jewry. It was reported that when Criminal Investigation Chief R. J. van den Bergh made reference to the raid in a speech, a voice from the audience cried: "Jews!" Van den Bergh's response was that foes of apartheid might indeed be "instruments of Jews."[29]

Around this time, the South African Jewish Board of Deputies, the umbrella representative body of South African Jewry, was approached by the pro-government, Afrikaans language newspaper *Dagbreek* and was asked why it was that so many of the white Communist plotters were Jews. Did this suggest that Jews were not happy in South Africa, and what was the official Board view on the matter? The Board's leadership were in an unenviable position. Their primary mandate was to protect the community from anti-Semitism, and any statement suggesting support for the liberation movements would most likely have provoked a strong anti-Semitic reaction. However, taking the government's side was also not an option. The Board's mandate did not extend to adopting political positions on behalf of all Jews, especially ones that went against the prevailing consensus. Most Jews certainly did not support the radical agendas of their Communist brethren, but neither did they endorse the hardline race policies of the ruling National Party. At election time, they overwhelmingly voted against the "Nats" and all Jewish Members of Parliament represented the comparatively more liberal Opposition. Ultimately, the Board issued a non-committal, middle-ground response: "The facts prove abundantly that the Jewish community of South Africa is a settled, loyal and patriotic section of the population. The acts of individuals of any section are their responsibility and no section of the community can or should be asked to accept responsibility therefore. If individuals transgress the law, they render themselves liable to its penalties. The Jewish community condemns illegality in whatever section of the population it appears."[30]

Mention has been made of three Jewish Communists who were elected to Parliament on the CPSA ticket. They were Sam Kahn, Brian Bunting (son of a Jewish mother and the non-Jewish founding father of the CPSA, Sidney Bunting), and Ray Alexander. Only the first two actually sat in Parliament; Alexander won the election but the tightened-up anti-Communist legislation of the day prevented her from taking up her seat.

Under normal circumstances, it would have been essentially impossible for a Communist Party candidate campaigning on a platform of full racial equality to be elected to Parliament by white voters. Even working-class whites overwhelmingly rejected it, and indeed had notoriously campaigned under the slogan "Workers of the World Unite and Fight for a White South Africa" during the various periods of industrial unrest that took place in and around Johannesburg during the century's early decades. However, there was one small loophole, in the form of the 1936 Representation of Natives Act. In terms of this measure, blacks in the Cape Province who qualified to vote were removed from the common rolls and, voting on a communal roll, were allowed to elect three whites to represent them in the 150-seat House of Assembly, two more in the Senate, and two on the provincial council.

Taking advantage of this, the CPSA was able to get a representative elected to the Senate and three successive candidates elected to the Assembly for the Cape Western constituency before the passage of the Suppression of Communism Act in 1950 and the subsequent amendments to it closed this avenue as well. The lawyer Hyman Basner, after standing unsuccessfully for the Senate in 1937, was elected by a 60 percent majority in 1942. He worked indefatigably within the rural constituencies he represented, striving to breathe new life into the country's tradition of rural resistance. His most conspicuous achievement was to secure a wage increase for black mineworkers whilst serving on the Witwatersrand Mine Natives Wages Commission.[31] Disillusioned by his inability to make real headway within a system designed to stringently limit black political rights, he resigned from the Senate in 1947.

Sam Kahn was elected to the House of Assembly in November 1948 and served until his expulsion in May 1952. While his career as an MP was unavoidably brief, he carved a noteworthy niche for himself in the annals of the anti-apartheid struggle. A superb orator with a memorable turn of phrase and biting wit, he launched devastating broadsides against laws that were as ludicrous in their conception as they were callous and unjust in their implementation. He even managed to get the full text of the Communist Manifesto inserted into the record of *Hansard*, ostensibly to demonstrate the true nature of the aims of the CPSA. Through this stratagem, a fundamental text of Communist theory otherwise banned in the country was made available to the public courtesy of the Government Printer.[32]

In his maiden speech, Kahn said that not only the CPSA but democracy itself was in jeopardy because of the National Party's policies. He told the House that the problem of race relations in South Africa would not be solved by stamping and branding every form of opposition to the government as "Communist." He concluded with a plea for the fair treatment of black South Africans, from whose ranks men of great professional and educational skill were emerging, despite the entrenched prejudice that faced them everywhere they turned.[33] An indication of the hostility to which Kahn was exposed is shown in the opening remark of a subsequent speaker, the National Party MP F. E. Mentz, who said, "I do not wish this afternoon to react to the voice of the Kremlin that has been heard for the first time in this House."[34] Moves were soon afoot to shut down this small window of opportunity for black grievances to be given expression. In March 1949, Minister of Justice C. R. Swart banned a series of meetings at which Kahn was scheduled to speak and also ensured that Kahn was constantly trailed by members of the Special Branch while he was in Johannesburg.[35] In May, following a devastating attack by Kahn on the Prohibition of Mixed Marriages Bill, the National Party representative for Kempton Park expressed the belief that Kahn and his ilk should be banned altogether: "[O]ne feels that the day must be hastened when we shall introduce legislation to prohibit the expounding of the ideology that he [Kahn] is preaching far and wide in this country."[36] Such legislation was promulgated the following year, in the form of the Suppression of Communism Act. However, because the CPSA had dissolved itself shortly before the bill became law, Kahn could not yet be expelled from Parliament for belonging to an illegal organization. In 1951, therefore, the Act was amended to establish the continued culpability of any person who had once been a member of the CPSA. Kahn ceased to be a Member of Parliament in March 1952. In his final address to the House, he said that it had been his advocacy of equal rights for all South Africans, black and white, and not his belief in socialism that had really brought him into conflict with the government. It was such multiracial equality that the regime wished to make "the modern blasphemy, the twentieth century heinous crime in politics."[37]

Brian Bunting, Kahn's successor, sat in the House for nine months, and likewise used that platform to eloquently confront the government on every piece of discriminatory legislation. His inevitable expulsion came in July 1953, when a parliamentary Select Committee found by a 19 to 2 margin that he had "advocated, defended and encouraged the achievements of the objectives of communism both before and after the promulgation of the [Suppression of Communism] Act." Sam Kahn himself said in a tribute to Bunting that he had "hastened his own expulsion by scarifying the nationalists for their . . . callous treatment of the African peoples . . . speeches fired with indignation."[38] Bunting had the unique distinction of being expelled from the South African parliament for being a Communist, only to be returned to the House forty-one years later following the country's first democratic elections.

Ray Alexander, the third Jewish Communist to be elected to parliament, was never allowed to take up her seat, thanks to another hasty amendment to the Suppression of Communism Act. She was forcibly prevented from entering the House of Assembly by a strong police presence strategically posted at all entrances to the building.[39]

By the end of the 1960s, a relentless series of draconian security measures, police raids, and court cases had effectively crushed all internal opposition to the apartheid state. Those Jewish activists who did not go into exile, in some cases after serving lengthy prison terms, were forced for many years to keep a low profile. Some died in exile and others never returned, even after the lifting of political restrictions by President F. W. de Klerk in early 1990 made it possible to do so. Many did return, however, and played a significant part both in negotiating an end to white minority rule and in building the new democratic society thereafter. They included Joe Slovo, Ronnie Kasrils, Norman and Leon Levy, Brian and Sonia Bunting, Denis Goldberg, Ray Alexander, Pauline Podbrey, Ben Turok, Violet Weinberg, and Gill Marcus. Marcus, Communist background notwithstanding, went on to show an expertise in financial management that culminated in her appointment as Governor of the Reserve Bank, a position she held with distinction. Lionel and Hilda Bernstein returned periodically to participate in various aspects of the transition, although they remained based in the United Kingdom.

From the mid-1970s onwards, a new generation of Jewish anti-apartheid activists arose, again comprising a significant component of whites involved in the anti-apartheid struggle, albeit not to so disproportionate an extent as previously. These were active in such organizations as the United Democratic Front, End Conscription Campaign, National Union of South African Students, Congress of South African Trade Unions, and the Detainees' Parents Support Committee. Within their ranks were certainly individuals of a strong leftist bent, but comparatively few identified outright as Communists. By then, the crumbling of the apartheid system was being accompanied by a parallel disintegration of the Soviet empire; clearly, Marxism was not the savior of humankind that it was once believed with such fervor to be by the previous generation. Even so, there were a few exceptions. The lawyer and academic Raymond Suttner worked underground for the ANC and SACP from 1971 to 1975, resulting in a seven-and-a-half-year prison sentence. After the SACP was unbanned, he served on its Central Committee, and later became a Member of Parliament.

The activities of identifiable Jews like Sam Kahn and Arthur Goldreich caused much anxiety within the mainstream Jewish leadership which, as we have seen, was sometimes challenged by government supporters to account for it. On one occasion, a delegation purportedly met with Kahn and urged him to tone down his anti-government rhetoric on the grounds that he was endangering the Jewish community. Kahn agreed that Jewish Communists caused anti-Semitism, but pointed out that Jewish capitalists did so just as much. He supposedly then said, "I'll tell you what gentlemen. As a gesture of concern for the Jews, let's enter into a bargain: you give up your business and I'll then give up politics."[40] It is a good story, but it may be apocryphal. Its source is Joe Slovo, whose antipathy toward the mainstream Jewish establishment has already been noted and who, as an ever-enthusiastic raconteur, may have taken dramatic license with the facts.

The rift between the Jewish mainstream and its left-wing activist fringe has never healed. Not without reason, the latter felt resentful at what they saw as the community leadership's belatedly embracing them as authentic Jewish heroes only after it became clear that white minority rule was on the way out. Where had the South African Jewish Board of Deputies, the rabbinate and the Jewish press been prior to that, when they had been taking such risks and making such sacrifices to confront the injustices of the apartheid regime? For their part the broad majority of Jews, also with justification, looked askance at those who had not merely turned their backs on the greater cause of Jewish peoplehood but often collaborated with the avowed enemies of world Jewry. The oppression of Soviet Jewry, it hardly need be pointed out, was never a cause Jewish Communists ever made the slightest attempt to identify with. Since the turn of the century, the relationship between Jewish leftists and the remainder of the community has, if anything, been even more soured by the virulent anti-Zionist campaigning of former Jewish activists, most notably Ronnie Kasrils. The latter, as Minister of Water Affairs and Forestry and later as Minister of Intelligence, exploited his high office as well as his impressive "Struggle" credentials to demonize Israel and discredit its local supporters to an extent that few other anti-Israel activists have been able to achieve.

Sam Kahn's unabashed insistence on his right to make political statements even if it made mainstream Jewry feel uncomfortable does not mean that the principle of freedom of expression was adhered to within the local Communist movement itself. Indeed, the contrary was true. Throughout its history, strict ideological conformity on the part of its members has been zealously enforced, with deviants from the Party line quickly finding themselves out in the cold. The history of the CPSA and its SACP successor is replete with cases of members being expelled for ideological deviations or acting contrary to Party directives. For those thus dealt with, the experience could be devastating, not unlike being declared a heretic under Catholicism or put into *Cherem* (excommunication) under Jewish law. At the social and professional level, expulsion had serious implications since the close-knit Communist community also acted as a surrogate family and support system for those within the fold. The emotional trauma of being expelled from the "family" should also not be downplayed.

One of these "heretics," Norma Kitson, referred to the guardians of doctrinal orthodoxy within the party as the *Khevra Kadisha* (Jewish burial society), since whatever they couldn't control, they buried.[41] Amongst those she specifically had in mind were Brian and Barbara Bunting (born Isaacman), who, according to another anti-apartheid veteran Paul Trewhella, had been "leaders of a small, tight exile apparatus in London between 1963 and their return to South Africa in 1991."[42] Brian's father Sidney, a principle founder of the CPSA, was declared to be a right-wing deviationist and expelled from the Party for disagreeing with Stalin's advocacy of an "Independent Native Republic" as the CPSA's principal slogan at the Sixth Congress of the Comintern in 1928. His son was careful not make the same mistake. In a career within the party lasting over fifty years, he was a meticulous follower and in due course enforcer of the Party line. For decades after going into exile, he was London correspondent for the Soviet news agency, Tass, and he never deviated from the current line of the Soviet Union.[43] As a long-serving member of the Central Committee and as an editor of the SACP journal, the *African Communist*, he exercised significant influence within the Party and the anti-apartheid movement in general.

An intriguing question that always arises when speaking about communism in the Western democracies is how its adherents reacted firstly to the progressive revelations of the oppressive nature of the Soviet regime and eventually to the dramatic collapse of Soviet Communism itself from the end of the 1980s. The first serious challenge to their hitherto unquestioned belief that the USSR was the "emblem of liberation" and hope for a better, socialist future for mankind was when news filtered through of Soviet leader Nikita Khrushchev's famous denunciation of Stalin at the Twentieth Congress of the Communist Party of the USSR.

Now, the cherished image of Stalin as the benevolent, beloved, and heroic leader of his people had to be adjusted. He had "made grave errors," and sometimes succumbed to flattery, even if his essential reputation as a great war hero, strong leader, wise statesman, and leading Marxist theorist remained secure.[44]

Gradually, a rift began widening between those within the Party who adhered to the "made-some-mistakes-but-still-fundamentally-sound" approach and those who gradually became more and more disillusioned with the Communist program. Ever-emerging evidence of the oppressive nature of the Soviet Union, including its iron-fisted control over numerous Eastern and Central European countries, could hardly be suppressed. Soviet apologists tied themselves in knots trying to justify the crushing of the Hungarian uprising in 1956 and the equally harsh suppression of the democratic Prague Spring in Czechoslovakia twelve years later.

The division between dogged Party loyalists and those who turned their backs on the Great Dream could be acrimonious in the extreme, never more so than in the case of the renowned husband-wife team of Ruth First and Joe Slovo. In 1954, First had been one of a group of prominent South African Marxists who visited the USSR and afterwards wrote up their impressions, published on their return, in a pamphlet entitled "South Africans in the Soviet Union."[45] Like her fellow tourists, she described what she had seen in glowing terms, even to the extent of interpreting at face value the fact that not one person she had spoken to had complained or expressed dissent about their situation. A woman of her considerable intelligence should even then have realized that while a society where many of its citizens were complaining obviously had a problem, a society where no-one complained at all clearly had a much bigger one. Later, to her credit, she was unequivocal in her rejection of the regime she had once championed. Described by her daughter, the author Gillian Slovo, as "the critic, the outsider who questioned orthodoxy,"[46] she differed sharply with her dogmatically loyal husband on the issue, and the bitter and often public confrontations they had were largely responsible for the breakup of their marriage. First was adjudged to be "deviationist" and dangerously undisciplined by her erstwhile comrades, with the result that by the time of her assassination by agents of the apartheid regime in August 1982, she had been completely marginalized within the SACP. This did not prevent the Party from embracing her as a martyr after her death.[47]

In general, it would seem that Jewish women were more likely to recognize the realities of what international Communism had become and distance themselves accordingly. In addition to First and Kitson, Pauline

Podbrey and Lorna Levy, wife of Leon, did so as well. Even Hilda Bernstein at one point fell afoul of Slovo for expressing concerns about the 1968 Soviet invasion of Czechoslovakia.

Slovo himself remained a committed Marxist to the end, even if he did eventually come to condemn Stalin and Stalinism. In his influential essay "Has Socialism Failed?"[48] written shortly after the collapse of most of the Communist governments of Eastern Europe in 1989, he insisted that socialism's practitioners had failed, not socialism itself. Moreover, those failures should not blind people to socialism's very real achievements:

> For our part, we firmly believe in the future of socialism; and we do not dismiss its whole past as an unmitigated failure. Socialism certainly produced a Stalin and a Ceausescu, but it also produced a Lenin and a Gorbachev. Despite the distortions at the top, the nobility of socialism's basic objectives inspired millions upon millions to devote themselves selflessly to building it on the ground. And, no one can doubt that if humanity is today poised to enter an unprecedented era of peace and civilised international relations, it is in the first place due to the efforts of the socialist world.

Slovo went on to denounce the perversion of the socialist enterprise by Stalinism, a term he defined as denoting "the bureaucratic-authoritarian style of leadership (of parties both in and out of power) which denuded the party and the practice of socialism of most of its democratic content and concentrated power in the hands of a tiny, self-perpetuating elite." This, he asserted, did not "flow naturally from the basic concepts of Marxism whose core is essentially humane and democratic and which project a social order with an economic potential vastly superior to that of capitalism."[49]

None of this is particularly convincing. It was all very well for Slovo to come out against the tyranny of the Soviet and Warsaw Pact regimes once they had collapsed, but it is a fact that he not only failed to do so when they were in existence, but was an active apologist for them. In a 1994 interview, he defended his failure to speak out against the gulags with the excuse that in the course of visiting the Soviet Union as part of official delegations, he and other participants were never in a position to investigate the truth of this themselves: "People said there were gulags, millions of people incarcerated there. We were assured there were no such things. We didn't have the opportunity to check."[50] But, as Campbell dryly observes, the culture of utter intolerance for independent thinking within the SACP, particularly when this took the form of criticizing the Soviet Union for its human rights violations, had very largely been brought about through Slovo himself: "Like the proverbial orphan pleading for clemency after murdering his parents, the circumstances that Slovo offered in extenuation were very much of his own making."[51]

It is also something of a stretch, to say the least, to credit the socialist world for the hopeful new era of peace that humanity was about to enter, given that it was the prior existence of socialist regimes that had surely prevented that era from coming about in the first place. Nor would many students of history today accord Lenin a particularly honored place in the pantheon of world statesmen.

That being said, Slovo's belief that the future of socialism lay in embracing a democratic mode of government was genuine. His vision, and that of the SACP, for a post-apartheid South Africa was that it would "guarantee all citizens the basic rights and freedoms of organization, speech, thought, press, movement, residence, conscience and religion; full trade union rights for all workers including the right to strike, and one person one vote in free and democratic elections." Such freedoms, he wrote, constituted the very essence of the Party's national liberation and socialist objectives and they clearly implied political pluralism. Experience having shown that an institutionalized one-party state had a strong propensity for authoritarianism, the SACP remained "protagonists of multi-party post-apartheid democracy both in the national democratic and socialist phases."[52]

In the four years following the publication of this article, Slovo played a central role in the complex negotiations between the ANC-headed liberation movements and the white minority government over the country's political future. Whatever his personal wishes might have been, he showed himself to be pragmatic and far-sighted, notably in his proposal of a "sunset clause" whereby the white political establishment and civil service would be given a substantial role in a future democratic transitional government. The administration that ultimately replaced the apartheid regime, even if it included within its ranks numerous senior members of the SACP, bore no resemblance to the totalitarian Marxist regimes of pre-1990 Europe. With its constitutionally entrenched Bill of Rights, independent judiciary, and extensive system of public involvement in the legislative process, it compared favorably with the most democratic systems of government anywhere in the world.

Some two decades have passed since that memorable transformation and, certain problems notwithstanding, South Africa's democratic consensus has endured. Within the ranks of those committed individuals of all races whose efforts and sacrifices brought it about were many Jews, and of these a significant number were inspired to take such action by their profound belief in the Communist vision. That vision proved to be an illusion, in large part a tragic one, yet it is only right that those veterans have been accorded a place of honor in the annals of South Africa's history. Sometimes, it is good enough simply to have done the right thing, even if it was not always done for the right reason.

Notes

1. *Manifesto of the Communist Party of South Africa.* Adopted at the inaugural conference of the Party, Cape Town, July 30, 1921. http://www.CPSA.org.za/docs/history/1921/manifesto21.html. Accessed Jan. 2, 2013.

2. The campaign for democracy against white minority rule was popularly referred to simply as "The Struggle," particularly in black political and white left-wing circles.

3. Norman Levy, *The Final Prize: My life in the Anti-Apartheid Struggle* (Cape Town: South African History Online, 2011), 72.

4. Helen Suzman, *In No Uncertain Terms: The Memoirs of Helen Suzman* (Johannesburg: Jonathan Ball, 1993), 289.

5. Levy, *The Final Prize*, 160.

6. Glenn Frankel, "The Road to Rivonia: Jewish Radicals and the Cost of Conscience in South Africa," in *Memories, Realities and Dreams: Aspects of the South African Jewish Experience*, eds. Richard Mendelsohn and Milton Shain (Johannesburg: Jonathan Ball, 2000), 192.

7. A journalist and lecturer, Ruth First was born into a well-to-do but nevertheless socialist Johannesburg family in 1925. After the war, she edited several left-wing newspapers, including the *Guardian* and its subsequent incarnations *New Age*, *Clarion*, and *Advance*. She was detained and held in solitary confinement for four months in 1963 and went into exile the following year. At the time of her assassination by an apartheid hit squad on August 17, 1982, she was Director of Research and Training in the Department of African Studies at the Eduardo Mondlane University in Maputo, Mozambique.

8. Lionel "Rusty" Bernstein was a founding member of the Congress of Democrats and served on the working group that drew up the famous Freedom Charter, a statement of principles that underpinned the philosophy and vision of the liberation movements from the mid-1950s onwards. Himself an accomplished writer, the actual wording of the Charter is his, although he never claimed credit for this. Bernstein was a founder of the ANC's armed wing, *Umkhonto we Sizwe*. He was detained for long periods during the early 1960s and was a defendant in

the Rivonia Trial. On his acquittal he and his wife, fellow activist Hilda Bernstein, went into exile in the United Kingdom.

9. Of these, only Bernstein and Goldberg actually stood trial in the end. Wolpe and Goldreich made a daring escape from police custody, Hepple was released on the understanding that he would turn state's witness and likewise managed to flee the country, and Festenstein was eventually not charged. Of the nine defendants at the trial, including Nelson Mandela, eight were sentenced to life imprisonment while Bernstein was acquitted for lack of evidence.

10. Of particular interest in this regard is Baruch Hirson's autobiography *Revolutions in my Life* (Johannesburg: Witwatersrand University Press, 1995), much of which focuses on the years he spent as a political prisoner in Pretoria Central. He records the often bitter ideological arguments that took place between proponents of Stalinism and Maoism and how distressing it was for him, as the only Trotskyite, to be frozen out by both factions. Hirson himself served nine years for his involvement in the African Resistance Movement's sabotage operations.

11. Gideon Shimoni, *Community and Conscience: The Jews in Apartheid South Africa* (Johannesburg: David Philip, 2003), 74, makes a distinction between "liberals," whom he defines as those who confronted the apartheid system only within the parameters deemed legal by the regnant white polity and "radicals," most but not all of whom were Communists, who went beyond those parameters.

12. See *Cutting through the Mountain: Interviews with South African Jewish Activists*, ed. Immanuel Suttner (Johannesburg: Viking, 1997). Suttner grapples very insightfully with the question in his Afterword; See also Glenn Frankel, *Rivonia's Children: Three Families and the Cost of Conscience in White South Africa* (New York: Continuum, 2001; Mark Israel and Simon Adams, " 'That Spells Trouble': Jews and the Communist Party of South Africa," *Journal of Southern African Studies* 26, No. 1 (2000): 145–62; Mendelsohn and Shain, eds., *Memories, Realities and Dreams: Aspects of the South African Jewish Experience*; and Shimoni, *Community and Conscience: The Jews in Apartheid South Africa.*

13. Rusty Bernstein, *Memory Against Forgetting: Memoirs from a Life in South African Politics, 1938–1964* (London: Viking, 1999).

14. Joe Slovo, *Slovo: The Unfinished Autobiography* (Johannesburg: Ravan Press, 1995), 31.

15. Suttner, *Cutting Through the Mountain*, 303.

16. Ibid., 305.

17. Nelson Mandela, *Long Walk to Freedom: The Autobiography of Nelson Mandela* (Randburg, SA: Macdonald Purnell, 1994), 66.

18. David Saks, *Jewish Memories of Mandela* (Johannesburg: South African Jewish Board of Deputies, 2011), 97.

19. They included Baruch Hirson, Lionel Forman, Sid Shall, Joe Slovo, and Monty and Myrtle Berman.

20. Cited in Shimoni, *Community and Conscience*, 90.

21. Levy, *The Final Prize*, 26.

22. Slovo: *The Unfinished Autobiography*, 28.

23. Richard Mendelsohn and Milton Shain, *The Jews in South Africa: An Illustrated History* (Johannesburg: Jonathan Ball, 2008), 130.

24. Shimoni, *Community and Conscience*, 76–77.

25. Hirson, *Revolutions in My Life*, 97.

26. Suttner, *Cutting Through the Mountain*, 605.

27. Ibid., 601.

28. J. T. Campbell, "Beyond the Pale: Jewish Immigration and the South African Left," in *Memories, Realities and Dreams*, 141–42.

29. "Escape Artists," *Time*, August 30, 1963, 31.

30. South African Jewish Board of Deputies—SA Rochlin Archives: Biog. 303 Goldreich A.

31. Campbell, "Beyond the Pale," 124.

32. Slovo, *The Unfinished Autobiography*, 41.

33. Union of South Africa, *House of Assembly Debates*, 27/1/1949, col. 187.

34. Ibid., col. 189.

35. David Saks, "Sam Kahn and the Communist Party," *Jewish Affairs* 51, No. 1 (1996): 25–29.

36. Union of South Africa, *House of Assembly Debates*, 24/5/1949, col. 6423.

37. H. J. Simons and R. E. Simons, *Class and Colour in South Africa, 1850–1950* (Harmondsworth, UK: Penguin, 1969), 593–94.

38. Levy, *The Final Prize*, 151.

39. Ibid., 153.

40. Shimoni, *Community and Conscience*, 113.

41. "Brian Bunting: Political Activist and Journalist," the *Independent*, London, July 19, 2008. http://www.independent.co.uk/news/obituaries/brian-bunting-political-activist-and-journalist-871771.html. Accessed Jan. 2, 2013. Kitson was specifically referring to the SACP leadership in exile, but her comment applied equally well to the situation in South Africa itself.

42. Ibid.

43. Ibid.

44. Levy, *The Final Prize*, 160.

45. The copy consulted by the author is housed in the Historical Papers Division, William Cullen Library, University of the Witwatersrand. Ref. AD 1812, Political Trials, No. Eq. 7.5.1.

46. Gillian Slovo, *Every Secret Thing: My Family, My Country* (London: Little, Brown and Company, 1997), 111.

47. Campbell, "Beyond the Pale," 153.

48. Joe Slovo, "Has Socialism Failed?" South African Communist Party, 1989.

http://www.marxists.org/subject/africa/slovo/1989/socialism-failed.htm. Accessed Jan. 2, 2013. Slovo followed this up with a paper entitled "Beyond the Stereotype: The CPSA in the Past, Present and Future," which essentially expanded on the points made in the previous essay. http://www.CPSA.org.za/docs/history/stereotypeJS.html. Accessed Jan. 2, 2013.

49. Joe Slovo, "Has Socialism Failed?."
50. Quoted in Campbell, "Beyond the Pale," 153–54.
51. Ibid., 154.
52. Ibid.

10

Conclusion

The End of a Dream

Matthew B. Hoffman and Henry F. Srebrnik

The Jewish Communist movement is now an historical memory, almost all those involved long gone. In a sense, this has been true of the Communist movement as a whole, largely replaced by identity politics and other varieties of radical politics, such as anti-Globalization, or even forms of militant Islam. Our book deals with the movement in the English-speaking world, though it was also very active in Belgium, France, and other European countries, as well as in Argentina, Brazil, Mexico, and Uruguay.

Matthew Hoffman looked at Yiddish-language Communists in the United States. Also in America, Jennifer Young provided a study of the Jewish People's Fraternal Order, while Gennady Estraikh examined the career of Paul Novick, the long-time editor of the Communist *Frayhayt*. Henry Srebrnik focused on the work of pro-Soviet Jewish organizations in Canada, while Ester Reiter concentrated on women in the Canadian Jewish Communist movement and on the political activities of the United Jewish People's Order. Stephen Cullen discussed the nature of Jewish involvement with Communism in Britain. Philip Mendes provided an overview of the organizations founded by Jewish Communists in Australia. Finally, David Saks described the political work of a number of influential Jewish Communists active in the struggle against apartheid in South Africa; some lived to see it finally toppled.

While the size and influence of the movement varied in each country due to differences in their Jewish communities and their relationships to that nation's politics, there is no doubt that there was an overall unity to the movement, based both on its role as a support group for the Soviet Union as well as providing a cultural enclave for Yiddish-speaking Jewish immigrants and their descendants.

The first main cause, then, for the decline of the Jewish Communist movement in the postwar years was that it proved unable to survive the twists and turns of Soviet policy toward the Jews. The Jewish Anti-Fascist Committee was disbanded in 1948 and not a single Yiddish publication was produced in the USSR between then and 1959. Jews had become, in Stalin's eyes, an unreliable and alien group. As a result, Jews disappeared from important political, diplomatic, and military positions. Many were dismissed under various pretexts. The number of Jews in the Supreme Soviet had also declined precipitously by 1950. The last Jewish schools in the country were shut down that year; and no Jewish schools were in operation in Birobidzhan after 1948. Israel was increasingly described as an American "colony" and satellite of Western imperialism, especially after it sided with the United States in the Korean War. The negative Soviet attitude toward its Jewish population would become more apparent when the country began to provide ideological, military, and economic support to Israel's Arab neighbors.

But much worse was to come. Most of the high-profile Soviet Jewish intellectuals who had been involved with western Jewish movements would, in the last years of Stalin's rule, be executed following show trials in which they were accused of plotting on behalf of "Zionism" and "imperialism." In 1952, Stalin decided to put fifteen former JAFC leaders on trial; included were the renowned Yiddish writers and intellectuals Peretz Markish, Leyb Kvitko, David Hofshteyn, Itsik Fefer, and David Bergelson. They were all falsely charged with a range of capital offenses, from treason and espionage to bourgeois nationalism, in order to create a connection to U.S. imperialism. Among the accused were former American ICOR activists Elias Wattenberg and Leon Talmy; both had immigrated to the USSR in the early 1930s and had become members of the JAFC during the war. Their years in America had made them vulnerable to charges of espionage. Along with Wattenberg's wife, Chaika Ostrovskaya, a translator for the JAFC, they were executed on August 12, 1952.[1]

That same year, fourteen Communist leaders were arrested for treason and espionage in Czechoslovakia, including the deputy premier and secretary of the Communist Party, Rudolph Slansky. The situation was exacerbated by anti-Semitic propaganda. Eleven of the fourteen arrested were Jewish; they were accused of being Titoist and Zionist agents in a conspiracy organized by an Anglo-American network. Of the eleven eventually executed, eight were Jewish. Similar show trials took place in East Germany, Hungary, Romania, and other Soviet satellite states.[2] The slightest deviation from the Soviet pattern was declared treasonable and tens of thousands of people were sent to slave labor camps. Foreign and international Jewish welfare agencies were expelled.

It was not until 1956, however, that the Jewish Communist movement received a mortal blow, in the form of the "secret speech" by Nikita Khrushchev at the 20th congress of the Communist Party of the Soviet Union, in which Khrushchev exposed the murderous deeds of Stalin and his henchmen. The report of Stalin's crimes against the Jews of Russia, with detailed revelations of anti-Semitic repression in the Soviet Union after 1948, including the murder of the cream of Yiddish writers and intellectuals in August 1952 and the so-called "Doctors' Plot" in early 1953, were published in the Polish press and elsewhere.[3] Nowhere was the crisis of faith more profound than among the Jewish Communists. For most, it became painfully clear that the Soviet Union was in fact a despotism and that its espoused ideals, which had inspired so many, were nothing more than cynical camouflage and window dressing. They now realized that, in their aspirations to build a democratic future without war and oppression, they had committed themselves to a social system that proved, in every sense, the negation of that vision. To have lived as a Communist had meant lying about, or at least living a lie in regard to, the main events in their own lives and in the history of their times.

The Birobidzhan project was also exposed as largely fraudulent and a complete failure. When Harrison Salisbury, the Moscow bureau chief of the *New York Times*, was permitted to visit the region in June 1954, he was constantly shadowed by Soviet MVD (later KGB) secret police agents. "Never, in my stay in Russia, had I experienced such surveillance," he wrote. Nonetheless, he managed to learn a great deal about the JAR, which seemed to have no particular Jewish character. "Established originally as a Jewish settlement colony in an obvious move to provide a counterweight to Palestine in the early thirties," he concluded, "it was plain that Birobidjan had lost its significance as a Jewish center a long time ago." It was now part of the Soviet gulag, "MVD-land."[4]

Stalin and his successor, Nikita Khrushchev, tried to blame the Jews themselves for the failure. Stalin "is supposed to have noted privately [at the Yalta Conference in 1945] that he was displeased with the Jews, who had failed to build up their own territory—Biro-Bidzhan."[5] Khrushchev told a correspondent for the French newspaper *Le Figaro* in March of 1958, "They do not like collective work, group discipline. They have always preferred to be dispersed. They are individualists."[6] Many years later, the Canadian Communist Joshua Gershman would remark that Birobidzhan disappeared from Soviet propaganda until it "was taken off the dusty shelves" following the 1967 Arab-Israeli Six-Day War. And even then, he continued, no Jewish writers were allowed to visit the region to report on it. When the USSR in 1975 marked the hundredth anniversary of Mikhail Kalinin's birth, not even the *Birobidzhaner Shtern* mentioned that Kalinin had been the "father" of the plan to make Birobidzhan a Jewish entity.[7] As has been widely shown, most of the leading Jewish Communist intellectuals and institutions distanced themselves from or explicitly left the Communist Party after 1956.

Yet to understand truly the "vanishing" of the Jewish Communist movement to which this volume's titles allude, one must look beyond the political fortunes of Communism and the sins of Stalin in the postwar era. From its inception, one of the common denominators of the Jewish Communist movement was its appeal to immigrants of East European origin. Especially in North America and England, and to a lesser extent in the other countries addressed in this book, the Jewish Communist movement constituted a distinctively Jewish Communist subculture, marked by an on-going commitment to Yiddish and a separate Jewish ethnic identity. Against this claim, some scholars, like Ezra Mendelsohn, have viewed Jewish Communist organizations "as halfway houses, positioned between the ultimately doomed ghetto and a future of universal brotherhood"[8] envisaging a future where Jews would assimilate into a universal culture and where they themselves would become superfluous. Yet, the movement addressed in these pages was so unique and noteworthy for precisely the opposite reason. The members of the Jewish Communist movement were decidedly not assimilationists and saw no need to renounce their Jewishness, unlike some Jews who were as individuals attracted to the mainstream, non-Jewish CPs. They often viewed proletarian Jewish culture, particularly in Yiddish, as the most authentic expression of being Jewish, of a secular *Yidishkayt* that helped define the milieu of Yiddish-speaking immigrants of the working-class left.

In the context of the Jewish Communist movement in the United States for example, many scholars have argued persuasively that it was this particularistic, ethnic cultural component that made Jewish Communism such a popular movement among Jewish immigrants, over against the strictly internationalist and theoretical Marxism underlying communism to begin with. In his seminal article, "Jews and American Communism," Paul Buhle rightly identifies that from the beginnings of Jewish socialism in America "a vital minority of Jewish radicals regarded the preservation of the language, culture, and traditions as the *sine qua non* of their self-identity and revolutionary fervor. Again and again over several generations, they resisted both the forced assimilation offered by the English-speaking radical movements and the defensive, conservative, and truly ethnocentric forms of identity available to the non-radical Jew."[9] Buhle argues that Yiddish-speaking radicals had "the sense of Communism as realization of 'national' (or ethnic) and international aspirations simultaneously. To Yiddish-speaking Communist recruits, Bolshevism did not imply 'national nihilism,' but rather the advance of cultural self-identity in a movement recast according to Leninist faith."[10] These Jews saw no contradiction in participating in pro-Soviet Jewish organizations that, by working for an international transformation of society, would also promote Jewish interests. In this sense, leading, Yiddish-speaking Communist intellectuals in the United States, like Moyshe Olgin and Kalman Marmor, forged what they believed to be a true union of Communism and *yidishkayt.* This holds true just as much for British Jewish Communists, such as Phil Piratin or Mick Mindel, for whom continued self-identification as Jews went hand-in-hand with a life-long commitment to communism.

Even while being part of a larger Communist "family," the extensive network of groups fashioned by the Jewish Communists enabled them to create a "communist-oriented subculture" that was largely independent of the Communist Party. The prevailing worldview of this subculture, which combined Communism, Yiddishism, and secular nationalism, was part of the ideological baggage that left Eastern Europe along with the massive immigration of Eastern European Jews, and was thus transferred to the countries discussed in this book. These groups both promulgated Communist ideals and provided radical, Yiddish-speaking Jews—many of whom were not necessarily identified as Communists—a common cultural experience. In his discussion of this Jewish Communist-oriented subculture, Arthur Liebman observed that for Yiddish-speaking Communists, "their immersion in a Yiddish Communist subculture had produced a rather loyal following for the Party in general and for Yiddish Communism in particular. The role of ideology and politics, however, in the post-World War II era was undoubtedly subordinate to the decades-long social network that they had forged."[11] In other words, the Jewish Communist movement depended both on the immersive cultural experience it offered its supporters and the political ideology it embraced. So, just as much as the collapse of the pro-Soviet Communist ideology that had animated this movement, the crumbling of the common cultural experience that undergirded Jewish Communism was equally responsible for its precipitous decline in the decades after World War Two.

The social and cultural element of the Jewish Communist movement was inherently linked to the immigrant enclave communities that most Jewish Communists lived in until the postwar period. As immigrant Jews and their descendants began to climb the path of upward mobility out of the working-class urban centers and into the professions and the suburbs, both the economic and the cultural—especially linguistic—underpinnings of the Jewish Communist movement unraveled. Indeed, the Jewish community in the immediate postwar world was a very different place than it had been in the 1930s and 1940s. Based on a variety of intertwining factors, the sociocultural trajectory of many Jews in the countries of the English-speaking world in those years was almost universally one of increasing assimilation and a gradual jettisoning of Yiddish language and culture as a defining marker of Jewish ethnic identity. This cultural shift resulted in the broad decline of secular Yiddish culture in all its variations, not just that of the Jewish Communist subculture; a drastic decline in Yiddish speakers and readers meant a dwindling audience for Yiddish cultural productions. For the Jewish Communist movement in particular, the loss of the linguistic and demographic foundation that provided the cultural core of this subculture made it almost impossible for ideology alone to maintain it. Even before the pro-Soviet Communist ideology that sustained the political vision of the movement became irreparably tainted by the revelations of Stalin's crimes in 1956, Jewish Communism as a mass movement on the Jewish street had begun to fade considerably.

There were several remnants of this movement that survived the 1950s, such as the YKUF (*Alveltlekher Yidishe Kultur Farband*) and its journal, *Yidishe Kultur* (published by Itche Goldberg until 2004) and the *Morgn-Frayhayt* (kept going by Paul Novick until 1988), but they increasingly became "one-man shows" cut off from a vital, living community and wider movement. These former Communist, pro-Soviet Yiddish organs, although still committed to a left-wing politics, became more focused on preserving the spirit of the secular progressive Yiddish culture associated with the movement during its heyday. There were a handful of other cultural and institutional relics of this former heyday of Jewish Communism that lasted beyond the 1950s as well, from cultural organizations to summer camps. However, in the end, the political abandonment of communism and the Soviet Union by increasingly larger majorities of former pro-Soviet, pro-Communist Jews, along with the mass exodus of Jews from the Yiddish-speaking immigrant enclaves that they had largely inhabited before the War, proved to be the death knell for the once-thriving Jewish Communist movement this book has chronicled.

Notes

1. The full transcript of the trials, translated into English, has been made available in *Stalin's Secret Pogrom: The Postwar Inquisition of the Jewish Anti-Fascist Committee*, eds. Joshua Rubenstein and Vladimir P. Naumov (New Haven, CT: Yale University Press, 2001).

2. See further Paul Lendvai, *Anti-Semitism Without Jews: Communist Eastern Europe* (Garden City, NY: Doubleday, 1971).

3. On January 13, 1953, the Soviets announced that a conspiracy had been unmasked among Jewish doctors in the USSR to murder Kremlin leaders. Mass arrests quickly followed. The "Doctors' Plot," as this alleged scheme came to be called, was Stalin's last anti-Semitic attack, as he died shortly thereafter. See Jonathan Brent and Vladimir P. Naumov, *Stalin's Last Crime: The Plot Against the Jewish Doctors, 1948–1953* (New York: HarperCollins, 2003). Simon Sebag-Montefiore, *Stalin: The Court of the Red Tsar* (New York: Alfred A. Knopf, 2004) provides portraits of Stalin and his entourage of sycophants.

4. Harrison E. Salisbury, *American in Russia* (New York: Harper & Brothers, 1955), 279–85.

5. Bernard D. Weinryb, "Antisemitism in Soviet Russia," in *The Jews in Soviet Russia Since 1917*, 3rd ed., ed. Lionel Kochan (London: Oxford University Press, 1978), 321.

6. Quoted in Amir Weiner, "Nature and Nurture in a Socialist Utopia: Delineating the Soviet Socio-Ethnic Body in the Age of Socialism," in *Stalinism: The Essential Readings*, ed. David L. Hoffman (Oxford: Blackwell Publishers, 2003), 268.

7. Joshua Gershman, "It Should Never Have Happened!" *Canadian Jewish Outlook* 15, No. 2 (February 1977): 3–5.

8. Ezra Mendelsohn, *On Modern Jewish Politics* (New York: Oxford University Press, 1993), 27–28.

9. Paul Buhle, "Jews and American Communism: The Cultural Question," in *Radical History Review* No. 23 (Spring 1980): 14–15.

10. Ibid., 18.

11. Arthur Liebman, *Jews and the Left* (New York, 1979), 315.

Contributors

Stephen M. Cullen is a Senior Research Fellow at the University of Warwick, England. He was educated at the University of Edinburgh; Nuffield College, Oxford; and Wolfson College, Oxford. He has written on fascism, communism, the Great War, and British government family policy, early intervention, and parenting. He is the author of *In Search of the Real Dad's Army; The Home Guard and the Defence of the United Kingdom*, 1940–1944 (Pen & Sword Books, 2011). Recent articles include "The Parenting Early Intervention Programme in England, 2006–11; a Classed Experience?" *British Educational Research Journal* 39 (6), (2013), 1025–043; "Strange Journey: the life of Dorothy Eckersley," *The Historian* 113, (2013), 18–23; " 'Jewish Communists' or 'Communist Jews'? The Communist Party of Great Britain and British Jews in the 1930s," *Socialist History* 12 (41), (2012), 22–42; and "Fay Taylour: A Dangerous Woman in Sport and Politics," *Women's History Review* 21 (2), (2012), 211–32.

Gennady Estraikh is Associate Professor of Yiddish Studies at the Skirball Department of Hebrew and Judaic Studies, New York University. His publications include *In Harness: Yiddish Writers' Romance with Communism* (Syracuse University Press, 2005); *Yiddish in the Cold War* (Legenda, 2008); and *Evreiskaia literaturnaia zhizn' Moskvy, 1917–1991* (*In Yiddish Literary Life in Moscow*) (European University Press, 2015). He is also the co-editor of *Dovid Bergelson: From Modernism to Socialist Realism* (Legenda, 2007); *A* Captive of the Dawn: The Life and Work of Peretz Markish (Legenda, 2011); *Translating Sholem Aleichem: History, Politics and Art* (Legenda, 2012); 1929: *Mapping the Jewish World* (New York University Press, 2013); *Uncovering the Hidden: The Works and Life of Der Nister* (Legenda, 2014); and *Soviet Jews in World War II: Fighting, Witnessing, Remembering* (Academic Studies Press, 2014), among many other publications.

Matthew B. Hoffman is Associate Professor of Judaic Studies and History at Franklin & Marshall College in Lancaster, Pennsylvania, where he teaches courses on Jewish history and culture. For the last several years his research has focused on the world of Yiddish-speaking Communists in America in the years before World War Two. Hoffman has published and presented a number of papers on this topic, including "The Red Divide: The Conflict between Communists and their Opponents in the American Yiddish Press," appearing in the journal *American Jewish History* (2010) and "From Czernowitz to Paris: The International Yiddish Culture Congress of 1937," in *Czernowitz at 100: The First Yiddish Language Conference in Historical Perspective*, ed. Joshua Fogel (Lexington Books, 2010). His first book is *From Rebel to Rabbi: Reclaiming Jesus and the Making of Modern Jewish Culture* (Stanford University Press, 2007).

Philip Mendes is an Associate Professor at Monash University in Melbourne and is the Director of its Social Inclusion and Social Policy Research Unit in the Department of Social Work. He has been researching Jewish Left history and politics for over twenty years, and is the author or co-author of eight books including *The New Left, the Jews and the Vietnam War, 1965–72* (Lazare Press, 1993), jointly edited with Geoffrey Brahm Levey; *Jews and Australian Politics* (Sussex Academic Press, 2004); and most recently *Jews and the Left: The Rise and Fall of a Political Alliance* (Palgrave Macmillan, 2014).

Ester Reiter is a Senior Scholar and Associate Professor Emerita in the School of Gender, Sexuality and Women's Studies in the Faculty of Liberal and Professional Studies, York University, Toronto. She is the author of *Out of the Frying Pan and Into the Fryer: A Study of the Organization of Work in the Fast Food Industry* (McGill-Queen's University Press, 1995). Her published works include articles on the Jewish left in Canada and she is currently completing a book on that topic.

David Yoram Saks is a writer, historian, and Jewish communal professional and has written extensively on South African Jewish, political, and military history for a wide range of local and international publications. He worked as curator of history at Museum Africa from 1990–1996 before joining the staff of the South African Jewish Board of Deputies. He is today Associate Director of the SAJBD and editor, since 1999, of the journal Jewish Affairs. His books include *Boerejode: Jews in the Boer Armed Forces, 1899–1902*

(Charlie Fine, 2010) and *Jewish Memories of Mandela* (South African Jewish Board of Deputies and the Umoja Foundation, 2011). He holds a Master's degree in History from Rhodes University, Grahamstown, South Africa.

Henry F. Srebrnik is Professor of Political Science at the University of Prince Edward Island, Charlottetown, PEI, Canada. As well as being the author of numerous scholarly articles on Jewish involvement in the world Communist movement, he has written *London Jews and British Communism, 1935–1945* (Vallentine Mitchell, 1995); *Jerusalem on the Amur: Birobidzhan and the Canadian Jewish Communist Movement, 1924–1951* (McGill-Queen's University Press, 2008); *Dreams of Nationhood: American Jewish Communists and the Soviet Birobidzhan Project, 1924–1951* (Academic Studies Press, 2010); and *Creating the Chupah: The Zionist Movement and the Drive for Jewish Communal Unity in Canada, 1898–1921* (Academic Studies Press, 2011).

Jennifer Young is the Director of Education at the Max Weinreich Center for Advanced Jewish Study, YIVO Institute for Jewish Research, New York. She is completing a doctoral dissertation entitled "American Jewish Communists, Anti-Fascism, and the Shaping of Ethnic Culture in the International Workers Order, 1930–1956" in the Department of History and the Skirball Department of Hebrew and Judaic Studies at New York University.

Index

www.ingramcontent.com/pod-product-compliance
Lightning Source LLC
LaVergne TN
LVHW050150080826
844660LV00002B/143

* 9 7 8 1 4 3 8 4 6 2 1 9 6 *